Play Therapy with Adolescents

Play Therapy with Adolescents

Edited by
Loretta Gallo-Lopez,
MA, RPT-S, RDT-BCT,
and
Charles E. Schaefer, PhD, RPT-S

JASON ARONSON
Lanham • Boulder • New York • Toronto • Plymouth, UK

Published by Jason Aronson
An imprint of Rowman & Littlefield Publishers, Inc.
A wholly owned subsidary of The Rowman & Littlefield Publishing Group, Inc.
4501 Forbes Boulevard, Suite 200, Lanham, Maryland 20706
http://www.rowmanlittlefield.com

Estover Road, Plymouth PL6 7PY, United Kingdom

British Library Cataloguing in Publication Information Available

The hardback edition of this book was previously cataloged by the Library of Congress as
follows:
    Play therapy with adolescents / edited by Loretta Gallo-Lopez and Charles E.
    Schaefer.—[2nd ed.].
        p.   cm.
    Includes bibliographical references and index.
    1. Play therapy. 2. Adolescent psychotherapy. I. Gallo-Lopez, Loretta.
  II. Schaefer, Charles E.
  RJ505.P6P55   2005
  615.8'5153'0835—dc22   2004023173

ISBN: 978-0-7657-0339-2 (cloth : alk. paper)
ISBN: 978-0-7657-0802-1 (pbk. : alk. paper)

♾ ™ The paper used in this publication meets the minimum requirements of American
National Standard for Information Sciences—Permanence of Paper for Printed Library
Materials, ANSI/NISO Z39.48-1992.

Printed in the United States of America

To my parents Catherine and Gus Gallo, who bravely weathered the storms of my adolescence, and taught me that family is life's greatest treasure. I miss you both.

—LGL

To my parents, William and Loretta Schaefer, for their love and support.

—CES

Contents

Part II Special Populations

· Preface ·

$\mathcal{M}$any people question why anyone would choose to work with adolescents. After all, adolescents are resistant, hostile, moody, resentful, defiant, frenzied, explosive, and difficult. Most psychotherapists working with adolescents know of colleagues who avoid adolescent referrals at all cost. Yet many of us are inexplicably drawn to this population. Perhaps it is because adolescents are also challenging, fascinating, creative, evolving, impassioned, spontaneous, intense, and unpredictable. And although adolescence is often marked by turmoil and inner conflict, it is also a time of growth and self-discovery. Adolescents, at times, present an external image masked in the guise of omniscience and self-assurance. However, below the surface, they are often fearful and full of questions. Our task as mental health professionals is to get past the facade, to help our young clients to examine their fears and search for answers. How do we accomplish this task? How do we get adolescents to "let us in"?

Play Therapy with Adolescents, the first book to offer a complete volume of play therapy approaches specifically geared toward adolescents, seeks to provide answers to these questions. This volume of chapters, written by experts in the field of adolescent play therapy, offers readers entry into the world of adolescents to make connections and forge alliances.

Each of the sixteen chapters contained within this volume provides a wealth of practical information that professionals can easily utilize in their work with adolescents individually, in family therapy, or in groups.

Part I invites the reader to explore a myriad of play therapy approaches. Each author provides specific guidelines and theoretical framework from such diverse orientations as sandtray therapy, filial therapy, poetry therapy, theraplay, gameplay, drama therapy, and the use of metaphor and transitional objects. Approaches range from client-centered, nondirective play therapy, to highly structured and directive, cognitive-behavioral play therapy.

Part II addresses issues related to specific problem areas especially significant in work with adolescents. Included are strategies for working with adolescents with attachment issues, delinquency issues, aggressive behaviors, and eating disorders, as well as adolescents in foster care.

Establishing trust and building relationships are the cornerstones to effective therapy with adolescents and are common themes running through each of the chapters. Authors identify strategies and offer insight related to making that all-important connection with adolescents entering therapy. Case illustrations are included in order to provide readers with examples of the practical application of the approaches presented.

Play Therapy with Adolescents is a unique volume of work that will be an invaluable resource for professionals faced with the challenging task of working with this exciting population. We hope you find yourself inspired, encouraged, and enlightened.

Loretta Gallo-Lopez
Charles E. Schaefer

I

PLAY THERAPY APPROACHES

An Introduction to Play Therapy with Adolescents

Claire Milgrom

$\mathcal{P}$lay therapy with adolescents is increasingly being addressed in the play therapy literature (Carroll, 1998; Cerio, 2000; Gil, 1996; Jernberg and Booth, 1999; Ray, Bratton, Rhine, and Jones, 2001; Straus, 1999). However, many referral sources, including social service personnel, do not think of referring troubled adolescents for play therapy, assuming that adolescents are too old to engage therapeutically in this manner. Indeed, many therapists would not choose this medium for working with adolescents, citing similar reasons. Adolescents themselves might view cynically the idea of participating in play activities with a therapist, because their primary developmental tasks include individuation, separation, and preparation for adult roles.

In one form or another even adults continue to play, negating the idea that adolescent developmental tasks should preclude participation in play for therapeutic purposes. Adult play behavior can be seen in their participation in sports, the arts, computer and video games, gambling, board games and card games, arts and crafts, and in their attendance of costume and theme parties. Huizinga (1955) observes that play is a cultural factor in life and that the spirit of playful competition is, as a social impulse, older than culture itself, pervading all aspects of life.

For adults, playing is frequently part of relationship building. Attending a recreational event or participating in a sport or game with other adults is often a prelude to more intimate interactions. Once a relationship is established, play for adults serves many purposes including ongoing relationship building, ongoing mutual assessment of the health of the relationship, skill development, recreation, and relaxation.

The role of play in therapy with adolescents is similar in many respects. Play by definition is generally fun, which in turn, makes it an ideal means of building relationships with many clients. This is especially true for building relationships with adolescents who might be wary of authority figures and resistant to engaging. Playing is likely to be far less threatening than "working on issues" verbally, especially if adolescents are not voluntary clients.

As part of therapy, play is an excellent way of assessing how adolescents function in the world. Imaginative play using a sand tray, dolls or puppets, for example, can reveal themes relevant to adolescents' lives. Imaginative play can also be an indication of an adolescent's ability and willingness to engage and to be spontaneous while simultaneously demonstrating the manner in which they relate to adults. The use of board games or card games can be used to assess adolescents' social skills, power and control issues (e.g., playing by the rules or not), feelings of self-esteem (e.g., need to win, negative self-talk) and relationships with adults. Arts and crafts can be used to assess adolescents' ability to express themselves and their creativity.

Rather than being contraindicated for use with adolescents, incorporating play into therapy allows adolescents to use the therapeutic relationship to move back and forth along the developmental continuum while striving for healthy individuation and separation from a nonabusive and nonpunitive adult (Cattanach, 1992). This is especially important for adolescents with attachment issues due to chronically abusive and neglectful home environments and/or histories of multiple placements in the foster care system. Within the safety of the therapeutic relationship, adolescents may be observed coloring and playing with Barbie dolls during one session, and discussing issues related to partners or moving out on their own in a subsequent session.

In terms of a rationale for using play therapy with adolescents, playing is a joyful experience. For adolescents with severe behavioral concerns, playing can maximize the number of positive interactions experienced with adults, which is often encouraged as a means of changing dysfunctional behavior patterns (Delaney, 1994). In the context of a caring relationship, play therapy can create special memories and experiences for adolescents who may otherwise have had a lifetime of overwhelming pain and loss. Jernberg and Booth (1999) provide a poignant illustration of this. They quote a young woman who revisited her Theraplay therapist as an adult. (Theraplay is a fun, activity-based and therapist-guided form of play therapy.) The young woman reportedly told her therapist that she was unable to remember anything about the time that they "just talked" but was able to remember "every detail of every active thing (they) *ever* did together" (Jernberg and Booth, 1999, p. 341).

STARTING PLAY THERAPY
WITH ADOLESCENTS

Playing is not "cool" for adolescents unless done on their own terms. So while it can be beneficial to conduct therapy sessions with adolescents in a playroom setting, it is important that therapists allow playing to be a choice. Nor should therapy be referred to as "play therapy." Adolescents must be allowed to decide for themselves how to engage in their healing process. Conducting sessions in a playroom setting gives adolescents the option of sitting and talking with the therapist, exploring the toys, engaging in play, or all three at different times. Toys can be kept beside the chairs in the playroom for adolescents who choose to sit and talk. Toys such as Play-Doh, Silly Putty, or a mini Etch-a-Sketch can provide a distraction from the potential intensity of an initial therapeutic encounter and help clients cope with anxiety or otherwise overwhelming feelings.

Sometimes adolescents are so overwhelmed by the idea of participating in therapy that their caregivers have a difficult time getting them to attend therapy appointments. Therapists can help to engage adolescents by initially meeting with them in their own "territory" where they are likely to feel more comfortable. This might include going to their homes, meeting them for coffee, playing basketball with them outside, or driving with them and talking in the car. Straus (1999) refers to this as "traveling treatment." Traveling treatment might occur at any point in the therapeutic process depending on the client's needs.

The therapeutic environment should invite play and validate and normalize any regressive tendencies that might be triggered in sessions. Suggested toys and materials are the same as those utilized with younger children with some modifications, and include the following:

- Arts and craft supplies such as paper, pencils, markers, paints, glitter glue, clay, and materials for craft projects such as pom-poms, popsicle sticks, felt, foam sheets, Styrofoam, thread, and beading supplies. Adolescents are sometimes capable of undertaking more advanced craft projects such as embroidery, knitting, crocheting, decoupage, and woodworking. If a particular project is planned, shopping for supplies together can be fun and exciting for adolescents, if time and budgeting allows. One adolescent, who was luckily the last client of the day, spent over an hour playfully yet intensely agonizing over her sticker choices for a decoupage project she planned. She giggled like a six-

year-old the entire time and continued to make fond references to the
shopping excursion in sessions over a year later.
- Sand tray.
- Cars, trucks, trains, and planes.
- Army and action figures, plastic domestic and wild animals.
- Barbie dolls. Since most North American girls seem to have been
  exposed to Barbie dolls during their childhood, it is especially useful to
  keep some in the playroom to stimulate memories of childhood play.
- Easy-Bake Oven. This is another toy that seems to stimulate memories of childhood play or childhood wishes if adolescents did not own
  one.
- Stickers. Many adolescents love stickers even though they may only
  admit it sheepishly. Stickers can also promote memories of childhood
  play. They can be used for arts and crafts projects and making collages.
  They can also be used for behavior modification charts with lower
  functioning adolescents. Some adolescents enjoy receiving a sheet of
  stickers with a theme they can relate to, such as animals or sports.
- Board games and cards. Adolescents may be cognitively capable of
  playing more sophisticated board games than children but they also
  may enjoy the sense of mastery and competence they get from playing
  games designed for younger children.
- Dollhouse with people, animals, and furniture.
- Stuffed animals.
- Puppets.
- Baby dolls and baby supplies.
- CD player and CDs. This is particularly important for adolescents
  because music is generally a significant part of their lives. Compilation
  CDs including a variety of artists are an excellent way of ensuring that
  individual client's tastes are found in the playroom collection. Music
  for dancing, classical music, and children's music such as lullabies are
  also good to have on hand both for stimulating and soothing emotions. Adolescents can also be encouraged to bring their own music to
  listen to during sessions.
- Guitar. A guitar in the playroom often fascinates children and adolescents. They enjoy trying to play it or singing songs along with the
  therapist if possible. Many popular songs are built around a few basic
  chords that are relatively easy for adolescents to learn, allowing them
  an opportunity for both pleasure and mastery of a new skill.
- Camera. A camera can be used both in the playroom and during "traveling treatment" for the compilation of life books of adolescents. The

therapist can keep a photo journal of adolescent's time in therapy to be given to the adolescent upon termination.

- Sports equipment. Playing sports such as basketball, "catch" with a baseball or football, jumping rope, sponge-ball tennis, or Frisbee is an excellent way to build relationships, especially with those who have poor verbal skills or those who feel particularly shy at first. Sports equipment might need to be adapted (e.g., using Nerf balls) to indoor play if sports sessions cannot be held outside. Sports activities allow adolescents some time to "warm up" to the therapeutic relationship, the opportunity to receive the undivided attention of an interested adult if they wish to show off some of their skills, to teach the therapist skills, and simply to have fun and relax.

Many adolescents may start to engage with a therapist upon recognition of toys in the playroom with which they had played at home or in foster care. Comments about playing dress-up with Barbies or creating battles in the sand with army figures can provide the basis for many discussions and play reenactments of both childhood and current issues. If such comments are not forthcoming from adolescents, therapists can ask about their favorite childhood toys and, if possible, provide them in the playroom in subsequent sessions.

No matter how inviting a therapeutic setting is, in order to encourage the use of play as a therapeutic tool, the therapist's attitude towards play must be inviting. Therapists can role model such an attitude by expressing enthusiasm and enjoyment for playing themselves. For example, challenge an adolescent to a game of Battleship and make missile noises when a ship gets hit. Suggest a game of catch with a football and allow the adolescent to teach the therapist how to "get just the right spiral." Greet the adolescent with a talking caterpillar made out of pompoms and jiggly eyes and have craft project materials ready for the adolescent to create his or her own caterpillar. Dance the "funky chicken" to music brought in by the adolescent. A sense of humor is essential when working with adolescents.

Therapists modeling playful behavior need to be prepared for an adolescent's reaction to their behavior, which may range from enthusiasm to indifference to disdain. The adolescent's reaction must be handled respectfully and, of course, playing should always remain the adolescent's choice. Sometimes feelings of self-consciousness, embarrassment, or lack of trust can influence an adolescent's initial response. Many adolescents become more playful as their feelings of comfort increase. Therapists can help this process by letting adolescents know that other children, adolescents, and even adults like to play when in the playroom, and by maintaining their own playful attitude. They can also acknowledge any feelings expressed by adolescents about feeling weird, silly, or babyish, but also express positive feelings about the act of playing and remind them of the confidential nature of therapeutic sessions.

SPECIAL ISSUES

Because of the unique developmental status of adolescents, neither child nor adult, play therapy with this population presents special issues that may not always be addressed specifically in child and adult therapy literature. Issues that may require special attention when using play therapy with adolescents include the use of directive versus nondirective techniques, confidentiality, interpretation of metaphor, developmental issues, caregiver response, and adolescent "culture."

Directive vs. Nondirective

Caroll (1998) believes that many adolescents respond to focused interventions more readily than nondirective techniques due to the sometimes overwhelming confusion and uncertainty that can characterize adolescence. She notes that adolescents may need the focus of directive methods if "therapy is not to submerge in their diffuse and ever changing feelings" (p. 137). Indeed, some adolescents entering into a therapeutic process with specific goals in mind may welcome therapists' ideas for helping them achieve their goals. However, some adolescents referred for therapy may be involuntary, demonstrating their reluctance to attend through refusal to talk or to engage in therapist-initiated activities. Even voluntary adolescent clients may need to exert their independence in a similar manner at times. Additionally, some adolescents, as with clients of all ages, may readily talk but avoid any emotional content or direct discussion of issues that resulted in their referral to therapy. In this context, Schaefer's "prescriptive approach" (2002) that suggests tailoring the individual therapeutic approach to the individual client's therapeutic needs, is particularly relevant. After gathering information from referral sources, caregivers, and the client, therapists can decide on the best way to meet treatment objectives, utilizing directive, nondirective, or a combination of both techniques. For example, with adolescents who are particularly difficult to engage, a nondirective approach may be most effective, at least during the initial stages of therapy. The therapist's unconditional acceptance of an adolescent may need to be well established before an adolescent is willing to accept any form of direction. A nonthreatening form of engagement that does not involve specific directions for treatment and does not require an adolescent to buy into "therapeutic language" is to inquire about favorite snacks and provide them if possible. Adolescents may feel more at ease with the "concreteness" of this type of questioning rather than more metaphorical questions (e.g., If you were an animal, what type of animal would you be?). Adolescents might consider the latter too "touchy-feely."

Listening to music together is another nonthreatening way of engaging reluctant adolescent clients. A study by Larson (1995) suggested that music is particularly important to adolescents and their emotional self-regulation. Specifically, the study indicated that adolescents frequently listen to music while thinking about the themes of songs in relation to their own lives. Listening to an adolescent's choice of pop, rap, or heavy metal songs during therapy sessions can help a therapist understand some of the themes relevant to the adolescent without direct questioning. A therapist's ability to listen to controversial lyrics can be instrumental in establishing his or her credibility as open, nonjudgmental, and nonpunitive.

Playing games chosen by the adolescent is yet another nondirective technique that allows adolescents to engage on their own terms. The beginning of an adolescent's ability to relinquish some control in the therapeutic setting may be demonstrated when he or she first allows the therapist to choose a game. More directive techniques such as making life books or sand tray work may then be gradually introduced.

In contrast to a nondirective approach or a gradual transition from nondirective to directive approach, Jernberg and Booth (1999) cite the use of directive Theraplay techniques to achieve treatment objectives with an adolescent experiencing difficulty with peer relationships. Whereas traditional talk therapy with this adolescent, described as talkative and pseudosophisticated, appeared to be ineffective, an abrupt change to Theraplay activities seemed to be more expedient in meeting treatment goals, that is, improved peer relationships. The regressive nature of the Theraplay activities, initiated and guided by the therapist, likely addressed the previously unmet needs of the client as a frightened little girl. This "catching up" of her developmental needs allowed her to relate more positively to her peers as an adolescent (pp. 338–41).

Confidentiality

Although this may seem obvious, it is extremely important to respect adolescents' confidentiality, especially if they are engaged in play therapy. Even when adolescents overcome their own defenses and allow themselves to play during a therapy session, they are generally keenly sensitive to the potential ridicule or insensitivity of others. Given this, adolescents need to be reassured both verbally and by direct observation of the therapist with others including their caregivers, that the therapist will not be talking to anyone about their play activities without their permission. If adolescents are nervous about someone entering the playroom unannounced or being unknowingly observed, they should be given permission to lock the door, cover a two-way mirror, or ensure that video recording equipment is turned off. Nevertheless, the therapist needs to maintain a positive attitude towards playing and a simultaneous acknowledgment that others may not be as understanding about it. Finally, adolescents need to know that they can choose to share as little or as much as they want about the content of sessions with others.

Caregiver Response

Caregivers often have a difficult time understanding the complex mixture of regressive needs and striving for independence that may underlie adolescents' confusing or difficult behavior (Jernberg and Booth, 1999). Because the inclusion of caregivers in the therapeutic process tends to increase the likelihood of a successful outcome (Ray, Bratton, Rhine, and Jones, 2001), it is important that they be given information about how best to respond to both types of needs in their adolescents. One mother, who had not been prepared for her fourteen-year-old to behave in a regressed manner during a therapy session—he cuddled a pillow and wrapped a blanket around himself—teased him about his "blankie." Caregivers need to be encouraged not to tease or make sarcastic comments about adolescents' play or regressive behavior in the playroom. They also need to know that adolescents may need to "try on" different behaviors in the playroom, that this is part of the therapeutic process, and that in this way previously unmet needs from the past, which may be impinging on current functioning, may be addressed.

Interpretation of Metaphors

One of the fundamental principles of play therapy is that playing allows children and adolescents to address issues through play, which can provide some emotional distance from painful or overwhelming feelings. When therapists interpret children's and adolescent's play behavior, usually during the reexperience and resolution phase of treatment according to Brems (1993), the therapeutic goal is to assist in the client's development of insight. Brems goes on to note that the development of insight requires a level of abstraction not necessarily available in children. She concludes that interpretation by therapists is not always necessary for child clients to have successful treatment outcomes. This may also be true for adolescents.

While playing provides some emotional safety from difficult issues, adolescents are obviously far more sophisticated and aware of metaphorical significance than are younger children. Often, if left unsaid, adolescents will choose to interpret their own metaphors during play. With highly defended adolescents, interpreting play themes too early in the therapeutic relationship can result in them feeling overwhelmed and vulnerable. In these instances, it may be appropriate to work within the metaphor without interpretation. For example, one fifteen-year-old girl who had been raised in a chronically chaotic and violent home reported to her therapist recurring dreams of a young girl being sexually assaulted. At that point in therapy, she had never disclosed any sexual victimization. Her behavior indicated a need to present as strong and unassailable. The adolescent chose to make a dream book about the assaults, expressing feelings and identifying ways to help the little girl. No disclosure of victimization was made during the process. The therapist worked within the metaphor without interpretation. Eventually the client reported an end to the dreams and expressed feeling confident in her ability to help girls who had been sexually assaulted. She appeared to have undergone an empowering and healing experience within the context of a metaphor that may or may not have been related to a direct or indirect real life event.

Developmental Issues

Gil's (1996) guiding principles for therapy with adolescents include decoding and supporting the intent of seemingly dysfunctional behavior that in many instances has its origins in earlier unmet childhood needs and cognitive distortions. Cerio (2000) notes that adolescents often choose to play during therapy because of unmet needs related to an earlier stage of development. Playing with a nonjudgmental, nurturing adult can be a reparative and cathartic experience for adolescents who may have been traumatized or neglected as children, giving them the opportunity to share painful experiences and memories from the past, and to process them therapeutically. Carroll (1998) notes that regressive play for adolescents offers an opportunity to "make up for missed experiences and provides the basis for an internal mechanism to understand experiences, promoting a more constructive response to daily life" (p. 137).

Despite the lower emotional functioning of some adolescents referred for therapy, adolescents' physical size and strength, and their heightened sexual awareness can present challenges to the dimensions of play therapy. Jernberg and Booth (1999) recommend using a team of cotherapists or a therapist who is the same gender as the client, when using Theraplay activities that have the potential to be sexually stimulating or to arouse sexual fantasies in an adolescent. In less directive play therapy with same-sex or opposite-sex therapists, alternative methods of playing out particular themes may need to be suggested to the adolescent when therapist-client boundaries feel like they may be violated. Therapists must set clear limits regarding the client's and the therapist's comfort and safety during sessions. For example, one thirteen-year-old girl with seductive behavior who liked to role-play dancing as a princess with her prince needed to be redirected to play out this scene with dolls. Another very large sixteen-year-old boy referred for problems with aggression at school needed to have a plan of action developed early in the treatment process for expressing his anger safely when it arose during sessions.

Adolescent Culture

Knowing what is important to adolescents is an excellent way of building and maintaining relationships with adolescent clients. Showing an interest in their taste in music, movies, television, and sports is validating for them as individuals. It is also an invaluable means of assessing the meaning they ascribe to their world. For example, therapists can learn what issues evoke certain feelings such as anger, sadness, joy, or shame by finding out the lyrics of songs that resonate with them, and they can discover to what their clients aspire by learning about their media idols. Adolescent clients are also much more likely to reveal their own issues once a media idol of theirs has acknowledged struggling with the same challenges such as alcoholism, childhood abuse, or the death of a significant person in their life. Introduction to the conversation of a Backstreet Boy's treatment for addictions or Eminem's anger towards his mother can stimulate discussion of the adolescent's own problems or concerns.

PLAY THERAPY TECHNIQUES
WITH ADOLESCENTS

In using a prescriptive approach to play therapy with adolescents, therapists will obviously be using whatever techniques seem to make the most sense for individual clients. The following are suggestions for approaching adolescents' issues that I have found to be effective for a number of different situations.

Creating Motifs and Metaphors for Individual Clients

When themes in an adolescent's life become apparent during therapy, either the client or the therapist can create motifs and metaphors to help explore the themes further. This underscores the adolescent's "specialness" and focuses on his or her specific needs. It also encourages continuity, connectedness in the therapeutic relationship, and creativity, while providing some protective emotional distance. A metaphor that arose for a seemingly tough, gang-affiliated sixteen-year-old girl was that of her "marshmallow heart," which she needed to keep a secret and protect at all costs. Once I let her know gently that I had discovered her secret when she told me about giving money to a street person, either she or I frequently invoked the marshmallow heart metaphor when issues needed to be explored. For example, I would ask her, "Do you feel comfortable enough with your new boyfriend to show him your marshmallow heart? Would he know how gentle he needed to be with such a heart?" She was eventually able to talk about her father beating her and her resulting need to build a wall around her marshmallow heart. On Valentine's Day, I gave her a chocolate covered marshmallow heart. The client commented that the heart had its own protective shell. She later acknowledged that she might even like the fact that I knew about her "marshmallow heart." The motif also provided a safe way of processing communication glitches, misinterpretations, and hurt feelings when they arose in sessions.

CHEAT

CHEAT is a simple card game that uses only half the deck if there are only two players. The half-deck is shuffled and dealt to each player face down. Players can arrange their cards in their hands from sets of highest to lowest cards. Play begins with the first player placing a card or cards face down and saying "One Ace" (or however many cards he or she has placed). If the player does not have any Aces, he or she still plays the card or cards but pretends they are Aces. Play continues in this manner with the next player placing a card or cards on the table and saying for example, "Four Twos." Play continues until Kings, then starts again with Aces. If the opponent does not believe that the other player has actually placed down the number and type of cards that he or she states, the opponent calls, "Cheat." If the opponent is correct, the player must pick up all of the cards already played. If the opponent is incorrect, he or she must pick up the cards already played. The winner is the first player to run out of cards.

Adolescents seem to like this game because of its "cheekiness." They can feel "in control" and accepted even when participating in supposedly "bad" behavior. They seem to enjoy the paradox that, in this game, the rules are to cheat. It is a great game for relationship building. Players are required to closely observe body language and facial expressions that requires significant eye contact and paying attention to the opponent. I have experienced depressed adolescents with a noticeably flat affect become joyfully animated and energetic while playing this game and I have seen angry, avoidant adolescents become giggly, make extended nonhostile eye contact, and become receptive to subsequent interventions after playing this game.

Stimulating Childhood Memories

As mentioned above, many adolescents begin to engage when they first notice a toy in the playroom that reminds them of childhood. Some adolescents respond to direct questions such as, "What did you like to play when you were a kid?" Some respond to comments such as, "I bet you were a really cute kid!" Sadly, many respond by saying things like, "No, I was a really bad kid—you would have hated me."

Therapists can encourage exploration of adolescents' perception of self in the context of childhood memories by asking them to bring to sessions old photographs of themselves and their families and by having them make collages and lifebooks. Jarratt (1994) makes excellent suggestions for the compilation of lifebooks for children who have suffered separation and loss through death, divorce, and multiple placements. Another effective way to help adolescents change their perception of themselves as responsible for childhood abuse, neglect or other family difficulties, is to help them write stories with their childhood selves as the main character. They can also be encouraged to nurture themselves by making something for themselves that they would have liked to have received when they were a child, such as a pretty poster, a picture frame, a felt doll, or a wooden car.

CASE ILLUSTRATION

Tanya was a sixteen-year-old gang-affiliated and streetwise girl living in a group home when she was referred for therapy by her social worker to address anger management issues. Tanya was my client with a "marshmallow heart." She had spent many years in the foster care system due to pervasive violence and substance abuse within her family of origin. She had previously been incarcerated for a serious assault on a group home youth care worker. Tanya swaggered in for her first appointment wearing sunglasses that she did not remove for the entire session.

Tanya did remove her sunglasses during our second session. Early sessions took place in a toyless counseling office and focused on developing a level of comfort and trust between therapist and client. Tanya talked extensively about the fights she had had and the people she had assaulted both in the past and the present, describing the incidents in vivid detail and with no apparent empathy for the people she hurt. Sometimes she became so loud and agitated during her narration that she stood up and enacted the scenes, using different voices for different people and gesturing wildly in the air with her fists or making a stabbing motion as if she had a knife in her hand. Tanya always quickly reassured me that she was never hurt and never cried when I expressed concern for her physical and emotional well-being. Sensing that she was not in a position to be challenged in any form about her violent behavior (group home staff were attempting to lessen her angry outbursts), I listened to her stories and gave her positive feedback about her fabulous story-telling style.

Tanya responded by continuing her detailed narratives but also by expanding her repertoire of stories to include incidents and memories that did not always involve violence. She also enthusiastically accepted my suggestions that we do some beadwork together. She was very good at it and made many small beaded creatures such as spiders, frogs, and snakes in her gang colors. Tanya seemed pleased when I gave her a small beaded guardian angel to watch over her and her fellow gang members, agreeing indirectly that they all needed someone to watch over them. While her violent narratives continued, her manner became noticeably calmer as she focused on her beadwork. One day, Tanya arrived with a story about giving some money to a homeless person. She laughed self-consciously but again seemed pleased when I commented that I had discovered her secret. That is, that underneath her cool, tough façade, she had a "marshmallow heart."

At about this time, I moved to another agency that only had playrooms and no "toyless" counseling offices. I was worried that Tanya would respond negatively to being in a playroom, feeling that she might think it was "too babyish" and "uncool" for her. Instead, Tanya immediately caught sight of the Barbie dolls and began to reminisce about childhood play with siblings and friends. Her half-hearted comments about feeling too old to play petered out by the time I had enthusiastically dumped the Barbie clothing on the floor and begun to brush Ballerina Barbie's hair. Tanya did not need a formal invitation to play.

Tanya's behavior continued to soften over the next several months in the playroom. We dressed Barbie dolls and styled their hair. We made pink and yellow heart-shaped Play-Doh cookies. We made collages with glittery stickers that she said she would have liked when she was younger. We decoupaged a lock box for Tanya to keep all her special keepsakes in, including pictures of herself when she was an adorable baby. We played in the sand tray. We played cards and *Junior Monopoly* that Tanya remembered playing with her sister when they were children.

While we played, we laughed and talked. Tanya reported about her day at school, her boyfriend troubles, and her arguments with family members and group home workers. We both used the "marshmallow heart" motif to talk about difficult topics and to smooth out her rumpled feelings when she became upset by something I said. Her narratives of violent acts became very rare and group home staff reported a significant change in Tanya's behavior. She sought alternative ways of dealing with conflict when it arose and, at times, was able to express concern for people that ended up on the receiving end of her angry outbursts. Tanya gradually began to connect her feelings of anger with her overwhelming feelings of childhood pain and powerlessness. Sometimes she cried. The first time she cried, she did not return for two sessions. When she did return, she refrained from playing or making crafts for a few sessions.

During one session when we were making Christmas decorations, Tanya accidentally cut herself. She began to cry in response to my fussing over her. She compared the caregiving she was receiving with the lack of caregiving she experienced as a child and how this affected the way she interacted with people in the present. She chose a Winnie-the-Pooh Band-Aid for her cut.

In the summer, Tanya and I went out for ice cream in a neighborhood where she had lived. She talked about fond memories of a kind, elderly neighbor who let her play in her garden. We used her memories to write a story about herself as a lovable little girl, not the horrible girl that she thought was so bad.

Tanya, now living on her own, working, and nearing adulthood, still comes to see me on a regular basis. Sometimes we play games or make arts and crafts. Sometimes we go out for a drive or a walk. Sometimes we just sit and talk. Recently she commented with a laugh that her "marshmallow heart" was no longer a secret because she was so nice to everybody that everybody just knew.

Play therapy may not be appropriate for all adolescents and not all adolescents will participate in play with a therapist. However, in my experience, some of the least likely candidates to play, that is the "coolest" adolescents, the angriest, and the most reluctant, have been the adolescents who seem eventually to play the most enthusiastically and benefit most profoundly from this type of intervention. Perhaps this most simple and basic of human activities is the most natural way of helping troubled adolescents heal.

REFERENCES

Brems, C. 1993. *A Comprehensive Guide to Child Psychotherapy*. Boston: Allyn and Bacon.
Carroll, J. 1998. *Introduction to Therapeutic Play*. London: Blackwell Science Ltd.

Cattanach, A. 1992. *Play Therapy with Abused Children*. London: Jessica Kingsley Publishers.

Cerio, J. 2000. *Play Therapy: A Do-It-Yourself Guide for Practitioners*. Alfred, NY: Alfred University Press.

Delaney, R. J. 1994. *Fostering Changes: Treating Attachment-Disordered Foster Children*. Fort Collins, CO: Walter J. Corbett Publishing.

Gil, E. 1996. *Treating Abused Adolescents*. New York: Guildford Press.

Huizinga, J. 1955. *Homo ludens*. Boston: Beacon Press.

Jarratt, C. J. 1994. *Helping Children Cope with Separation and Loss*. Boston, MA: The Harvard Common Press.

Jernberg, A. M., and P. B. Booth. 1999. *Theraplay: Helping Parents and Children Build Better Relationships through Attachment-Based Play*. San Francisco: Jossey-Bass Publishers.

Larson, R. 1995. Secrets in the bedroom: Adolescents' private use of media. *Journal of Youth and Adolescence* 24: 535–50.

Ray, D., S. Bratton, T. Rhine, and L. Jones. 2001. The effectiveness of play therapy: Responding to the critics. *International Journal of Play Therapy* 10(1): 85–108.

Schaefer, C. E. 2002. Prescriptive play therapy. *International Journal of Play Therapy* 10(2): 57–73.

Straus, M. B. 1999. *No-Talk Therapy for Children and Adolescents*. New York: Norton.

Adolescent Sand Tray Therapy
Theresa Kestly

$\mathcal{W}$hen adolescents come into a therapy office where there is a sand tray, they find it difficult to keep their hands out of the tray. Although they sometimes think that playing with toys is just for children, playing with sand in a small tray is a different matter. Even when they say they do not want to play with toys, they still run their hands through the sand, tunneling, shaping, drawing designs, burying, patting, and sifting it through their fingers. Beyond this casual play, many adolescents are eager to engage with sand and miniatures in intelligent ways as they sort through the issues that brought them into therapy.

BACKGROUND OF SAND TRAY THERAPY

The first description of sand tray therapy as a unique therapeutic tool came from a British pediatrician, Margaret Lowenfeld (1939), but it was the children in her clinic who actually created the process. When Lowenfeld first set up her clinic for children in London around 1930, she was convinced from her experiences of working with trauma victims during World War I that words were inadequate for children to express their traumatic experiences and to reveal the inner workings of their minds. Although Lowenfeld spoke seven languages fluently, she knew that children needed a means of therapeutic expression that did not rely on words alone. Remembering a book written by H. G. Wells (1911) on play with miniature toys, Lowenfeld decided to include a box of miniature toys in her clinic. In addition she put two small zinc trays half filled with sand for molding and shaping to give children tactile experiences. She also provided areas of water play. Naturally, the children combined these play areas pouring water in the sand and using the toys to build scenes in the trays. When the children began referring to their "worlds,"

Lowenfeld recognized that she had a tool that would allow children to reveal their worldviews. She eventually wrote a book, *The World Technique* (1979), to describe in detail this method of play.

The Swiss analyst, Carl Jung was impressed with the sand tray method when he heard Lowenfeld present her technique at an international conference in 1937 (Mitchell and Friedman, 1994) Years later, Jung recommended the method to his student Dora Kalff who traveled to London to study extensively with Lowenfeld. Upon returning to Switzerland, Kalff adapted the Jungian principles of therapy to the sand tray process. Kalff then traveled to the United States during the 1960s to present her version of sand tray therapy, called "sandspiel," the German word for sandplay. She presented her methods primarily in California where the technique became quite popular as a Jungian-oriented method of therapy with clients of all ages including adults.

Lowenfeld (1979), however, did not limit the use of the sand tray to one theoretical orientation. She pointed out in her book that Freudians would easily see the sexual themes in sand tray worlds, Adlerians, the power complex. She also said Jungians would love the sand tray process because of its deep symbolic potential. Lowenfeld actually saw the sand tray both as a tool for healing and for doing research to understand how the minds of children really worked. She also believed it was an avenue of expression essential to the developing child. Thus, Lowenfeld brought to professional therapists a tool suitable for both the healing aspects of therapy and the ongoing diagnosis and research that are vital to therapeutic practice.

Therapeutic Rationale of Adolescent Sand Tray Therapy

In the context of individual and group therapy, the sand tray is helpful to adolescents in several ways. It helps them: (1) to work on the conflict of transitioning from childhood to adulthood, (2) to use nonverbal thinking processes, (3) to engage creativity and imagination to develop a sense of identity, and (4) in the context of group sand tray therapy, to work on peer relationships.

Transition from Childhood to Adulthood

Sand tray therapy invites and allows the young person to explore the world that lies between childhood and adulthood. Adolescence is a time of conflict between growing up and staying a child. Youngsters often bring to adolescence a number of unresolved childhood experiences, and yet they must move forward developmentally. In sand play, the adolescent can explore oncoming adult roles while simultaneously retreating toward the safety of childhood because the sand tray allows the builder to play simultaneously at more than one developmental stage.

In the Eriksonian stages of development (table 2.1), the primary task of adolescence is identity versus role confusion. If the adolescent has not accomplished earlier developmental tasks from prior stages it is difficult, and sometimes impossible, to work on identity issues. Regardless of age-appropriate stages and prior accomplishments, humans tend to move back and forth across the range of developmental tasks. For example, Jeffrey, eligible to be class valedictorian of his large urban high school, suddenly began to deteriorate academically. He lost interest in schoolwork and peer activities, and he began to feel depressed about a number of things. Jeffrey began to question his future and whether he even could succeed in college. In one of his sand

Table 2.1   Erikson's Developmental Stages and Developmental Tasks

Adolescence (twelve to eighteen): *Identity vs. Role Confusion*		
Physical Maturation Sexual Relationships Membership in Peer Groups Emotional Development Formal Operations		
Latency Age (six to twelve): *Industry vs. Inferiority*		
Friendship Concrete Operations Skill Learning Self-Evaluation Team Play		
Infancy (birth to two): *Trust vs. Mistrust*	**Toddlerhood** (two to four): *Autonomy vs. Shame and Doubt*	**Early School Age** (four to six): *Initiative vs. Guilt*

Social Attachment
Maturation of Sensory
  Perceptual and Motor
  Functions
Sensorimotor Intelligence
  and Primitive Causality
Understanding the Nature
  of Objects and Creation
  of Categories
Emotional Development
	Elaboration of Locomotion
	Fantasy Play
	Language Development
	Self-Control
		Sex-Role Identification
		Early Moral Development
		Self Theory
		Group Play

Note: After B. Newman and P. Newman, 1995.

play sessions, he created a world with a deep ravine separating a small village of children at a playground from a young man riding a horse along a ridge. Jeffrey expressed great sadness about the chasm between the village playground and the young man on the horse.

As he described his experience of the chasm that separated the boy from the village, Jeffrey began to talk about a similar chasm between himself and his older brother, George, who was in a great deal of trouble. His older brother dropped out of college a year earlier due to excessive use of drugs and irresponsible behavior. The parents were disappointed and very anxious about their oldest son. Growing up, Jeffrey and George had been very close. They did everything together, but during the sand tray session Jeffrey recounted that it was very painful for him now because George was distant and not much fun. Jeffrey worried that his academic achievements were creating even more distance between himself and George. Jeffrey felt guilty about his achievements in light of his brother's failures, and he felt isolated from his peers and family as the time approached for him to leave home for college.

Although it was clear that Jeffrey successfully resolved the earlier tasks of initiative versus guilt during his early school age, he needed to revisit this developmental task as he encountered his high school graduation, his academic honors, and his future success in college and adulthood. Could he claim his academic success or would he have to forego his success in order to regain closeness with his brother? Jeffrey was able to resolve the conflict quickly in therapy, but it was necessary for him to span the stages as he worked through his depression. In the sand tray he could bring in the earlier developmental stages (the playground) as he worked on his identity related to the young man on the horse. Sand tray play allows for this simultaneous expression of stages, ideas, feelings, historical periods, and so on. Everything relevant to the solution of a problem can be presented at one time, in one container, often with apparent ease. The disparate pieces come together at many levels, and thus, potential for integration is greatly enhanced.

NONVERBAL THINKING PROCESSES

Following her experiences in orphanages during and after World War I, Lowenfeld was convinced that trauma could not be expressed through words alone. She believed there was a region in the brain that did not obey the ordinary laws of reality. Even before science documented the function of the right hemisphere, Lowenfeld realized that the brain used a thinking process that did not depend on language. She was convinced of this because of her observations of children. She refuted the commonly held belief of her contemporaries that infants could not think or remember experiences since they did not have language. Lowenfeld recognized that there was a nonverbal thinking process and that humans recorded these nonverbal experiences as information to be accessed throughout the life span. She also understood that human experience, especially preverbal experiences, needed an avenue of expression that was not limited to words. When the children showed Lowenfeld how the sand tray worked, she saw it as a tool well suited to the expression of experience because of its multidimensional qualities.

When humans experience events, they do so through all of the senses simultaneously—sight, sound, smell, touch, and taste. It is not possible for the language system to convey these experiences adequately because language is linear; experiences are multidimensional. The sand tray incorporates color, tactile dimensions, relationships among objects, depth and height, seen and unseen, feelings, and many other dimensions all simultaneously. This capacity to process elements simultaneously is far closer to experience than the linearity of language. Thus, the nonverbal aspects of the sand tray are very useful in the therapy process to help adolescents explicate and integrate their life experiences.

CREATIVITY AND IMAGINATION IN IDENTITY FORMATION

Identity versus role confusion is a life-long task, but rarely is it more challenging than during adolescence. During this time of initiation into adulthood, adolescents must explore what fits and what does not fit as they move from childhood and family experiences into their own sense of self and what the future holds for them.

Adolescence is often a time of rebellion. Unfortunately, many adolescents have no means of envisioning the future, and so they are left with simply throwing off the past as they try to separate and individuate. This can create a void with ensuing despair and loss of identity. The sand tray is well suited as a container for these dramatic explorations, and it provides a means for developing a vision of the future. In the sand tray the adolescent can blow up, annihilate, and discard what they no longer need within the safety of well-contained play. However, they also can create what they do need. This destructive tendency of adolescents, if channeled properly, is crucial to clear the way for new life, to create new ground for a vision of what they want to become. Adolescents need avenues for creation of identity as they tear down parts of the old to rebuild the new. Play serves this purpose well. Play is a wonderful avenue for this revisioning process of adolescence. Since play is usually a time of relaxation, it allows the young person to concentrate effectively and efficiently on the reorganization process—rejecting what no longer works and creating what is needed now—without fear of failure, ridicule, blame, or criticism.

PEER RELATIONSHIPS IN GROUP SAND TRAY THERAPY

As age increases, adolescents spend more and more time with peers and less time with their parents and other family members. Peer-group membership does not replace the function of family attachment patterns or the adolescent's need for family closeness. Rather, peer groups serve to help adolescents extend their sense of belonging into the larger society through the development of meaningful peer-group relationships. In learning how they do or do not fit into particular peer groups, adolescents explore and refine questions of personal identity. They search for their belonging in the larger world beyond their personal families. With peers they test values, clarify commitments, explore status, power, cultural heritage, and a host of other things that help them to resolve questions of where they do or do not fit.

Group sand tray therapy allows adolescents to explore the questions of group identity, not only at the verbal level but also at the image-thinking level. Youngsters can often figure out how to connect with peers in a group sand tray process through use of images even when words have previously failed. For example, at the end of the school year a school social worker asked one group of five eighth-grade boys to build sand tray worlds about how it felt for them to leave middle school and move on to high school. Through their sand tray images the boys were able to visualize and then talk about their fears of moving on to high school. Through their shared images, they developed empathy for one another because they were able to visualize the common ground they held together. At the end of the session one boy said to another boy from a rival peer group, "It's not you I have a problem with. It's your group." Through their common play and their common vision, they could see that they were connected, not separated and alienated (personal communication, Romero, 2002).

It is not uncommon for adolescent group members to build actual bridges or connecting structures from one world to another when they are working in individual trays. After five or six group sessions of building in individual trays, they often request one larger sand tray where they can build as a community. Building in the community tray brings up challenges of sharing territory, negotiating themes, and deciding how to talk about what they have made. Frequently after building in the community tray, some of the group members will want to return to building in individual trays. This request provides opportunities for group decision making. In addition, it allows all the group members to flow back and forth between the desire for individuality and desire for group connection. When facilitators help adolescents to honor both individuality and group connection, it allows adolescents to see how their individuality is enhanced in the context of the larger community. They also see how the community benefits from the contribution of each individual member. This flow between group connection and individuality is very visible in the sand tray building process, and youngsters often use the visual contrast intelligently as they integrate "sense of self" within the larger community.

SAND TRAY METHOD

Professionals need to consider several things when implementing a sand tray program for adolescents: (1) organizing the sand tray apparatus so it is consistent with methodology and (2) acquiring the therapeutic skills of witnessing and processing sand tray building.

Sand Tray Apparatus

Following is a brief summary of sand tray equipment and supplies. Additional sources of information are readily available about the sand tray apparatus in books, journal articles, and from trainers.

Sand Trays Typically a sand tray is approximately 20 by 30 by 3 inches in size. The dimensions vary by a few inches from one orientation to the other, but it is important to design the tray so that the builder can see the entire surface of the sand tray without unnecessary head movement. These dimensions allow clients to have physical and visual control over the space by enabling them to reach all areas of the tray easily. This access is important to builders, especially to builders who have physical or sexual abuse issues or other trauma. Since traumatic events often leave victims with a sense of having lost control over their lives, it is essential to offer them ways to reestablish their sense of control. The miniaturized world of the sand tray, serving as a microcosm of the real world, affords builders the opportunities to reclaim mastery over their real life situations. For youngsters, a deeper tray—four to five inches—is helpful as they often become vigorous in their play, and the higher sides help to contain the sand. Some therapists object to a tray that is too deep because it can intimidate some clients who fear going too deep into their process.

Most therapists provide two trays, one wet and the other dry, so that builders have a choice. Some builders are averse to working with wet sand, and some get frustrated with the dry sand because it will not hold a shape. From a Jungian point of view, the wet and dry sand also have symbolic significance. The inside of the tray is painted blue to represent water on the bottom and blue sky on the sides.

Collection   The sand tray office contains a collection of small figurines including people (male, female, adults, babies, children, families, siblings, soldiers, religious figures, and so on), wild and domestic animals, insects, vegetation, fences, gates, bridges, buildings, transport (land, sea, and air), fantasy animals, fantasy people, outer space objects, symbols of the four elements (fire, earth, air, and water), and other miscellaneous objects. Natural objects such as rocks, shells, feathers, twigs, driftwood, and seedpods are also useful. Figures need to include a variety of colors, sizes, cultural heritage, and historical eras. Additionally art materials such as clay, paper, glue, and string, along with scissors and paints, provide the builder with possibilities for creating objects that are not available in the collection.

The collection of miniatures is usually arranged on shelves or in drawers or baskets in some logical order by categories. There is no standard method for arranging the miniatures, and therapists can exercise their own style and creativity. Lowenfeld organized her miniatures by categories in a cabinet with drawers. Many therapists use a combination of shelves and containers. Many books and articles on sand tray therapy explain how to build an appropriate collection. Catalogues, specific to sand tray therapists, are available, and most trainers provide these kinds of resources. A rule of thumb is to provide a good selection of the kind of objects representative of the world of the client. For example, adolescents who come in contact with cigarettes, drugs, and alcohol need to have figurines representing these kinds of experiences.

Sand   There are many sources of sand, both commercial and natural. Some sand, especially sand from building supply stores, may not be safe for play. Sand marked as "safe for children" or natural sand that comes from a known source are good choices. The tray is filled about half way with approximately thirty pounds of sand, depending on the size of the tray. There is some controversy about the color of sand suitable for therapy. Some therapists use only a neutral color while others like to offer a variety of colors. If there is limited space for only two trays, strong colors such as black or orange should be avoided since some people have aversions to these colors.

Group Space   Ample floor space is necessary to promote a good experience for adolescent group sand play. Cramped space makes it difficult for adolescents to move freely. Ideally, the room should be big enough to hold a large community tray, approximately five feet (a round or square container), and five or six individual trays that can be arranged in a circle or some other configuration that supports group cohesion.

THERAPEUTIC SKILLS

It is relatively easy to learn about the sand tray apparatus and to organize a sand tray area for clinics, schools, or hospitals. The more challenging task is acquiring the witnessing and processing skills required to do sand tray therapy effectively. Dora Kalff (1980) and Margaret Lowenfeld (1993/1979) both cautioned against the use of interpretation. Untrained therapists often assume, however, that interpretation is the crux of the sand tray method. Unfortunately, clients are hurt by this approach because it betrays the safe and protected space of play. Kalff was adamant that the therapist's primary role was creating a free and protected space for sand play therapy. Lowenfeld described the sand tray process in terms of energy. She believed that creative energy is activated during the building and processing of trays.

Although many therapists tend to follow either the Lowenfeld approach or the Kalff method, it is advantageous to integrate their ideas. When integrated, the sand tray serves as a container or a channel for the flow of creative energy that comes when the sand tray builder plays. The sand tray is a container at the physical level, and the therapist is an extension of the physical container at the psychological level. As a witness to the sand tray, the therapist must contain the play in the miniature world without judgment or efforts to control or interpret the play. The play itself is a form of energy. Sometimes the play is very destructive, violent, and provocative. It also can be tender, profound, and loving. Adolescents "play out" their life experiences, and the therapist's task is to hold whatever energy comes with equanimity and interest.

Holding the energy of adolescent play, both negative and positive, requires the therapist to work with transference and countertransference issues. In visual form, countertransference is often much stronger with sand tray images than it is in verbal therapy. The images of sand tray play can be a powerful way to communicate life experiences. For example, an adolescent who has experienced the trauma of sexual abuse can portray through sand tray images a very graphic scene that captures the pain and helplessness of being a victim. These kinds of scenes can touch and stimulate unresolved issues in the therapist. The therapist needs to know how to respond to this kind of material. Otherwise, an adolescent interprets the therapist's inability to contain the images as a rejection or a judgment, and in effect, a rejection of him or her.

When adolescents build sand trays, they use figurines to represent their experiences. In the sand tray building, they are free to explore the elements of their life experiences. They "try out" things, as adolescents must do, to see if they fit or not. They "play it" in miniature form. In the miniaturized version of their worldview they can, in a short time, with no harm to self or others, see what it would look like if their experiences were this way or that. They can play with danger, fear, love relationships, career, family, intimacy, self-image, ideals, future, culture, and all the other things that adolescents must deal with as they transition from childhood to adulthood.

The miniature world is a way for adolescents to create in external form the mental models by which they live their lives. A well-trained therapist can help adolescents contain and integrate the experiences they portray in their sand tray worlds. Through the process of these integrating experiences, youngsters can actually revise the mental models by which they live. The sand tray gives them a way of looking at who they are, and this is very helpful as they work on the developmental tasks of identity.

TRAINING RECOMMENDATIONS

Sand tray therapy sounds deceptively simple from its name. Therapists sometimes hear or read about the process and then proceed with using the technique without any training. At a minimum, training should include didactic contact hours with a qualified sand tray trainer, a personal experience of building trays with a qualified therapist, and supervision with several in-depth cases. Study of the history and origins of sand play, including both Lowenfeld and Kalff, and study of play behavior in general are also extremely helpful.

If the therapist wants to use the group sand play process with adolescents, it is essential to be trained in group sand play therapy also. Initial work with individual cases is good preparation for group work, but it is not a substitute for actual training in group sand tray therapy (DeDomenico, 1999). The therapist should also have personal experience as a group member in sand tray building before attempting facilitation of sand tray groups. Understanding the sand tray images and the witnessing process is complicated with individuals, and it is even more complicated with groups.

CONCLUSION

Providing a safe space for sand tray work is a challenge for the therapist whether it is individual therapy or group therapy. The environment of safety is essential for success. Once adolescents know they have a safe place, they will open up to the experience of sand tray play in remarkable ways.

Jennifer, an eighth grader, built a shimmering tray with gemstones and other shiny objects in the school counselor's office. Jennifer had a reputation for negative acting-out behavior at school and at home. When she finished her tray, she asked the counselor if Mr. Wilson, the school principal, was going to see her tray. The counselor replied quickly, "Oh no, this is confidential." Noting the young girl's disappointed look, the counselor asked, "Do you want the principal to see it?" Jennifer answered, "Yes." The counselor invited the principal in to look, and when he saw Jennifer's world, he said to her, "Wow, this is very bright." "Yes," Jennifer replied, "That's how I am inside. Hardly anybody sees it." Mr. Wilson replied, "Yes, I've seen that in you." Jennifer simply beamed.

Fortunately, the principal was receptive and nonintrusive. He thanked Jennifer for showing him her world. This event was crucial for this young lady. Her tray gave her a visual image of how she felt on the inside, and it gave her a way of communicating an aspect of herself that was difficult to show to most people because she was caught in her own reputation of being a negative, acting-out adolescent. Through having her "bright" world witnessed by important adults at her school, she was able to begin acting in ways that were more consistent with her positive qualities. Gradually she was able to release the negative acting out as she claimed more and more of her inner resilience (personal communication, Dickerman, 2002).

Adolescents appreciate the chance to use the sand tray modality. Some of them have to get by the obstacle of playing with toys, but once they do, they are astounding in their ability to resolve problems through creative play. Sand play helps to reduce the stigma often associated with adolescent therapy. Words can be embarrassing to an adolescent, and words can also retraumatize youngsters who have experienced various kinds of abuse. Most of the time adolescents will simply refuse to talk rather than engage in verbal communications that increase their sense of defectiveness. In contrast, play provides a safe distance from the reality of life experiences. It creates an environment free of anxiety where adolescents can address the most serious issues in a productive and vital manner. To the untrained therapist, this idea of a "safe distance from reality" seems counterproductive. For those who are trained, however, the protected place of sand tray play is a special environment unlike any other. Adolescents can use it intelligently, and they are very grateful for the opportunity to develop themselves through using the sand tray process.

REFERENCES

DeDomenico, G. 1999. Group sand tray-worldplay: New dimensions in sandplay therapy. In *The Handbook of Group Play Therapy: How To Do It, How It Works, Whom It's Best For*, ed. D. Sweeney and L. Homeyer, 215–33. San Francisco: Jossey-Bass Publishers.

Dickerman, L. E. 2002. Personal communication.

Erikson, E. 1968. *Identity, Youth and Crisis*. New York: Norton.

Kalff, Dora. 1980. *Sandplay: A Psychotherapeutic Approach to the Psyche*. Boston: Sigo Press.

Lowenfeld, M. 1939. *The World pictures of children: A method of recording and studying them*. *British Journal of Medical Psychology* 18(pt. 1): 65–101. Presented to the Medical Section of the British Psychological Society, March 1938. Reprinted (1988) in *Child Psychotherapy, War and the Normal Child*, ed., C. Urwin and J. Hood-Williams, 265–309. London: London Free Association Books.

———. 1979. *The World Technique*. London: George Allen and Unwin. Reprinted under the title, *Understanding Children's Sandplay*, by the Margaret Lowenfeld Trust, 1993.

Mitchell, R. R., and H. S. Friedman. 1994. *Sandplay: Past, Present and Future*. New York: Routledge.

Newman, B., and P. Newman. 1995. *Development through Life*. California: Brooks/Cole Publishing Company.

Romero, R. 2002. Personal communication.

Wells, H. G. 1911. *Floor Games*. London: Palmer. Reprinted 1976. New York: Arno Press.

Theraplay with Adolescents

Evangeline Munns

$\mathcal{A}$dolescents have often been regarded as a challenging population for mental health practitioners. It is widely recognized that the adolescent is in a state of transition from being a child to being an adult, often resulting in feelings of confusion, uncertainty, over and/or under reactions, unpredictability and a sense of being lost not only for the adolescent, but also for the parents who have to find ways of adapting to the changing status of their child. It is a time of withdrawal from parental control; a seeking of new ideals, values, and loyalties; and a striving to become their own unique selves. In this struggle adolescents often end up in conflict with their caretakers, teachers, and peers. In the normal situation, parents and children somehow weather this stormy period, but when there are long standing difficulties with the parent/child relationship as happens when there are earlier insecure attachments, then families often need a therapist's aid. When an adolescent is referred to a mental health practitioner, he/she frequently comes reluctantly and with resentment. Regardless of the treatment method used, the therapist will need three key ingredients: understanding, patience, and a sense of humor.

Theraplay offers a number of features that can be attractive for the adolescent—it emphasizes building up a child's self-esteem (adolescents need a lot of this)—it is nonverbal (child does not have to talk about his/her problems or feelings)—it enhances the parent/child relationship or attachment (most common referral problem), and it is engaging and playful (appealing to adolescents because it is fun).

The difficulties with Theraplay are there as well. In some activities there is a lot of physical contact—the therapist must move carefully and gently, respecting the child's "nos." The therapist must also be "in tune" and react appropriately to an adolescent's heightened state of sexual awareness. This usually calls for a modification of some activities and/or an exclusion of other activities that might be quite appropriate for a younger child, but not for an adolescent.

First, Theraplay will be described in its traditional form and then guidelines will be reviewed for working with adolescents. A case study of doing Theraplay with a thirteen year old will also be included.

WHAT IS THERAPLAY?

Theraplay is a form of play therapy that is structured (led by the therapist), short-term (usually lasting approximately eight sessions), and is applicable to a wide age range (from infants, preschoolers, latency-aged children, adolescents, adults to the elderly). Its primary purposes are to enhance parent/child attachment and/or relationships, improve the self-esteem of both child and parent, and to increase trust in others. It has been found helpful for a wide variety of personalities—from aggressive, acting out, impulsive children to inhibited, withdrawn, fearful children. It is particularly useful for those who have attachment and/or relationship issues typically found in adopted or foster care children, step-children, children who have come from orphanages, and autistic children.

Theraplay is a nonverbal form of treatment where problems are not discussed, bizarre behavior is ignored, and no interpretations are made, although reflections of how the child is feeling might be made. "Johnny you're looking a little sad today" (but no further, probing questions are asked). The focus is on the healthy, positive aspects of the client. There is an underlying belief that every child has a potential for inner healing and growth.

No toys are used. The emphasis is on interactions first between the therapist and the child and then the parents and child. Parents are actively involved, first as observers through a one-way mirror or in a corner of the room, with an accompanying interpreting therapist (if one is available). Later, (in the fourth or fifth session) parents participate directly with their child under the guidance of the therapist. [In our center the half-hour session of Theraplay is followed by a half hour of parent counseling]. Theraplay replicates normal parent-child interactions that are playful, physical, and fun.

THEORY

Theraplay is based on attachment theory. It is believed that the first relationship the child has is the most important one in his/her life because it forms the template for later relationships. If that relationship is not a strong or healthy one then all other relationships will be skewed in some way. Theraplay goes back to that first relationship and tries to make it more sound by replicating what a normal parent might do with a normal, young child. At times regressive activities are used, such as rocking the child in the therapist's or parent's arms while singing a special song about the child, lotioning or powdering his/her "hurts" on hands or feet, feeding the child potato chips, grapes, and the like, and sometimes even feeding the child with a baby bottle if it is felt that the attachment difficulty began in infancy. Theraplay goes back to the roots of connectedness and tries to make that connection a more positive and stronger one. Early perceptions and feelings are revisited in a caring and accepting atmosphere. As the child progresses emotionally, less regressive activities are used and more age-appropriate activities are included.

In Theraplay, there is an emphasis on building self-esteem of the child and the parent, therefore, both start feeling better about themselves and are then able to become more aware of each other and more in tune with each other's feelings and needs. The empathic responsiveness of the parent to the child's cues is especially essential to the child's changing view of himself as a valued, important human being and growing sense of being securely attached to his parents (Jernberg and Booth, 1999).

RESEARCH

There is considerable research regarding the importance of early attachment patterns to later social and emotional adjustment (Fonagy, 1994; Freeman and Brown, 2001; Karen, 1994; Lyons-Ruth, 1996; Main, Kaplan and Cassidy, 1989; Solomon, George, and DeJong, 1995). (For a thoughtful and analytical review see Goldberg [2000].) Research pertaining specifically to the influence of early attachment on later adolescent adjustment has been explored in relation to later problem-solving coping styles (Greenberger and McLaughlin, 1998); to identity development (Samuolis, Layburn and Schiaffino, 2001); to self-image (Dunlop, Burns and Bermingham, 2001; O'Koon, 1997); to self-esteem (Patterson, Pryor, and Field, 1997); and to depression and suicidal ideation (de Jong, 1992; DiFilippo and Overholser, 2000; Milne and Lancaster, 2001). Attachment patterns not only have long-lasting effects in the life-span of an individual, but also these patterns are often transmitted across generations (Zeanah, 1994; Zeanah and Zeanah 1989).

In Theraplay there is a lot of physical contact because early parent/child interactions are predominantly physical. As Dr. Clyde Ford (1993) states:

Early emotional life is physical, not verbal. We learn by being handled. Bonding, separating, feelings and needs and their fulfillment, are first experienced through the body. How, when, and why we are picked up, put down, held close, or pushed away determine the quality of our early emotional existence. . . . What we learn then, for better or worse, forms the template of our subsequent emotional life. . . . What we learn then governs the functional and dysfunctional patterns of our relationships as children, adults, and parents . . . and what we learn then, we learn through our body. (p. 22)

Research regarding the importance of physical contact is growing (Field, 1998; Field, 2000; Smith, Clance, and Imes, 1998) in regards to the physical, emotional, social, and intellectual development of the child and well-being of the adult. Moreover, internationally recognized clinicians working with sexually and physically abused children (James, 1994; Hindman, 1991) emphasize the importance of touch in the healing of these children. Psychobiologists conclude from their research, (Marcellus, 1998; Shore, 1998) that more attention needs to be paid to using nonverbal or preverbal methods of therapy in the treatment of traumatized, deprived, or poorly attached children, because the memories of trauma are stored in the more primitive parts of the brain and often not easily accessible to verbal or cognitive psychotherapies that depend on cortical or higher functioning parts of the brain. Theraplay is a nonverbal and preverbal method of therapy.

Although the clinical use of Theraplay is practiced around the world today (Munns, 2000), research using Theraplay is not extensive and clearly needs more studies. However, there has been some important research. Ritterfeld (1991), using Theraplay with language disabled children, found that those receiving Theraplay not only increased their social emotional scores significantly, but also increased their language scores significantly as compared to two control groups—one receiving traditional speech therapy and another receiving arts and crafts activities. Five other research studies (all accepted as Ph. D. thesis projects at accredited universities) used Theraplay with various populations: Bernt (2000) concentrated on failure-to-thrive clients; Rubin (2000) on homeless mothers and their children; Talen (2000) on at-risk preschool children attending a primary health unit; Martin (2000) and Zanetti, Matthews, and Hollingsworth (2000) on group Theraplay within school classrooms. Dr. Morgan (1989) using pre- and post-ratings of children in a clinic setting (no control group) found that two-thirds of her subjects improved in their self-confidence, self-esteem, cooperation, and trust after receiving Theraplay. Munns (1996) found, in two separate pilot studies (no control groups) using the Auchenbach child behavior checklist, that the aggressive factor significantly decreased in children receiving Theraplay.

MAIN DIMENSIONS OF THERAPLAY

After making hundreds of observations of normal parent-child interactions with their young children, Dr. Jernberg (1979), the founder of Theraplay, categorized these events under four main dimensions: Structure, Challenge, Engagement, and Nurture. A fifth dimension, Playfulness, was later added. These dimensions characterize normal parent-child relationships and guide the activities a therapist would use in doing Theraplay with troubled children of all ages. The specific dimension emphasized in the Theraplay session is dependent on the individual needs of the child. All activities with the children are done in a positive, playful manner. Games are often used that engage a child easily, but all have a clear underlying purpose.

Structure

In the traditional situation there is a regularity or a structure to a child's life such as regular meals, play and sleep times, rules regarding behavior of what is permitted or not permitted, and so forth. Parents structure the child's world so the child develops a sense of orderliness and predictability of life events and a sense of safety. The therapist preplans and structures the Theraplay session by leading it. Sessions have a definite beginning and end. The therapist purposefully introduces games where there are clear rules and guides the child and parents to follow those rules. Children who are impulsive, act out, and have poor inner controls as well as children who are "tyrants" at home, who come from chaotic backgrounds, or who have inner chaos (psychotics) need structure, and this dimension would be emphasized in their Theraplay sessions.

Challenge

Children ordinarily love challenge if it is offered in a way in which they can succeed. In the mastery of challenging activities, the child has to take some risk, but if successfully completed, the rewards are tangible. The child's self confidence and self-esteem grows. Parents challenge even the infant—to reach a little farther for that toy, to try to sit or walk alone. Challenges increase as the child becomes older. If this is done in a way in which the child does not experience repeated failures, then the child's sense of independence and personal achievement is strengthened. If the child has been pressured too early or too often, which frequently happens in our North American society where independence and achievement are strongly valued, then the child can feel overwhelmed and may withdraw or overcompensate. The clients coming to Theraplay vary—some need more challenge in their lives, but at an appropriate level (those who are timid, fearful, overprotected at home), and some need less (those who have too much challenge in their lives—the "super" or overachieving children). Challenging activities such as thumb or arm wrestling, hopping or running races, paper punching, and so forth are also tension releasing and are sometimes used with aggressive children to "let off steam." Challenging activities are recommended for withdrawn, fearful, overprotected children or those who are very rigid in their ways (autistic children).

Engagement

Most parents have the ability to engage their children in many delightful and joyful ways. The mother may play "Peek-a-boo" or "Pat-a-cake" with her young child. The father may lift the child up high and then down to touch noses in a "hello-goodbye" game. The child likely responds with excited giggles. In these engaging games there is often intrusion into the child's space, but it is done in a manner that is enjoyable to the child. The parent must be attuned to what the child finds pleasurable or not pleasurable and be guided by the child's cues. The child learns more about himself or herself and body boundaries. In Theraplay the therapist playfully engages the child in a variety of activities that are full of fun and surprises and so the child learns not to fear change—that instead the unknown can be a source of adventure and excitement. Children who are withdrawn, defensive, rigid or avoidant, or those who protect themselves from any kind of intrusion can benefit from engagement. Engaging activities must be carefully geared to the child's responsiveness, especially when working with abused children. The therapist must stop and/or modify the activities honoring the child's "nos" or signals of reluctance or fear.

Nurture

All children need nurturing. Parents show their love and caring through the nurturance of their children. From the gentle handling that a newborn needs, to feeding, bathing, powdering, lotioning, rocking, cradling, caressing, kissing, soothing, singing, and hugging the child in ways that give the child the message that he or she is cherished. These experiences build an inner representation of being important and valued. In Theraplay nurturing activities are given to all children, but it has been found that the aggressive, tough, "macho" adolescent who acts out and finds himself or herself in trouble in most areas of his life at home, school, and with peers, is often the child who needs the most nurturing. However, nurturance may be resisted by these very same children as being too "babyish," so the skills of the therapist are truly tested in finding ways of nurturing that are acceptable to the child. This is true as well of the "pseudomature" child or the parentified child who will often want to "take care" of the therapist rather than the other way round.

Appropriate Subjects

As previously stated, Theraplay is appropriate for all ages—from infants to the elderly. It has been used for a wide range of difficulties—from the acting out child to the withdrawn child. In addition to being helpful for children with attachment or relationship issues, it has also been used with suicidal and homicidal children, obsessive-compulsive children, psychotic children, autistic children, learning and/or physically disabled children, and developmentally challenged children. Theraplay is particularly suited for children with attachment issues such as adopted and foster children. Sexually abused or physically abused children have also been helped by theraplay, but activities usually have to be modified for them and the therapist has to be especially sensitive to their cues and respond in a respectful fashion so the child feels empowered. Parents who have difficulty managing their "tyrant" children have also benefited from Theraplay.

Inappropriate Subjects

Children who recently have been traumatized or abused need time to recuperate. A child who has been traumatized because of a loss of a family member or a close friend needs time to grieve. Children having had recent surgery or serious illness need quiet time to heal. The exuberance and fun of theraplay may be appropriate at a later date. More traditional forms of play therapy such as nondirective play therapy should be attempted first. After they have formed some trust with the therapist, the nurturing part of Theraplay that they so desperately need can be offered slowly and gently. These children need to be desensitized to physical touch or their complete healing will not take place (Hindman, 1991; James, 1994). Theraplay offers a safe way of achieving this since there is caring, appropriate physical contact in many of the activities. However, the timing and nature of contact has to be carefully considered.

FORMAT FOR FAMILY THERAPLAY

In the first session the child's thorough developmental and family history is taken along with the parent's own childhood history. The parents' marital relationship is also discussed. Family interactions are assessed in the second session using the Marschak Interaction Method (MIM), which consists of a series of simple standardized tasks that the parents perform with the child under the observation of the therapist through a one-way mirror or from a corner of the room (Di Pasquale, 2000). These interactions are videotaped (with previous written consent from the parents) and on the third session, a video feedback is given to the parents with visual examples showing strengths and problem areas of the family. Goals are formulated and agreed upon with the parents. An initial verbal contract is established for eight Theraplay sessions with an option for additional sessions if needed. Another MIM is sometimes given at the end to help evaluate treatment changes. Four checkups during the year are also included. Because the treatment plan is very clear right from the beginning and positive changes often occur quickly, the attendance rate of the clients is usually very high.

As previously mentioned, parents observe the first three or four sessions through a one-way mirror or corner of the room (with an interpreting therapist if one is available) while the therapist interacts with the child. During this period parents start seeing their child in a new light especially since the therapist is modeling new positive interactions with their child and focusing on his/her positive attributes. Usually during the fourth session (and subsequent sessions) the parents observe the start of the session for five to ten minutes then come into the room and join the therapist and the child in relaxing, fun activities that are enjoyable for everyone. Gradually the direction of the activities is given to the parents in later sessions —for instance, "hey, Mom, could you lead us in the game "Simon Says?" (a game that the mother would have observed in previous sessions). The therapist coaches and supports the parent in leading the activity so that everyone follows the rules. Parents are asked to do "homework" with their child and adopt the activities they are comfortable with into weekly Theraplay sessions at home. Very often, when parents are asked a week in advance to lead two or three activities of their choosing for the next session, they will practice these activities at home first and thus generalization of what is happening in the clinical setting is transferred to the home setting.

At the end of the treatment sessions a party is planned where favorite activities are included, party hats are exchanged, parents bring their child's favorite foods, and souvenirs from sessions (body outline, powder handprints, etc.) are given along with a small present from the therapist to the child. The last session is treated as a celebration of the child's growth. An appointment is made for the final MIM and feedback (this is optional). An appointment for the first checkup is also made. The checkup is similar to a Theraplay session and is usually scheduled one or two months after the MIM feedback. If additional services might be needed, this is discussed before the last Theraplay session. (Note that additional measures of pre- and post-treatment changes are often used besides the MIM, such as the Parenting Stress Index, etc.).

If the parents are unable to participate in Theraplay then the child can still benefit from Theraplay. However, parents are included whenever possible so that generalization of positive changes in the child can take place within the home more easily. If the child is institutionalized or placed within foster care, then a residential staff member or foster parents can be included. Theraplay is a relationship-based treatment method. Its purpose is not only to have the child learn to relate to the therapist (who in essence is modeling for the parent) but mainly for parents and child to relate more positively to each other.

The agenda for each session is preplanned and follows a format where the child is welcomed warmly and then quickly engaged into the room. A definite beginning (such as a welcome song or rap or a creative handshake) starts the session followed by an inventory or checkup of the child's positive features (for instance, "I see you've brought your sparkly blue eyes, your nice curly hair, your rosy cheeks, and I see you have some freckles"—therapist might count the freckles, etc.). This can be followed by a powdering or lotioning of the child's "hurts" (bruises, scratches, etc.) on the hands or feet of the child. The therapist leads the other activities focusing on structuring, challenging, engaging, or nurturing activities depending on the child's needs. Feeding the child some kind of snack (chips, pretzels, grapes, etc.) is always included because some form of nurturing is unquestionably a part of every session for every child. There is a mixture of activities that involve close contact versus giving the child space and allowing large movement activities. Boisterous and calm activities, as well as cooperative and competitive ones are balanced, depending again on the child's needs. There is a definite end to the session with a simple closing song.

The Theraplay session is often followed by one-half hour of parent counseling (this is optional). If the child is old enough he/she can be included in the counseling. The Theraplay session is discussed with the parents, along with information regarding the child's progress at home and school. Homework Theraplay activities are discussed as well.

WORKING WITH THE ADOLESCENT

A number of general guidelines need to be remembered when working with the adolescent:

1. Keep the session structured—add more activities where there are clear rules. This is especially true for acting out, impulsive adolescents.

2. Add more challenging activities—this is often needed to maintain the interest of the adolescent. However, the therapist must balance the difficulty of the activity so that the client can feel success most of the time, but not feel the activity is so easy that it is devalued. Adolescents need to "save face," so they don't take kindly to failure and their frustration tolerance can be low. On the other hand, they love to "prove themselves," so the right amount of challenge can be intriguing to them.

3. Sexual awareness is heightened for the adolescent, therefore, physical contact can be easily misconstrued into having sexual overtones even though the therapist has been very circumspect and proper in his/her actions. Some conditions help such as: The therapist's gender should usually be the same as that of the adolescent. Having an older therapist can make things easier. Avoid (or modify) activities that may be too intimate—for example, do not have a young, attractive female therapist cradle a male adolescent, instead let the parents do this. In any activity, avoid going near erogenous zones (this is true for all clients). Be respectful of the client's feelings and occasionally monitor their comfort level by asking: "Is this okay for you?" or "Are you comfortable?"

4. Videotape all sessions if possible. Get written permission from the parents for videotaping. This helps to safeguard the therapist from being falsely accused of inappropriate touch.

5. Be honest and straightforward. Therapists have a much better chance of being accepted and trusted if they are genuine in what they say and do.

6. Adolescents need acceptance and praise, but don't "overdo" it because they generally recognize and won't accept false praise.

7. Be patient, use humor, and give a sense of accepting them. Adolescents often come in a hostile mood, ready to reject everything. Try to give them the feeling that you accept them as they are—including their feelings of anger.

8. Be prepared. Adolescents may reject the very thing they need most—nurturance. Attempting to nurture a child who is emotionally a "baby" inside, but has a "pseudo-adult" manner and appearance can test the skills of the most seasoned therapist. The therapist often has to modify the activity so the adolescent can accept it—that is, the client may not want his "hurts" to be powdered deeming this

as too "babyish." The therapist never forces this, but simply finds an activity that is still nurturing, but more acceptable. In one option the therapist may say, "I think I can tell your fortune. (Therapist takes child's hand.) I'm going to put some powder on the palm of your hand so the lines are clearer. Okay, now this is what I see." (Therapist proceeds to create a positive fortune for the child.) The main intent of this activity was to nurture the child through powdering his hand. (For the child, it is the fortune he wants to hear.) After similar activities like this one—powdered hand prints, tracing letters or numbers on the powdered palm of a child, and so on—the adolescent learns that having his hands touched can be a positive experience and then allows his "hurts" to be taken care of. He has learned that touch can be safe and bring a sense of comfort.

9. Be confident, "upbeat," and full of surprises and fun. If the adolescent picks up on the therapist's anxiety it will only add to the child's own fears, and resistance is likely to increase.

10. "Stick with it." The adolescent will probably resist somewhere during treatment (most often near the beginning). Use redirection, paradox, humor, and be creative in finding something that will engage the client. The adolescent needs to feel that the therapist will be supportive no matter how much resisting he does. Often an adolescent will come into treatment after parents, teachers, and others have "given up" and have dismissed him as a "bad kid." The adolescent often has adopted this perception of himself as well. The therapist tries to turn this around by seeing and commenting on the positive qualities of the client. The adolescent must feel the therapist's hope for positive change—the belief in his potential to grow and heal and that the therapist will not give up on him.

11. Learn their "language" and idioms to minimize misunderstandings.

12. Don't allow any physical hurts and don't get into any physical power struggles. If there is any attempt of physical aggression, immediately stop the action by saying "no hurts—in this room we do not hurt each other" (in a firm, definite tone). The therapist then redirects the adolescent so the situation is defused. However, if the client continues to try to be physically aggressive then the session is stopped. "We'll try again next time, but this session is ended!" [Note: The author happens to be a small woman, and in her thirty-five years of working with children she has been kicked only once—by a four-year-old autistic child—and she has never had to end a session because of a child's aggression.]

CASE STUDY: THERAPLAY
WITH AN ADOLESCENT

Although he was only thirteen years old, Ricky was the tallest boy in a residential setting for emotionally troubled children. He was placed in residence because his single mother could not manage him and was afraid of his hostility. Ricky's mother was divorced and disclosed that she had left her marriage because her husband was alcoholic and had been physically and verbally abusive. Ricky had observed this abuse and had learned to verbally abuse his mother. At times he would also be physically aggressive with her. When Ricky was four he had been separated from his mother for about one-and-a-half years because his mother had fled from her husband's violence. When she came back for her son, the husband had not allowed access. After prolonged court proceedings, a joint-custody agreement was reached. The agreement allowed Ricky to live with his mother and maternal grandmother and have regular visits with his father and father's girlfriend.

In residence Ricky could become explosive to the point of kicking holes in the walls. His violent reactions were major concerns for his mother and delayed any plans for Ricky to come back home. Ricky was doing reasonably well in school, and he was of average intelligence. During his second year in residence, he was referred for Theraplay.

After taking a thorough history, the Marschak Interaction Method was administered. Ricky and his mother performed twelve standardized tasks that were observed and videotaped. The video was replayed with mother in the following session, giving her feedback on the strengths and weaknesses in her interactions with her son. Mutual goals were formulated. The Marschak revealed a child and mother who were tense and uncomfortable with each other. In spite of mother's valiant efforts to engage her son, Ricky was so unmotivated and uncooperative that he almost brought his mother to tears. She contained herself but did state, "I can't do this anymore." Ricky realized he had brought his mother to the limit of her endurance, and then he started to be more cooperative. During the rest of the Marschak both started to relax more, and in the end, mother and son were actually starting to enjoy each other. Both showed a potential for being in tune and responsive with each other's needs. However, his mother tended to be achievement oriented and put some pressure on her son to be successful.

Goals in Theraplay

1. To boost self-esteem for both child and mother
2. Help mother to accept her son unconditionally, as her expectations

for his good behavior and school achievement were unrealistically high

3. Help mother to structure and manage her son
4. Help mother to be more nurturing
5. Enhance the positive attachment between mother and her son

A verbal contract for eight Theraplay sessions was agreed upon. Toward the end of the first cycle of eight sessions the therapists and mother felt that another eight sessions would help to consolidate their gains. The agendas were always preplanned each week, keeping the previous goals in mind along with any other needs that came to the fore. A typical session during the beginning, middle, and end of therapy is outlined below.

Session 1   In the first session Ricky came in nonchalantly, wearing dark sunglasses, a leather jacket and sporting the latest hair cut. He gave the sophisticated air of the "cool dude." He cooperated with activities but maintained an emotional distance. His mother observed through a one-way mirror with an interpreting therapist.

Session 2
>   Entrance: Follow the leader.
>   Welcome: A short welcome song.
>   Inventory: Comments on Ricky's color of hair and eyes, nice, strong shoulders. His height and arm span were measured and found to be equal in length. His smile was measured.
>   Powder Hurts: Cuts and scratches were gently powdered on his hands.
>   Cottonball guess: (therapist touches spots on his face head, hands, and feet while Ricky has his eyes closed and guesses where he is being touched with a cotton ball).
>   Cottonball blow: Lying on the floor face down and looking at each other, therapist and Ricky blow cottonballs to each other, each trying to keep the balls in the other person's area.
>   Cottonball fight: Therapist and Ricky face each other in a sitting position while throwing as many balls as they can at each other.
>   Cottonball Soothe: Therapist moves a cotton ball around on Ricky's face commenting on his special features.
>   Tracing patterns on back and back-rub: Therapist outlines shapes, letters, and numbers with his finger on Ricky's back while Ricky guesses what the shapes are. The therapist rubs Ricky's back in between the shape outlines.
>   Paper punch and basketball throw: The therapist holds a newspaper

sheet tautly while Ricky punches a fist through the paper—tearing it in half. This is repeated until there are a number of pieces of paper that are then crunched into small balls which Ricky throws into a loop made by the therapist's arms.

Feeding of Chips: Therapist places a chip, one at a time into Ricky's mouth, commenting on the crunching noises he is making.

Goodbye Song: "Goodbye Ricky, Goodbye Ricky, Goodbye Ricky, we're glad you came to play."

Ricky became more animated in this session particularly with the tension releasing activities where he could get rid of some of his aggression in an acceptable manner. He was intrigued that the span of his arms equaled his height. He liked the comments regarding his strong shoulders, although he tended to shrug off any compliments. He allowed his "hurts" on his hands to be powdered and looked interested. He came to life in the challenging activities such as cottonball blow and fight. He was a little bit uncomfortable with cottonball soothe, but tolerated it. He really enjoyed paper punch and basketball throw and started "showing off" with his prowess in throwing. He appeared neutral to tracing of shapes on his back, but cooperated. He liked eating the chips, but was still uncomfortable with the idea of someone feeding him.

The past week had been a rough one for Ricky. He had been physically restrained several times in the residence, and the tentative plans for visits home were put on hold.

Session 5 Mother joins in this session as she had in session four.

Entrance: Enter as your favorite animal.

Welcome song: Ricky and mother created a rap song that they taught to the therapists.

Inventory: Notice special features of Ricky—mom comments as well.

Play-Doh trophies: Therapist and mom make Play-Doh impressions of Ricky's fingers, hands, and ears.

Lotion hurts: Mom helps to lotion Ricky's hurts on his hands.

Barber Shop: While Ricky sits on a chair in front of a mirror, mom and therapists comb his hair and "shave" him using hot towels, shaving cream, and popsicle sticks for shaving.

Feather blow: Participants lie down on their backs with their heads touching while therapist drops a small feather in the air which they try to keep up in the air by blowing hard.

Licorice race: Mom holds an end of a licorice string in her mouth and

Ricky holds the other end in his mouth. On the word "go," both try to eat the licorice as fast as possible meeting in the middle where they touch noses.

Peanut-butter-jelly: Leader says "peanut-butter," and group mirrors back "jelly" in whatever tone, pitch, or speed of voice that leader used.

Feed Chips: Mother helps in feeding of chips, but she gets fed as well.

Goodbye song

Mother and son had a good session—nice positive feelings and spontaneous affection between them. There was a lot of nurturing in the barbershop activity during which Ricky just sat back and took it all in. Mom fully participated under the coaching of the therapists. Everyone really laughed while engaged in the feather blow game and was quite relaxed during and accepting of the intimacy of the licorice race.

Ricky's first home visit went well. Ricky was generally cooperative, and there were no aggressive incidents. Mom worried about how much freedom she should allow Ricky to visit with neighborhood friends while on home visits. This was explored with her.

Session 7

Entrance: Leapfrog in.

Welcome song: The rap song that mother and Ricky had created in a previous session was sung again.

Inventory: Comment on special features, measure length of arm and compare to length of leg, and so on.

Lotion hurts.

Family portrait of powder handprints: Mom and son powder each other's hands, make handprints, and compare handprints.

Clap patterns: Leader claps a sequence that others imitate; each time creating longer sequences of clap patterns. Leader also gradually includes touching body parts of neighbor—for example, clap hands together, touch shoulder of neighbor, and then clap hands together again.

Three-legged race: Mom and Ricky tie legs together and put arms around each other and pretend to race.

Food preferences: Ricky sits in mother's lap with eyes closed while mom feeds various pieces of food—such as raisins, candy, bread, pretzel, grapes, and the like, Mother then guesses what child likes best from the expression on his face.

Rock in Blanket: Ricky is rocked in a blanket held by therapists and mother while everyone sings a special song about him—"Rock-a-bye Ricky in the tree-top . . ."

Cradle in arms with lollipop and sing special song: Mother sits against a wall while cradling son in her arms and feeding Ricky a lollipop. Therapists help her sing a special song about him.

Feed chips.

Goodbye song

Ricky cooperated well. There was increased eye contact with his mother and more smiles and laughter. In food preferences Ricky sat in his mother's lap and happily cuddled in. Both mother and son were attuned to each other. Ricky loved being rocked in the blanket and later said this was his favorite activity. He seemed very content in his mother's arms sucking a lollipop that she held for him.

In the parent counseling session the therapists and mother decided that another cycle of eight sessions would be beneficial. Although Ricky and mother were making good progress in the Theraplay sessions, he was still being defiant during home visits.

The next eight sessions went very well, with full cooperation from Ricky and excellent attendance. He was always glad to see the therapists and looked forward to his special time with his mother. Therapists encouraged his mother to try Theraplay activities at home, but she did not do so consistently. For a while it seemed that Ricky would be able to go home permanently. However, every time that date came near, mother would change her mind due to fear that Ricky would return to his former unmanageable behavior. Ricky would feel betrayed and would act out, justifying mom's fears. The therapists confronted mother with this sequence of events and explored why she was so reluctant to have Ricky return home when he was showing good behavior in the residence and at school. Mother revealed that the situation at home was not ideal—the maternal grandmother was alcoholic. Discussion centered on mother's issues at home and also that her fear of her husband's previous abuse might be projected on to her son. Her unrealistic expectations for perfect behavior before Ricky came back home were also discussed. At the end of Theraplay, mother and son felt closer in their relationship, and their affection and enjoyment of each other had increased. Mother was able to structure and limit Ricky more effectively. Ricky was showing a lot more control over his impulses and anger. Check-ups indicated that Ricky and his mother fluctuated in their progress, but their positive relationship continued to be strong enough that Ricky remained at home and his school progress was satisfactory and at grade level.

REFERENCES

Bernt, C. 2000. Theraplay with failure-to-thrive infants and mothers. In *Theraplay: Innovations in Attachment-Enhancing Play Therapy*, ed. E. Munns, 117–37. Northvale, NJ: Jason Aronson.

DeJong, M. 1992. Attachment, individuation, and risk of suicide in late adolescence. *Journal of Youth and Adolescence* 21(3): 357–72.

DiFilippo, J., and J. Overholser. 2000. Suicidal ideation in adolescent psychiatric inpatients as associated with depression and attachment relationships. *Journal of Clinical Child Psychology* 29(2): 155–66.

Di Pasquale. 2000. The Marschak Interaction Method. In *Theraplay: Innovations in Attachment Enhancing Play Therapy*, ed. E. Munns, 27–51. Northvale, NJ: Jason Aronson.

Dunlop, R., A. Burns, and S. Bermingham. 2001. Parent-child relations and adolescent self-image following divorce: A ten-year study. *Journal of Youth and Adolescence* 30(2): 117–34.

Field, T. 1998. Massage therapy effects. *American Psychologist* 53: 1270–81.

———. 2000. *Touch Therapy*. New York: Churchill Livingston.

Fonagy, P. 1994. Crime and attachment: representation of attachment relationships in a severely personality disordered prisoner group. Paper presented at the International Conference on Attachment and Psychopathology, Toronto, Ontario, October.

Ford, C. W. 1993. *Compassionate Touch: The Role of Human Touch in Healing and Recovery*. New York: Simon and Schuster.

Freeman, H., and B. Brown. 2001. Primary attachment to parents and peers during adolescence: Differences by attachment style. *Journal of Youth and Adolescence* 30(6): 653–74.

Goldberg, S. 2000. *Attachment and Development*. London: Arnold.

Greenberger, E., and C. S. McLaughlin. 1998. Attachment, coping, and explanatory style in late adolescence. *Journal of Youth and Adolescence* 27(2): 121–38.

Hindman, J. 1991. *The Mourning Break*. Ontario, OR: Alexandria Associates.

James, B. 1994. *Handbook for the Treatment of Attachment—Trauma Problems in Children*. New York: Lemington.

Jernberg, A. 1979. *Theraplay*. San Francisco: Jossey-Bass.

Jernberg, A., and P. Booth. 1999. *Theraplay: Helping Parents and Children Build Better Relationships Through Attachment-based Play*, 2nd ed. San Francisco: Jossey-Bass.

Karen, R. 1994. *Becoming Attached*. New York: Warner.

Lyons-Ruth, K. 1996. Attachment relationships among children with aggressive behavior problems: The role of disorganized early attachment patterns. *Journal of Consulting and Clinical Psychology* 64(I): 64–73.

Main, M., N. Kaplan, and J. Cassidy. 1989. Security in infancy, childhood and adulthood: A move to the level of representation. In *Growing Points in Attachment Theory and Research*, ed. J. Bretherton and E. Waters, 66–106. *Monographs of the Society for Research in Child Development* 50(29).

Marcellus, J. 1998. The Neurodevelopmental sequalae of child maltreatment: Implications for assessment and treatment. Paper presented at the Post Conference Institute of the Long Shadows of Trauma Conference, Toronto, Canada, November.

Martin, D. 2000. Teacher-led theraplay in early childhood classrooms. In *Theraplay: Innovations in Attachment Enhancing Play Therapy*, ed. E. Munns, 321–37. Northvale, NJ: Jason Aronson.

Milne, L., and S. Lancaster. 2001. Predictors of depression in female adolescents. *Adolescence* 36(142): 208–22.

Morgan, C. 1989. Theraplay: An evaluation of the effect of short-term structured play on self-confidence, self-esteem, trust and self-control. Unpublished research, York Centre for Children, Youth and Families, Richmond Hill, Ontario.

Munns, E. 1996. Theraplay and the aggressive factor. Unpublished research, Blue Hills Child and Family Services, Aurora, Ontario.

———. 2000. *Theraplay: Innovations in Attachment-Enhancing Play Therapy*. Northvale, NJ: Jason Aronson.

O'Koon, J. 1997. Attachment to parents and peers in late adolescence and their relationship with self-image. *Adolescence* 32(126): 471–82.

Patterson, J., J. Pryor, and F. Field. 1997. Adolescent attachment to parents and friends in relation to aspects of self-esteem. *Journal of Youth and Adolescence* 24(3): 365–76.

Ritterfeld, U. 1991. Theraplay and Language Disabled Children. Austria: Ph.D. Thesis at Heidelberg University, personal communication.

Rubin, P. 2000. Multifamily theraplay groups with homeless mothers and children. In *Theraplay: Innovations in Attachment Enhancing Play Therapy*, ed. E. Munns, 211–34. Northvale, NJ: Jason Aronson.

Samuolis, J., K. Layburn, and M. Schiaffino. 2001. Identity development and attachment to parents in college students. *Journal of Youth and Adolescence* 30(3): 373–84.

Shore, A. 1998. Early trauma and the development of the right side of the brain. Paper presented at the Conference on the Long Shadows of Trauma, Toronto, Ontario, November.

Smith, E., P. Clance, and S. Imes, eds. 1998. *Touch in Psychotherapy*. New York: Guilford.

Solomon, J., C. George, and A. DeJong. 1995. Children classified as controlling at age six: Evidence of disorganized representational strategies and aggression at home and at school. *Development and Psychopathology* 7: 447–63.

Talen, M. 2000. Using theraplay in primary health care centers: A model for pediatric care. In *Theraplay: Innovations in Attachment Enhancing Play Therapy*, ed. E. Munns, 339–61. Northvale, NJ: Jason Aronson.

Zanetti, J., C. Matthews, and R. Hollingsworth. 2000. Adults and children together (ACT): A prevention model. In *Theraplay: Innovations in Attachment Enhancing Play Therapy*, ed. E. Munns, 257–75. Northvale, NJ: Jason Aronson.

Zeanah, C. 1994. Intergenerational Transmission of relationship psychopathology: A mother-infant case study. Paper presented at the International Conference on Attachment and Psychopathology. Toronto, Ontario, September.

Zeanah, C., and P. Zeanah. 1989. Intergenerational Transmission of maltreatment: Insights from attachment theory and research. *Psychiatry* 52: 171–96.

· *4* ·

Activity Filial Therapy with Adolescents
Christopher J. Brown

$\mathscr{B}$ernard and Louise Guerney created filial therapy in the 1960s (Guerney, 1964) to facilitate the emotional growth of emotionally disturbed children by enhancing the parent-child relationship. Parents were trained in child-centered play therapy skills to have special play time with their children. The Guerneys were not the first to utilize a playtime between a parent and a child for therapeutic value. As early as 1909, Freud (1959) instructed the father of "Little Hans" in conducting play times with his child. Freud successfully treated the young boy's phobias through teaching the father to develop quality play times at home.

One of the earliest examples of the application of child-centered play therapy principles and skills to a parent-child relationship was Natalie Rogers Fuchs' (1957) work with her daughter who was having difficulty with toilet training. Fuchs was instructed by her father, Carl Rogers, via mail during the period she had play times with her daughter. Fuchs' play times with her daughter eventually resulted in an alleviation of the toilet training problem.

Guerney's introduction of filial training (1964) represented a departure from previous models of parent training. Filial therapy training included an emphasis on play times and supervision. As in the case of other forums of parent training, filial therapy training utilized regular group training and didactic instruction from a professional. However, in other parent training models, parents did not share their experience in a support group format, parents were not taught relationship skills that focused on the child's play communication, nor were parents taught to respond to children in a way that allows them to solve their own problems (Landreth, 1991).

THERAPEUTIC RATIONALE

The rationale underlying filial therapy training is explained in the eleven tenets laid out by Guerney (1964): (1) All maladjustment in the life of the child should be understood in the perspective of relationships that the child is engaged in. Patterns of conflict have been engendered to this child through these family relationships. (2) Two traditional paths have existed in treating childhood emotional problems: individual therapy with the child, or family therapy/consultation including the parents and child. Change is sought in the network of the child's life that influenced and reinforced maladjusted patterns. (3) The primary considerations of change in the child's life are permissiveness and understanding, either on the part of the therapist in an individual setting, or by the parents in a family setting. (4) In the filial model the parents are not only inspired to be helped, but can actually be of help. (5) Parents can be expected to learn the role of play therapist for their child reasonably well. (6) The process of learning the skills of play therapy often provides parents with insight into personal issues that they were not aware of previously. (7) The process, even for a short time, of changing roles can serve to weaken old dysfunctional roles by the parent. (8) The parent can gain a much greater understanding of the child in the process of practicing special play times with the child. (9) The attention by the parent to the child can prove to be therapeutic, even if for a short period of time. (10) The role of the parent as therapist will multiply the weight of therapeutic progress for both the child and parent as well as for the child-parent relationship. (11) The lessons of filial therapy can serve the parent long after formal therapy has ended. Basically the tenets of filial therapy rest on the assumption that the parent, if able to learn the skills of child-centered play therapy, can be infinitely more effective than a therapist attempting to perform the same function.

According to Guerney (1964) the nature of the play session seeks to: change the child's perceptions or misperceptions of the parent's feelings, attitudes, or behavior toward the child; allow the child to communicate thoughts, needs, and feelings to parents that have previously been kept from the parents; and bring the child a greater sense of self-respect, self-worth, and confidence.

Landreth (1991) developed a condensed ten-week filial therapy training model based on Guerney's (1964) filial model. Landreth suggested that filial therapy training enhances parents' sensitivity to their child as they learn how to create a nonjudgmental, understanding, and accepting environment through which a child is able to explore new aspects of self and new ways of relating to their parents. This training takes place in a small group of up to six to eight parents in which the skills and application of child-centered play therapy principles are taught through discussion, videotape, demonstration, and role-playing.

According to Stover and Guerney (1967) there are several advantages to the use of filial therapy training with parents. Utilizing filial therapy with parents and children is the most effective use of the professional counselor's time. Parental fears and rivalry that might develop as the child bonds with the therapist and withdraws from a parent are reduced in filial therapy training. Parental guilt, commonly associated with resorting to an outside professional for help in dealing with a child's problems, is reduced in filial therapy because the parent is trained to become the agent of change in the child's life. Another benefit is that the parent develops appropriate responses to new child behavior patterns and avoids problems that might otherwise be aroused had the parent not been prepared by filial therapy training.

Van Fleet (1994) identified three central constructs in the practice and application of filial therapy. She suggested that filial therapists must recognize the value of play in childhood and acknowledge play as the primary avenue for understanding children's worlds. Van Fleet also believed that filial therapists must also trust that parents are able to learn the skills of filial therapy. If the filial therapist does not believe in the parent's ability, then it is unlikely that the parent will ever achieve understanding and mastery of the skills of conducting play times with a child. Finally, she maintained that filial therapists prefer an educational model to a biological and behavioral model when interviewing and evaluating children and families. Van Fleet identified the central goals of filial therapy as: (a) eliminate presenting problems at their source; (b) develop positive interactions between parents and their children; and (c) increase families' communication, coping, and problem-solving skills so they are better able to handle future problems independently and successfully.

RESEARCH IN FILIAL THERAPY

Stover and Guerney (1967) utilized filial therapy training with mothers and found a significant increase in the observed frequency of reflective statements and a decrease in directive statements. Positive change in the parent-child relationship and the child's general emotional development was supported by self-report. This study did not use a control group. Oxman (1972) utilized the data from Stover and Guerney (1967) as an experimental group and matched a volunteer control group on demographic data. Statistical analysis revealed that the treatment group made significantly greater enhancement in their children's behavior.

Using the filial model set forth by Guerney (1964), Stollak (1969) trained college students to conduct special play times with children. Twenty volunteer college students received ten weeks of training and then conducted play times with referred children through an on-campus clinic. No control group was used, and only children with severe mental retardation, severe emotional disturbance, or brain damage were excluded from the study. Stollak found that as a result of the filial training the undergraduates made significant improvements in reflection of content and clarification of feelings. He reported that the college students demonstrated a competence level in conducting play sessions equal to and greater than many graduate students who received similar training. Stollak suggested that college students represented an untapped resource in using child-centered play therapy to treat children.

Guerney and Stover's (1971) study of the effectiveness of filial therapy with fifty-one mothers and their children confirmed their earlier findings. Significant increases were found in both studies—confirming that mothers could learn to reflect feelings, allow their children self-direction, and demonstrate appropriate involvement in the affective behavior and expressions of their children. Clinical assessments revealed improvement in the psychosocial adjustment and symptomatology in all fifty-one children. The children also reported significant increases in several areas: increased interaction with their mothers, appropriate expression of aggression, appropriate sharing behaviors, and decreased dependence.

A follow-up of research participants from B. Guerney and Stover (1971) by L. Guerney (1975) revealed significant longitudinal findings: only one of the forty-two children required treatment after the filial training; thirty-two mothers reported continued improvement, while four reported regression, and one reported deterioration; 64 percent of the mothers attributed the continued growth to their own ability to understand their child; and the mothers reported an overall positive evaluation of the filial therapy training program. This follow-up study confirms the effectiveness of filial therapy training after a three-year period.

Boll (1972) examined the effectiveness of filial therapy training with a group of parents of mentally retarded children. A group of parents trained in traditional filial therapy, a group trained in filial therapy and given additional instruction on specific reinforcement and extinction techniques, and a control group were compared in this study. Both groups trained in filial therapy reported improvement in their children's socially adaptive behavior, with the most change occurring in the traditionally trained group. Boll suggested that the difference was due to group dynamics in the traditional group as compared to the other treatment group.

Guerney, Coufal, and Vogelsong (1976) examined the effectiveness of filial therapy as a treatment for emotionally disturbed children. They reported that children in the treatment group achieved significant improvement in social adjustment and reduction in conflicts with parents, teachers, and peers.

Symptoms of emotional dysfunction were decreased as well as mothers' dissatisfaction with their children. Socioeconomic background, type and degree of child maladjustment, maternal attitude, and personality variables were not considered to be determinants.

Ginsberg (1976) examined the effectiveness of filial therapy with foster parents, single-parent families, and families with different socioeconomic status. All groups reported positive results. Specifically, mothers in low socioeconomic groups experienced positive change as reported by parent report, school progress, and sibling and peer interaction. Foster parents reported reduced stress and an enhanced ability to build a mutually satisfactory relationship with foster children.

In an attempt to control potential differences between parents who seek professional help and those who do not, Sywulak (1977) utilized a design in which participants served as both the control and treatment group for a study of filial therapy. Thirteen mother/father pairs and six single-mother participants completed assessments four months prior to training, at a two-month midpoint in training, and after four months of training. The study revealed significant improvement in child adjustment and parental acceptance after two months of training, and this improvement was maintained after four months of training.

Sensue (1981) conducted a three-year follow-up study of the Sywulak (1977) study in which it was reported that filial therapy significantly increased parental acceptance and perceived child adjustment in a treatment group after four months of training. Positive results were confirmed after three years: parents and children reported positive change as a result of filial therapy training, and children who were formerly diagnosed as maladjusted were as well adjusted as the control group children.

Wall (1979) examined the efficacy of play therapy provided by three groups: masters-level trained play therapists, untrained parents, and by parents directed and observed by masters-level trained play therapists. Parents trained by masters level students improved their empathic communication ability with their children. Wall suggested that the parent's ability to accept negative feelings might have a more powerful effect on the children than the same acceptance from a therapist.

Lebovitz (1983) conducted a similar study that compared the effectiveness of a filial therapy group, a group conducting supervised play sessions, and a control group. Parent's filial skills were assessed, and parents, teachers, and independent observers assessed change in children's behavior. Assessments of children in both the filial group and the supervised play session's group revealed fewer behavioral problems as compared to the control group. Parents in the filial therapy group experienced several significant improvements over the supervised play session's group: greater decrease in children's problem behavior; parents communicated more acceptance of feelings, allowed children more self direction, and exhibited more involvement with their children; and the children demonstrated a greater decrease in dependence on their parents.

Payton (1980) studied the effectiveness of filial therapy between three groups: parents, paraprofessionals, and a control group. Parents in filial therapy training reported significantly higher scores on parenting attitude and improvement in children's behaviors as compared to the other two groups. Payton reported that parents are more effective in affecting personality adjustment in their children's personality than are paraprofessionals.

Kezur (1980) studied children who concurrently received filial therapy sessions with their parents and play therapy sessions with a therapist. Communication patterns between mother and child, and their impact on the relationship were examined. The study revealed that the mothers developed more effective communication patterns; children who expressed anger with the therapist became more open to expressing anger with their mother; mothers developed more insights into their communication; mothers who developed personal insights changed with their children in a positive direction; mothers were able to better meet their children's needs when they first met their own needs; and positive change in the mother child relationship occurred as both gained self-esteem.

Glass (1986) studied Landreth's (1991) ten-week filial therapy model and found that parents who received the training reported a significant increase in unconditional love for their children, a decrease in the level of conflict between parent and child, and an increase in their level of understanding of their children's play as compared to a control group. Other benefits reported were positive changes in parental acceptance, respect for children's feelings, recognition of children's need for autonomy, and closeness between parents and children.

Landreth's (1991) ten-week filial therapy training model was used with parents of chronically ill children by Glazer-Waldman (1991). There were no significant discoveries in pre-test and post-test measures of acceptance and anxiety for the parents. Five parents in the study did report positive change in them and in their children. Tew (1997) also used the Landreth (1991) ten-week model in working with families with chronically ill children. She found significant differences in strengthened and enhanced parent-child relationships, decreased parent stress, increased attitude of acceptance by the parent, and a significant decrease in problematic behavior of chronically ill children.

Lobaugh (1991) studied the effectiveness of Landreth's (1991) ten-week filial therapy training model with incarcerated fathers. The fathers were trained once a week during two-hour training meetings. The fathers in the treatment group demonstrated significantly increased parental acceptance, appreciation of the child's unique makeup, recognition of the child's need for independence and unconditional love, as well as significantly reduced parenting stress as compared with a control group of incarcerated fathers. Parents observed and reported that children in the treatment group benefited from an increased self-esteem and a decrease in problematic behavior. The Landreth (1991) ten-week filial therapy training model has also been used in a prison system to positively impact incarcerated mothers relationships with their children. Harris and Landreth (1997) reported filial therapy to be an appropriate intervention in working with incarcerated mothers in a five-week, biweekly training model. This experimental study showed significant change in the mothers' empathic interactions with their children, in the mothers' attitude of acceptance toward their children, and a reduction in the number of problems with children' s behavior in comparison to the control group.

Bratton and Landreth (1995) examined the use of Landreth's (1991) ten-week filial therapy model with single parents in an experimental, control-group design. They reported that single mothers developed healthier parenting skills and the weekly training group sessions provided needed emotional support. Parents in the treatment group showed significant increases in both attitude of acceptance and empathic behavior. Parenting stress was significantly reduced in the treatment group as well, and parents reported significantly fewer problems with their children's behavior.

Bavin-Hoffman, Jennings, and Landreth (1996) examined the longitudinal effects of Landreth's (1991) ten-week filial model on familial relationships that were outside of the play therapy relationship. Significant findings three years after participation in filial therapy training indicated that family functioning was increased in the areas of improved parent-child communication, improved partner communication, and improved child behavior. Other findings suggested that a side effect of filial therapy training was increased couple unity and value. This study suggests that when parents are more unified in parenting goals and strategies, there is greater marital harmony and reduced parenting anxiety.

Recent studies have investigated the effectiveness of the Landreth (1991) ten-week filial therapy model with various cultures. In a quantitative study of Native American parents and their children, Glover (1996) utilized filial therapy with parents on the Flathead Reservation in Montana and found significant results in increased level of empathy. Child participants experienced significant increases in level of desirable play behaviors with parents. Measures showed positive trends in parental acceptance, parental stress levels, and children's self-concept. Chau and Landreth (1997) examined the effectiveness of filial therapy with Chinese immigrant parents and their children. They reported significant findings including increased empathic interactions, increased attitudes of acceptance, and reduced parenting stress as compared to a control group.

Yuen (1997) also utilized the Landreth (1991) ten-week filial therapy training model with Chinese immigrant parents. Participants met for two weekly one-hour training sessions and met with their child for a thirty-minute weekly playtime. This experimental research study found a significant increase in treatment group participants level of empathic behavior, level of acceptance of the child, as well as a significant decrease in level of stress related to parenting, and in perceived problems in their children.

The Landreth (1991) ten-week filial therapy training model has also been effective with children experiencing learning difficulties. Kale (1997) found that filial therapy training significantly increased parent acceptance and decreased parenting stress with parents of children experiencing learning difficulties as compared to a control group.

Costas (1998) investigated the effectiveness of the Landreth (1991) ten-week filial therapy training model as a method of intervention for children who had experienced sexual abuse and their nonoffending parents. The fourteen experimental group parents evidenced a significantly increased level of empathy and acceptance toward children, as well as reduction of parental stress as compared to the twelve control group participants.

IMPLEMENTATION

The traditional model of filial therapy described previously represents the history and research in the field of filial therapy. The model outlined presents an adaptation of the Landreth (1991) ten-week model by including children in the adolescent stages of development and by incorporating a more *activity-oriented* play approach. This model differs from traditional filial therapy in that it seeks to meet the adolescent child in their natural mode of communication. Similar to the way children naturally communicate their wants, needs, and desires through play, adolescent children communicate through a combination of motoric activity and verbal discourse. Either modality exclusive of the other does not meet the adolescent child's communication needs. This model is based in the filial therapy model and thereby also follows child-centered theory and tenets. The underlying goal of the sessions is to facilitate the self-actualizing process within the parents as well as within the children. This serves the therapeutic needs of the adolescent child by meeting them in their developmental framework. This adaptation of the filial model seeks to provide a structured training program for parents as well as developmentally appropriate interventions with adolescents.

ACTIVITY FILIAL THERAPY (AFT)

A few issues should be addressed before examining the content of the AFT model. (Author's note: This model is based on the Landreth [1991] ten-week model and is adapted with permission. All quotes are directly attributed where appropriate, but the principles and the procedure are based on Landreth's work, writing, and personal communications with this author.) The issues that will be examined a priori are the group format of the meetings, the contents of the AFT kit, and finally, the process.

The implementation of this model can take place between one therapist and up to six parents. The therapeutic alliance can be quite different between a one-on-one situation and a one-on-four; it is recommended that beginning therapists start slow and practice this model with one parent and gradually increase the number of parents from there. It is the author's personal experience that the one-on-one session allows a more in-depth exploration of themes in the special times with the child and a greater examination of parenting dynamics and pitfalls. Group selection is a process of exclusion and inclusion and is crucial to the formation of an effective AFT group. First, be aware of any parents whose needs seem so great that they would benefit more from a one-on-one encounter on an ongoing basis. L. Guerney (1976) also suggests excluding parents who are severely mentally ill: psychotic, homicidal, and suicidal, as well as those with severely reduced intellectual functioning. Inclusion of parents can be based on natural group rules and process. This method is appropriate for most parents experiencing parenting difficulties with their adolescent, a decreased adult-adolescent connection, as well as for building and rebuilding connection with a distant parent.

The contents for the AFT kit are identified individually for their therapeutic value to address the needs of the parent-adolescent relationship. The toys selected are not arbitrary or random; each has value in facilitating communication. Great care should be taken regarding adding toys or other items to the kit. Bratton and Ferebee (1999) suggest the following items:

> Creative: Play-Doh, crayons (eight-count), paper, blunt scissors, expressive arts and media, toys useful for symbolic acting out, manipulative skill building materials and equipment, games that encourage movement, and commercial board games

Landreth (1999) suggests the following items:

> Nurturing: nursing bottle, doll, small blanket, tea set for two, doctor's kit
>
> Aggressive: rubber knife, dart gun, toy soldiers (ten to fifteen), punching bag, 5 feet of rope, toy snake
>
> Dramatic: family of small dolls, dollhouse furniture, lone ranger type mask, hand puppet, plastic animals (two domestic, two wild)
>
> Other: small plastic car, tinker toys, ball (soft sponge type) wood working tools, metal working tools, leather working tools, plastic work items, block printing items, model projects, art and drawing supplies, clay, games, puppets, sand, house keeping equipment, craft items, dress-up items, general supplies, and replacement supplies

The items selected for the AFT play times should closely resemble this list and can be added to throughout the ten-week meeting process. The items can often be purchased at resale shops or second-hand stores. This author recently purchased a cornucopia of play items that would almost complete the required items for about $40 at a community resale shop. The items should be stored in a special place and should only be used for the special AFT play times.

Meeting with a parent for any type of training is an extremely precarious balance. Let's consider the level of frustration and hopelessness that the parent has arrived at to call and seek out a professional's help. It is crucial that the therapist treat the parents with the appropriate respect and humility in this teaching and counseling environment. The attitudes of the therapist towards the client will be pervasive and should communicate warmth, acceptance, and caring (Rogers, 1951).

Session 1

Parents who come in for the first AFT meeting will be unsure, scared, and probably looking for some answers. The first session should address all their concerns. Greet the members of the group, use nametags, and give a brief overview of AFT. This overview should include: the nature of activity therapy as a motoric use of toys for communication while facilitating verbal discussion; the importance of tuning in to the feelings of the adolescent; the role of the parent during these times as a facilitator, not a problem solver; and the goals of having a closer relationship and less stress as a parent. (Note to leaders: this is a crucial time to lay the theoretical ground work for working with adolescents; the parents must be aware that you trust them and they can, in turn, trust their child.) The therapist must be aware of the process within the group and the time; this session lays the groundwork for the next nine weeks. Next, the group members introduce themselves and are encouraged to include what lead to their interest in AFT, background of family, and the one child of focus. Make connections between parents by generalizing comments to other group members: "Does anyone else feel overwhelmed in dealing with . . ."

The therapist also provides the basic agenda for AFT. This includes weekly meetings with the group for about an hour and a half, videotaping or audiotaping of sessions so the group can offer feedback, demonstrations and role plays in the group, and discussion of the goals of filial therapy: self-responsibility, self-control, self-esteem, and identifying and owning own emotions (Landreth, 1999). The leader may use the analogy of learning a new language. This is all new for the parents in the group. Although they may already trust their child, they have not had these kinds of special play times with the child and may feel uncomfortable with the skills and format. The leader should remind them it is a learning process, and they only have to do it for thirty minutes once a week. They may ask if they can use these skills outside of the sessions; however, they should be encouraged to *only* focus on the sessions for the ten weeks. The skills will naturally overlap with their parenting, but translating the skills to every day can be overwhelming.

The final task for the therapist in the first session is to teach reflective listening to the parents. Watching the clock is a foundational skill for AFT, and proper time should be allocated. The leader may role-play with a group member, using basic reflective listening skills and being sure to stay away from interpretation and complex reflection of themes. Leaders should let the group members role play, and process how it went. Landreth (1999) states that reflective listening follows the client's direction and does not direct, does not ask questions, and tunes into feelings, patterns, and behaviors. Some find it very useful to show a video for the last five minutes of the first session to show the parents some idea of what they will be doing with their child. The leader can either create a video with an adolescent child or use a commercially available video such as "Relationship Play Therapy with Clark Moustakas, A Clinical Session." Finally, the leader may give the homework assignment: journal about feelings you see in your child and use one reflective listening technique this week and come ready to share about it.

Session 2

The second session serves to cover the remaining questions concerning the format of the sessions and to use some of the basic skills in a role play. The goal of this session with the parents is to utilize the skills while emphasizing the relational nature of the AFT process. These skills should be used with understanding and compassion, not as a manipulative attempt to get into the secret world of a child. The leader should be sure to address the homework. If the parents know they are going to be asked about it, they will get in the habit of completing homework.

The setting for the special times with their child should be private and uninterrupted. This means no cellular phones, no other children barging in, and no breaks to take care of other needs. The parent should communicate the four central messages of child-centered therapy (Landreth, 1991, p. 182).

1. I'm here.
2. I hear you.
3. I care.
4. I understand.

These messages should be present in every word and deed during the special playtime. This is the one thirty-minute period during the week where the parent does not preach, teach, or correct.

It is incumbent upon the parent to orient the child to AFT session. The parent should introduce the child to the special time, state the amount of time that they will have together, and what is permissible during this time together. It may sound like this, "This is our special play time. We'll have about thirty minutes together today. This is a place where you can play with all of the toys in a lot of the ways you'd like to." Landreth (1991) emphasizes the structuring nature of an introduction to the playtime. It sets the stage to give permission to play, but recognizes that there are some limits here. Note that it says "you can play with all of the toys in a *lot* of the ways you'd like to but perhaps not all of the ways." Only those limits that are absolutely necessary are set, and limit setting will be covered in the third meeting.

It is important to recognize that not all adolescents will be willing to spend a special activity "play time" together. Since not all adolescents will engage in times with the toys listed, it is important to have some alternative activities. While some children are more likely to engage verbally at an early age, some engage easily with the playthings well into adolescence and this model allows for that difference. Note that some of the language suggested identifies the play set as "things" rather than toys. The leader may have to try a few activity times before using alternative strategies. If there is no way that a child will participate in the activity times, then the leader can use an alternative activity such as a special date. A variety of activities can be used, but the skills remain the same. The activities include baking cookies, going to a special place, building a project, redecorating their room, and the like. Anything from a weekly trip to the batting cages, to a cooking time where the child chooses the menu and leads the cooking is appropriate. The underlying tenets apply either way: let the child lead, use reflective statements to understand, and be accepting. The four messages of I'm here; I hear you; I understand; and I care (Landreth, 1991) can be communicated over lasagna as well as during building a bookshelf. The rules for the Activity Filial Sessions still apply: same time every week, allow the child to lead, and use the skills to understand. This is not a time to teach; this is a time to understand and build relationship.

When the group has processed all their questions surrounding format and process of AFT, the final activity for the second session is to do a role-play. One suggestion is that the leader play the part of the therapist and have a parent volunteer to play the child while role playing for about five minutes. Use the reflective listening skills as well as the basic tenets covered up to this point. At the end the parents should be allowed to process what they saw and heard the therapist doing (Landreth, 1999). It is important to address body language in communicating these core issues in the special time together. The body posture should be open and comfortable. Lastly, the homework assignments are given. A suggested homework activity is creating a journal about what areas you would like to see your child different at the end of the next eight weeks as well as how you would like to be different as a parent; use two tracking response to reflect understanding, acceptance, or caring this week. Come back ready to share about your experiences.

Session 3

This is the last session before the parents have their first special time with their child, and it is now appropriate to cover limit setting, some remaining principles of AFT, and answer questions. This is a particularly stressful session, and it is important to cover the following material and leave time for processing of last-minute questions.

The last major skill to discuss is limit setting. This is a skill all parents wish they knew, and are usually excited to hear that they can set a limit and trust the child to follow it. One recommended limit setting is based on Landreth's (1991, p. 209) model: ACT. Three simple steps outline the process of allowing the child to bring self under control, Acknowledge, Communicate, and Target. The first and usually most difficult thing to do is to acknowledge the child's feelings, "I can tell you are angry with your brother." The second step is to communicate the limit, and this gets a bit tricky because it is not the way parents are accustomed to setting limits. The idea is to let the child know that "people are not for hitting." The underlined sections can change according to the situation, but the format is the same. This new model recognizes the child's ability to choose and allows him/her to choose. Then the target can be identified, "your pillow can be for hitting." This is a brand new skill and can be a bit overwhelming, so give parents time to role-play this in the training session. As with all of the skills outlined in the AFT model, it will be tempting to go setting limits 682 times a day. Help your parents to understand that this is for use in the thirty-minute special times together for the ten-week training time. This allows them the freedom to only focus on their new parenting skills for just one short period during the week.

Landreth (1991, pp. 77–78) revised and expanded Axline's (1947) tenets of child centered therapy:

1. The therapist is genuinely interested in the child and develops a warm, caring relationship.
2. The therapist experiences unqualified acceptance of the child and does not wish that the child were different in some way.
3. The therapist creates a feeling of safety and permissiveness in the relationship so the child feels free to explore and express self completely.
4. The therapist is always sensitive to the child's feelings and gently reflects those feelings in such a manner that the child develops self-understanding.
5. The therapist believes deeply in the child's capacity to act responsibly, unwaveringly respects the child's ability to solve personal problems, and allows the child to do so.
6. The therapist trusts the child's inner direction, allows the child to lead in all areas of the relationship, and resists any urge to direct the child's play or conversation.
7. The therapist appreciates the gradual nature of the therapeutic process and does not attempt to hurry the process.
8. The therapist establishes only those therapeutic limits that will help the child accept personal and appropriate relationship responsibility.

These principles should permeate the teaching, role-playing, and role modeling in AFT. This list of principles can be used as a discussion tool in the training session to examine which principle the participants have the most difficulty with. This discussion can facilitate a deeper understanding of the principles as well as the participants' expectations of the process, the child, and of themselves.

Filial therapy principles should also be examined and reviewed in this session. Landreth (1991, pp. 346–47) outlined the following guidelines for filial sessions, and they fit for AFT.

DON'T
1. Don't criticize any behavior.
2. Don't praise the child.
3. Don't ask leading questions.
4. Don't allow interruptions of the session.
5. Don't offer information or teach.
6. Don't preach.
7. Don't initiate new activities. (1–7 are taken from Guerney, 1972)
8. Don't be passive or quiet.

DO
1. Do set the stage.
2. Do let the child lead.
3. Do track behavior.
4. Do reflect the child's feelings.
5. Do set limits.
6. Do salute the child's power and effort.
7. Do join in the play as a follower.
8. Do be verbally active.

The remaining time in the training session should be spent answering questions and doing role-plays to examine possible future difficulties in their special times during the next week. The ground rules (no interruptions, no phones, the same time each week for the meetings, the items for the AFT sessions are to be used only for that one session each week, etc.) should be reviewed. Parents are encouraged to put a sign on the outside of the closed door when they are engaged in their special time with their child and to orient and tell their child that they are taking a class to learn how to spend time with their children (Landreth, 1991). One parent will need to volunteer to videotape the session, and all parents should be reminded to keep notes about their special times with their children.

Sessions 4 to 9

The emphasis of this session (and the rest of the training) is processing how the sessions went and questions that arise along the way. All parents report on their sessions and share:

1. What went well.
2. What didn't go well.
3. What they would like to do differently next time.

Parents must be reassured of their skills. One way to do so is to use a ratio of two positive comments for each area of growth identified. This way the parent's are encouraged, but also challenged. A session is viewed by the group, processed, and a new volunteer is solicited for the following week. The subsequent sessions follow the same general format with reports from the parents, discussion of relevant AFT principles, and viewing videos of sessions.

Session 10

Graduation! This session is spent reviewing what has been learned, how the parents are different, how the child is different, and where they go from here. This is an important time for the parents to examine the process and to explore the implications for this training. The parents are encouraged to sign a contract stating that they will continue the special activity filial therapy times with their child for one year. This can be a contract written by them and signed by the child and the parent. This session is also a time when parents who still need some help can schedule continued experiences with the therapist.

CASE PRESENTATION

Fifteen-year-old Frank and his divorced parents, Jennifer and Mike, came into my office for an initial visit due to Frank's recent problems at school. Frank had been getting into fights, had been sent to detention several times, and was now in an alternative setting. Jennifer and Mike were both frustrated with their son's behavior and unsure of how to help him. Frank had lived with each of his parents several times and was currently living with his mother. Jennifer had never remarried, but has had several long-term relationships. Frank had remarried, but subsequently divorced.

I saw Frank for several individual sessions in which we processed the stressors in his life. He was willing to participate in counseling, but reluctant to discuss his feelings. He asked that I not use the phrase, "It sounds like you feel . . ." as his last therapist had. I agreed.

We processed several issues related to the appropriate expression of anger, boundaries, and family dynamics. A history of alcoholism in the family was revealed, as well as Frank's own current alcohol abuse. These topics were addressed in biweekly parent consultations with Frank present. Whenever the client was able, he addressed the issues of concern with his parents. Through the process of about sixteen sessions the presenting problems subsided: Frank was back in regular classes, had appropriate self-control, and was able to process feelings.

The next therapeutic issue was the irregular relationship with Frank's parents as he moved from home to home. In an attempt to foster greater attachment and relationship security, Frank and his mother, Jennifer, agreed to participate in Activity Filial Therapy (AFT). The first week was spent examining the tenets of AFT with Jennifer and discussing the goals of this new phase of treatment. Jennifer was reluctant at first but agreed to try the activities listed in the materials. Frank was also somewhat reserved about having "special times" each week with his mother, but also agreed to try it for four weeks.

The second week was spent discussing the materials in the process of AFT. Jennifer was reserved about the format, but agreed to give the activity model a try with the agreement that an alternative setting such as in the "special date" could be used if needed. I offered to lend the parent an AFT kit just in case the activity model did not fit. She agreed. During the role play the parent quickly engaged in the child role and used the expressive arts materials.

The third week was spent covering all the remaining materials in order to prepare for the pending session with Frank. The parent reported that while Frank was apprehensive about the "special time" together, he was amused and comforted that his mother wanted to build their relationship and that she was coming for this training. Having completed another role play (this time as the parent) and in possession of the loaner kit, the mother was ready to give it a try.

As session four approached I was curious to hear how things went. Jennifer reported that the "special time" was a huge success. The start had been a little awkward but she and Frank were soon involved in a clay project that kept them busy for the remaining time. The session was then wrapped up so they could continue the following week. The mother informed me that she would return the loaner kit next time because she had collected her own kit.

As the AFT training and supervision continued over the next six weeks, Jennifer and Frank were able to build relationship skills. Jennifer learned several parenting skills on setting limits that she could live with and learned to relate to her son without "being a nag." Frank realized that his mother was not perfect and that she wanted to know him but could also allow him space to be himself.

Frank has visited me sporadically during the last year and a half. He reports that the "special times" still occur although sometimes they go out and do something, and sometimes they just do an activity together. He is passing all of his classes and is still living with his mother. Jennifer also checks in and while she still has some problems, she reports decreased parenting stress and an increased ability to resolve issues with her son.

CONCLUSION

This model represents a molding together of the tenets of filial therapy with clinical practice of the author; it is a work in progress. I hope this gives you some structure and direction in including parents in the process of growth and change in the life of their child. This model is designed toward my favorite goal of therapy: the goal of therapy is to end therapy. Through the utilization of this model parents become empowered to positively impact their relationship with their child and their parenting skills and style. I welcome feedback and personal experiences as you use, modify, and adapt this model in your work with parents and adolescents. The author can be contacted at cb29@swt.edu.

REFERENCES

Axline, V. M. 1947. *Play Therapy.* New York: Ballentine Books.

Bavin-Hoffman, R., G. Jennings, and G. Landreth. 1996. Filial therapy: Parental perceptions of the process. *International Journal of Play Therapy* 5(1): 45–58.

Boll, L. 1972. Effects of filial therapy on maternal perceptions of their mentally retarded children's social behavior. Unpublished doctoral dissertation, University of Oklahoma, Norman, Oklahoma.

Bratton, S. C., and K. W. Ferebee. 1999. "The use of structured expressive art activities in group activity therapy with preadolescents." In D. Sweeney and L. Homeyer, eds., *The Handbook of Group Play Therapy: How to Do It, How It Works, Whom It's Best For* (pp. 192–214). San Francisco: Josey-Bass Publishers.

Bratton, S., and G. Landreth. 1995. Filial therapy with single parents: Effects on parental acceptance, empathy, and stress. *International Journal of Play Therapy* 4(1): 61–80.

Chau, I. Y., and G. L. Landreth. 1997. Filial therapy with Chinese parents: Effects on parental empathic interactions, parental acceptance of child and parental stress. *International Journal of Play Therapy* 6(2): 75–92.

Costas, M. B. 1998. Filial therapy with nonoffending parents of children who have been sexually abused. Unpublished doctoral dissertation, The University of North Texas, Denton, Texas.

Freud, S. 1959. Analysis of a phobia in a five-year-old boy. In *Collected Papers*, 149–289. New York: Basic Books.

Fuchs, N. R. 1957. Play therapy at home. *Merrill-Palmer Quarterly* 3: 89–95.

Ginsberg, B. G. 1976. Parents as therapeutic agents: The usefulness of filial therapy in a community mental health center. *American Journal of Community Psychology* 4(1): 47–54.

Glass, B. 1986. Parents as therapeutic agents: A study of the effects of filial therapy. Unpublished doctoral dissertation, North Texas State University, Denton, Texas.

Glazer-Waldman, H. 1991. Filial therapy: CPR training for families with chronically ill children. Unpublished doctoral dissertation, University of North Texas, Denton, Texas.

Glover, G. J. 1996. Filial Therapy with the Salish and Kootenai Indians. Unpublished doctoral dissertation, The University of North Texas, Denton, Texas.

Guerney, B., Jr. 1964. Filial therapy: Description and rationale. *Journal of Consulting Psychology* 28: 304–10.

Guerney, B., and L. Stover. 1971. Filial therapy: Final report on MH 18254–01. Unpublished manuscript: The Pennsylvania State University.

Guerney, B., J. Coufal, and E. Vogelsong. 1976. Filial therapy used as a treatment method for disturbed children. *Evaluation* 3(1–2): 34–35.

Guerney, L. 1972. *Play Therapy: A Training Manual for Parents*. Mimeographed Report.

———. 1975. *Brief Follow-Up Study on Filial Therapy*. Paper presented at the Eastern Psychological Association, New York, New York.

———. 1976. Filial therapy program. In *Treating Relationships*, ed. D. Olson, 67–91. Lake Mills, Iowa: Graphic Publishing Co., Inc.

Harris, Z. L., and G. L. Landreth. 1997. Filial therapy with incarcerated mothers: A five week model. *International Journal of Play Therapy* 6(2): 53–73.

Kale, A. L. 1997. Filial therapy with parents of children experiencing learning difficulties. Unpublished doctoral dissertation, The University of North Texas, Denton, Texas.

Kezur, B. 1980. Mother-child communication patterns based on therapeutic principles. Doctoral dissertation, The Humanistic Psychology Institute. *Dissertation Abstracts International* 53(8): A2691.

Landreth, G. L. 1991. *Play Therapy: The Art of the Relationship*. Munice, IN: Accelerated Development Inc. Publishers.

———. 1999. Outline and handouts for the ten-week filial therapy training model. Unpublished manuscript, University of North Texas, Denton, Texas.

Lebovitz, C. 1983. Filial therapy with incarcerated parents. Unpublished doctoral dissertation, The University of North Texas, Denton, Texas.

Lobaugh, F. A. 1991. Filial therapy with incarcerated parents. Unpublished doctoral dissertation, The University of North Texas, Denton, Texas.

Oxman, L. 1972. The effectiveness of filial therapy: A controlled study (DAI 32/11B). Unpublished doctoral dissertation. Rutgers University.

Payton, I. 1980. Filial therapy as a potential primary preventive process with children between the ages of four and ten. Unpublished doctoral dissertation, University of Northern Colorado, Dissertation Abstracts International.

Rogers, C. R. 1951. *Client Centered Therapy*. London: Constable.

Sensue, M. E. 1981. Filial therapy follow up study: Effects on parental acceptance and child adjustment. *Dissertation Abstracts International* 42(01A): 148–A.

Stollak, G. E. 1969. The experimental effects of training college students as play therapists. In *Psychotherapeutic Agents: New Roles for Nonprofessionals, Parents, and Teachers*, ed. B. Guerney, 510–18. New York: Holt, Rinehart and Winston, Inc.

Stover, L., and B. Guerney. 1967. The efficacy of training procedures for mothers in filial therapy. *Psychotherapy: Theory, Research, and Practice* 4(3): 110–15.

Sywulak, A. 1977. The effect of filial therapy on parental acceptance and child adjustment (DAI 38/12B). Unpublished doctoral dissertation, Pennsylvania State University.

Tew, K. L. 1997. The efficacy of filial therapy with families with chronically ill children. Unpublished doctoral dissertation, The University of North Texas, Denton, Texas.

Van Fleet, R. 1994. *Filial Therapy: Strengthening Parent-Child Relationships through Play*. Sarasota, Florida: Professional Resource Press.

Wall, L. 1979. Parents as play therapists: A comparison of three interventions into child's play (DAI 39/11B). Unpublished doctoral dissertation, University of Northern Colorado, Greeley, Colorado.

Yuen, T. C. (1997). Filial therapy with immigrant Chinese parents in Canada. Unpublished doctoral dissertation, The University of North Texas, Denton, Texas.

Transitional Objects in Play Therapy with Adolescents
Johanna Krout Tabin

IDENTIFYING TRANSITIONAL OBJECTS

At Ground Zero in New York City there are many teddy bears and other comforting stuffed animals—notably more than the number of lighted candles—that people have brought to express their feelings about the victims of the terrorist attacks on the World Trade Center on September 11, 2001. (Suzanne Gassner, personal communication, January 22, 2002). This placement of familiar transitional objects dramatizes the role of transitional objects throughout the life cycle.

We may speculate that whatever individual meanings the particular stuffed animals held for those who left them at the site, to some degree the animals represented a part of the memorialists themselves. The horror of the tragedy and sense of loss pushed these people back to a time when transitional objects were a comfort. As I will detail in this chapter, my understanding of transitional objects lies in their value as extensions of the self, reassuringly proving one's personal continuity, and giving a sense of control. In the context of treating an adolescent, the patient's use of transitional phenomena not only gives us specific information about fantasies, but also identifies a significant pattern for coping.

What transitional objects mean to a person, when they are used, and how they relate to a person's psychosocial development, are all important. Emphasis in the literature has been on the interpersonal value of these objects, particularly in terms of connection to the mother. This was Winnicott's emphasis when he first described the phenomenon (Winnicott, 1953). From the typical scene of a small child holding the mother's hand on one side while carrying a transitional object in hand on the other side, the implication is that the transitional object has a self-meaning. I have come to believe that this is its most basic importance: that transitional objects establish a sense of personal continuity as one moves from space to space and control over a self-representation as one submits to the control of another. Both elements occur when a child uses such an object for help in falling asleep (Wolf and Lozoff, 1989).

Adolescence is a transitional phase. Taken for granted are transitional phenomena, such as identity through dress, that characterize this phase of development. When an adolescent requires psychological treatment, transitional phenomena that appear inform therapists about the youth's self-imagery in trying to bridge the gap between childhood and becoming an independent adult.

INFORMATION FROM THE LITERATURE: DEFINITIONS OF TRANSITIONAL OBJECTS

Wulf (1946) was the first to discuss early childhood fixations on inanimate objects. He explored such choices in relation to later manifestations of fetishes in adults. His ideas inspired Winnicott (1953) to consider more broadly what it meant for children to choose such objects. Winnicott identified a transitional space between a child's sense of its own body and recognition of not-self. Therefore he called a child's highly cathected use of objects to deal with this space "transitional objects and phenomena." He saw an infant's babbling or singing on the way to sleep as transitional phenomena in this sense, but he tried to understand the behavior in terms of a child's relationship to the mother. Winnicott emphasized qualities of transitional objects and other transitional phenomena as comforting substitutes for the mother. In the background is that frequent scene of child holding a transitional object in mother's presence.

Some of the muddle in definition is revealed in Winnicott's (1953), Coppolillo's (1967), and Greenacre's (1969) treating the mother herself as a transitional object in some cases (as discussed by Ekecrantz and Rudhe, 1974). On the other hand, Winnicott also stated clearly that when the mother was present, she was secondary to the child's use of a transitional object (Ekecrantz and Rudhe, 1974).

Winnicott was a pioneer in developing general understanding of the infant/child-mother interrelationship. In particular, he developed the idea that psychologically the infant only gradually emerges from a fused state with the mother. By the 1980s, however, interest was growing in the demonstrable ways that even very young infants indicate awareness of personal boundaries

(Lichtenberg, 1983; Stern, 1985; Tabin, 1985). This awareness occurs long before an infant is able to form a cohesive sense of self.

Among other implications from early sensing of self, an infant's choice of a transitional object can provide feelings of security that are connected with selfness rather than as a substitute for comforting figures, such as mother. Accordingly, Passman (1987) and Tabin (1992) pointed out the role of control in the use of a transitional object. Here is an object which the child controls as adults may control the child.

Based on all these observations, there is a consensus that runs through the literature. As Triebenbacher (1997) underscores, transitional objects and other transitional phenomena function to reduce anxiety. They are clearly not part of the child, and yet they help the child comfort himself or herself without requiring another person.

INCIDENCE OF TRANSITIONAL OBJECTS

To appreciate the meaning and significance of transitional phenomena in our adolescent patients, we need the framework of knowing, in general, how often transitional phenomena appear and with what relationship to mental health. Most studies of incidence are difficult to interpret because they relied on parental sources or low rates of return on questionnaires. There is a tendency to find greater use of transitional objects among middle-class children compared to inner-city or rural children, and flaws in the studies make interpretation difficult. Middle-class parents, in any case, seem to be more likely to respond to questionnaires.

Fortunately, the question has been explored in some well-designed studies. Shafii (1986) used a questionnaire to survey 230 adolescents aged thirteen to fourteen years old—the entire eighth grade of a public school district. The subjects were evenly divided by gender. Seventy-one percent of the boys and 86 percent of the girls reported having used special objects for comfort at sometime in their lives. Most remembered starting to use transitional objects as toddlers and feeling that they no longer needed them when they were between five and seven years old. By the age of ten, it was no longer normal for transitional objects to be in frequent use. However, a surprising 73 percent of the girls and 45 percent of the boys reported that they still knew the whereabouts of the transitional objects they had used. Twenty-one percent of the girls and 12 percent of the boys reported they still made use of transitional objects at thirteen to fourteen years of age.

Ekecrantz and Rudhe (1974), working in Sweden, gathered their data by interviewing mothers. Nonetheless, it is a valuable study because the population was large (N = 390). Ekecrantz and Rudhe interviewed three groups, namely, families with three children apiece who were either six months to two-and-one-half year-olds, two-and-one-half to thirteen year-olds, or twelve to sixteen year-olds. Across the groups and with no significant differences according to sex, 74 percent of the children use or had used transitional objects. At age twelve, 20 percent still used them; by age sixteen, only 9 percent still used transitional objects. Only very few children (4 percent) changed their choice of object over the years.

Germane to the purpose of this chapter, Ekecrantz and Rudhe investigated ego state in relation to use of transitional objects. They found a slight but significant association between the use of transitional objects and independence. There also appeared to be a strong relationship between frustration tolerance and breadth of interests by these children. An important side note is that the mothers of children who used transitional objects tended to report positive attitudes toward the pregnancy and delivery of the particular child. It is possible to speculate that mothers with minimal ambivalence toward the child were comfortable with the child's growth toward self-sufficiency.

Triebenbacher (1997) studied attitudes toward transitional objects in seventy-five sets of mothers and fathers. She found very high correspondence between the parents in their reported observations about their children's use of this mechanism. Overall, the higher the educational level of the parents, the more accepting they were of children's continuing use of transitional objects, perhaps predictably, with fathers favoring an earlier time of termination than mothers. It is interesting that for both parents, the mean age at which they believed that children should no longer need a transitional object was two to three years earlier than when they recalled themselves to have given up an object. This might indicate a desire by the parents for their children to feel complete within themselves faster than the parents were able to do.

Speculation is also necessary in trying to evaluate racial and cultural factors that influence the occurrence of transitional objects because of the limitations previously mentioned in design or completion of most studies. Black, Hispanic, and racially mixed couples comprised 25 percent of the subjects in Triebenbacher's survey. She found no significant differences among these parents' reports compared with the reports of White parents.

These normative data omit an important question about incidence of transitional object use, after Wulf (1946), Dickes (1963), and Sperling (1963) raised the issue of fetish-equivalence. While Triebenbacher found oral involvement with transitional objects in 31 percent of the cases, there were no instances of anal involvement, and only one case of genital behavior with the objects. That this was true regardless of the ages of the children suggests that transitional objects may be precursors of fetishism only with the rarity that such pathology appears in the general population. It may be appropriate to consider fetishes as part-objects that represent other than the self (or why not simply masturbate?) while transitional objects represent aspects of the self. Greenacre (1969) differentiated objects used as fetishes from transitional objects by considering a fetish as a nonself object in contrast to the self-object quality of a transitional object.

THE DEVELOPMENTAL CONTEXT OF TRANSITIONAL OBJECTS

This chapter is about adolescents; but, of course, every adolescent was an infant/toddler first, striving to create an integrated ego. Given that most children adopt transitional phenomena during this phase, it is worthwhile to explore the initial adoption of transitional phenomena.

Triebenbacher (1997) notes that many children first demonstrate interest in a transitional object during weaning. She comments that this would support the idea of seeking a substitute for the mother. It seems to be a reasonable interpretation, especially for the 27 percent in the population she studied who demonstrated oral behavior with their transitional objects. On the other hand, Anna Freud pointed out that adult resistance to a baby's thumb-sucking reveals a rejection of the baby's first demonstration of self-soothing (Freud, 1954). Orality in use of a transitional object can be understood also as evidence that the child is dealing with its tensions through a self-created mechanism. The importance of a transitional object in spite of a mother's presence (which Triebenbacher's data show as an indifference to whether or not mother is present) would seem to require further interpretation. It makes sense that children may use objects to deal comfortably with transitional space as their perceptions develop, including self-perceptions/otherness. Children sense their growing ability for autonomy in various ways, perhaps indicated by the mother's (or the child's) recognition of the time for weaning. In other words, weaning and adoption of transitional objects may both reflect the child's nascent sense of selfness.

Toddlerhood is the period when a sense of self rapidly coalesces. The studies of both Ekecrantz and Rudhe (1974) and Shafii (1986) establish toddlerhood as the most common time for adopting transitional objects. Winnicott (1953) observed children who were from eighteen months old to three years old in making his landmark interpretation. His observations showed him how objects and rituals to which he gave the name *transitional phenomena* were a child's way of protecting a relationship with the mother, while moving toward greater independence from her. The role played by transitional objects in the process of ego formation was noted by Litt (1981) and Tabin (1992). The limitations of a child's mind during this period combine to make transitional objects a likely mechanism for dealing with anxiety (Tabin, 1985, 1992). At this stage, the child must rely mostly on prelinguistic abilities. Galenson, Miller, and Roiphe (1976) underscored the concreteness of mentation, so that a palpable object is a logical choice for managing difficult feelings. With *pars pro toto* symbolization, another characteristic of the age, the child can attribute to inanimate objects a whole range of feelings. The child's associations can give a toy the whole significance of a relationship or an event.

As with much in the marvelous efficiency of the unconscious, meanings are overdetermined. There seem to be at least three ways in which transitional objects serve the youngster in toddlerhood and later. The first one is to represent a caregiver, typically the mother or other beloved person, now under the child's control and wish for availability. The most frequent selections of a transitional object, diapers (before the advent of disposable ones), and the earliest blanket, provide reliable connections with the soothing and familiar that are particular to the child. The diaper offered an additional quality of connectedness: it was a container for material that emerged, connected with the body and yet feeling alien. The second is to reinforce qualities of the child's own being with which the child imbues the chosen object (Tolpin, 1972). The third is the self-objectifying use that gives a sense of personal continuity and control when the child must respond to transitions (Tabin, 1992). Underlying all of these and any other possible meanings is the transitional object or phenomenon as a coping mechanism. It is a mechanism that stems from the period in life—toddlerhood—when children become capable of clearly distinguishing themselves as unique individuals. This, concrete objects and rituals, in keeping with the mentation of the age, are natural choices for dealing with anxiety.

Kernberg (1974) and Arkema (1981) considered the capacity for transitional relatedness a pivotal developmental point in character development. In comparing two groups of adolescents, Lobel (1981) found that the existence of a transitional object in their histories characterized the healthy group. The data bore out Winnicott's belief that existence of a transitional object is a visible index of a certain developmental achievement.

When an adolescent presents transitional objects and phenomena in treatment, it is, above all, a sign of an emerging autonomous ego. Furthermore, it indicates that a deep level of emotional experience is being reached. The constant questions in all treatment, of course, apply: Why is the transitional object or phenomenon appearing now? What aspects of this adolescent's experience does the transitional object or phenomenon help the youngster to integrate? How can this indication of growth further serve the process of therapy?

Therapy is a process by which the adolescent can find conscious tolerance for thoughts, fantasies, and feelings that disrupt one and make one seem strange to oneself. Therapy is thus an integrative process, a method to achieve what adolescents of the 1970s used to call "getting my head together."

CASE EXAMPLES

Nora

Nora was a thirteen-year-old girl whose father had recently gained an important new job, necessitating that the family move across the country. An only child, Nora had close friends in the town where she lived before the move. Both parents reported that Nora was a successful child in every way.

Gradually, Nora seemed to change in her new surroundings. She always seemed independent for her age. Now she became fearful whenever she was separated from her mother. The mother began to work outside of the home at this time and Nora would call her from school several times during each day, begging for reassurance that her mother would really be there to pick Nora up after school.

In a conference held before I met Nora, the father said (in front of the mother) that the mother had become inexplicably strict with Nora since the move. He felt that his own relationship with Nora remained the same as ever, in spite of his now frequent absences because of business trips. The mother concurred that although she did not understand why herself, that she felt tension with Nora and found herself exerting control over matters with which she previously had felt relaxed, insisting that Nora attend to her table manners, for example.

Nonetheless, the parents believed that Nora's difficulties really escalated as she became friends with Brandy, one girl in her class. Brandy seemed obsessed with death and constantly talked about it with Nora. Now it seemed to them that Nora's fear that something would happen to her mother resulted from Brandy's preoccupation with ghastly themes. They were reluctant to interfere with Nora's friendship, relieved as they were that she formed at least one peer attachment at last. They did seem to realize that Nora's vulnerability to Brandy's fears must have something to do with Nora's inner concerns, in any case.

When I met Nora, I was impressed quickly with her intelligence and willingness to talk. At the same time, she seemed young for her age. She told me about her anxiety that something terrible might happen to her mother. I asked her when she first noticed this fear, and it became apparent that the fear followed leaving her mother when they were angry at each other. I said, "When we are children, it sometimes seemed that our angry thoughts could make mischief when we were feeling angry with someone." Nora smiled. Then she noticed that in an adjoining room through an open doorway, paper and colored markers were on a table. Checking with me that it was all right, she proceeded to go there and started painting.

The first paintings were feminine dress designs. Nora showed me some that were sexy, up-to-the-minute teenage outfits. She exclaimed that her mother wanted her to wear such things but that she was uncomfortable in them. It was one of the things that they fought about. Indicating the casual, loose fitting shirt and pants that she was wearing, she told me that was how she liked to dress.

I was dubious about the assignment of attitudes, but Nora seemed candid in complaining about her mother's restriction of Nora's television watching. It was one of the things that left her feeling angry with her mother and prone to imagining her mother being killed in a car accident.

In subsequent sessions, Nora confirmed her father's description of their having a joyful relationship. I was reminded of her mother's complaint that the father played with their only child as if a child himself. Gradually, it became plausible to me that Nora's mother wanted Nora to grow up faster so that she would stop being the father's playmate. I also learned that the family move placed them very near where the father's own mother lived and separated them from the mother's mother.

In this context, I began to hear about the household cat, Sunshine. Sunshine had been Nora's to cuddle with for as long as she could remember. When they moved to their present home, however, her mother declared that Nora was too irresponsible to take care of the cat. The transitional quality of the cat was perhaps important for the mother in terms of her forced separation from her own mother when the family moved. In any case, Nora believed that when her mother took over care of the cat, she was excluding Nora from the cat's care to shift the cat's affections to herself.

Connecting her points of anger with her mother and the intensity of her fears diminished Nora's need to check on her mother's condition throughout the school day. She began to feel less intimidated by and identified less with Brandy in Brandy's preoccupation with death, and started making friends with other girls in her classroom.

At this point, Nora appealed to me for a way to persuade her mother to let Nora arrange her room so that Sunshine's needs would be met there and Sunshine would be Nora's again. Simultaneously, as she used me to prompt her figuring out how this might be accomplished, she began to notice ways in which I physically resembled her maternal grandmother, a very strict lady. It seemed to me that as Nora felt freer to accept her anger toward her mother without so much fearing destructiveness of angry thoughts, she needed me to represent a higher power even than her mother. On this basis, she could summon inner permission to gain for herself what Sunshine represented.

One thing Sunshine meant to Nora was connectedness with the easier days before the family move, when Nora's mother seemed much more relaxed with her. The cat was both a symbol of the good and comforting mother and a symbol of Nora's ability to gain comfort without her mother. The quality of autonomy that Sunshine confirmed for Nora also enabled Nora to deal more realistically with her mother. She no longer was so compelled to provoke her mother into arguments nor to be preoccupied with angry feelings that must mean her mother's consequent death. I believe that my role in supporting Nora's plan for exhibiting autonomy and ego strength by becoming responsible for the cat helped her. Sunshine subsequently provided an opportunity to explore sexual feelings and Nora's place in the family triangle. With Sunshine, Nora found comfort in the transitional space created by the family move and adolescence.

Fred

Fred was a fourteen-year-old boy whom the school referred to me because he stretched himself out on the hallway floors in such a manner that other youngsters would almost have to step on him in order to pass through the hallway. In meeting with his parents before I first saw Fred, I sensed a rigid, sterile atmosphere. The parents did not seem to be too worried about Fred as long as he did as he was told. They followed through obediently, however, with the school's recommendation for his treatment.

Fred was large for his age, with a well-padded bulky frame. He shuffled into my office and sat down clumsily. He looked at me with his blue eyes half-shuttered. He did not speak, but apparently heard what I said. The most important statement Fred made was to a side table when he brushed against it as he rose from the chair. He apologized to the table.

As time rolled by, Fred gradually came to feel a degree of safety with me. He began to tell a little about his experiences in school. One day, he told me that he had been elected to a minor office in the student government. He seemed pleased. I, however, felt wildly joyful. Both his achievement and his willingness to confide in me seemed like milestones in his progress. I burbled my congratulations to him, proclaiming how glad I was at the news. Fred opened his eyes wide. "You're welcome," he said to me. The incident was a sharp lesson on the delicacy of ownership of feelings. Fortunately, we had come far enough that after another two sessions, Fred began to speak once more.

Five weeks later, Fred brought an object out of his pocket. At first, I thought it was a clump of dirty old strings. Then I could see that it was a small doll made out of knotted yarn. "I like to hold it," Fred said. "It was lost, but I found it." Fred did not remember who gave it to him. It seemed to him that he had it for longer than he could remember. He knew that he liked to have it with him always. It was not clear when he lost track of the doll. He was able to say that he was very sad when it was lost.

My belief is that the doll originally belonged to him when he was very young. It was the kind of object that a little boy might likely be given between the two or three year old period, when transitional objects are typical. Fred's losing track of it reminded me of the lack of self-worth that characterized him when we began together. I think that it may have been helpful to him to see that I learned how fragile his sense of importance was in what he did. He subsequently may have recognized I truly respected him and did not wish to take over his mind.

Fred's mood brightened. He began to give me examples of a growing sense of agency on his part. We were still a long way from enabling Fred to deal with his angers and establishing trust in his own controls and ability to cope. For a long time, the little androgynous doll continued to be a tangible sign to him that he was a person in his own right.

Discussion

Both Nora and Fred allowed me to know about their transitional objects at a point in the work when they began to deal with issues of individuation. This became possible when an opportunity occurred for them to test my belief in their right to autonomy (Weiss, 1993). Nora used me as a Supra-Mother/Superego in order to safeguard her use of Sunshine as a connector between her interrupted childhood and her present need for self-comforting. In Fred's case, we lost ground briefly because my spontaneous reaction to his good news felt to him like an effort on my part to engulf him. Fortunately, that could not have happened before he trusted me enough to tell his good news, so we already had a basis to get back to where he could feel I finally earned at least a little of his confidence.

Benson (1980) referred to transitional phenomena as guardians in adolescence of future possibilities for the self. In the cases he discussed, the transitional phenomena his adolescent patients brought into the treatment had to do with the process of adjusting from great, fantasized expectations (e.g., becoming a star athlete) to comfortably accepted realistic expectations. Horton (1976) went so far as to suggest that encouraging the use of transitional objects is useful when patients, whom he referred to as personality disordered, cannot seem to give personal meaning to the surrounding world. Transitional objects can safeguard the sense of self while exploring various interactions that must be experienced transitionally.

The examples of adolescent use of transitional objects in treatment were selected to illustrate the connection with the issues of transitional space during earlier childhood. Another important derivative is in the meaning of drug use. This all too frequent component in treating adolescents has some of the qualities of transitional phenomena. Honoring personal autonomy is part of the adolescent's motivation. The frequent factor of peer pressure can enhance autonomy in respect to parents.

A still deeper effort toward personal autonomy has to do with an urge for a greater sense of personal wholeness. By ingesting street drugs, including alcohol, the adolescent gains inner permission for reaching otherwise inaccessible fantasies. The practice can be a way of being in touch with long-repressed material that surges dangerously toward consciousness in the turmoil of adolescence.

It is often observed that those using street drugs find it difficult to label their feelings. It is perhaps not far-fetched to presume that—notably for bright children—when a child is unable to associate appropriate words to feelings, a repressive process must be in operation from an early time in life. In development, a sense of self and verbal facility occur simultaneously. Children who avoided integrating knowledge of feelings with a sense of themselves, later, during the upheavals of adolescence, must need a mechanism for gaining access to certain feelings without conscious responsibility for them. Using street drugs can be a transitional phenomenon that allows for ownership of feelings and fantasies with obvious roots in formulations from very early childhood. It is one of the hopes for therapy to offer mechanisms for helping the adolescent feel safe with innermost feelings.

CONCLUSIONS

The appearance of transitional objects and other transitional phenomena in the treatment process signals a renewed coalescence of self. Transitional objects and phenomena are connectors with past feelings of being able to cope. In the treatment relationship, they express at least an incipient trust that the therapist is willing to respect another's autonomy, even while they may mitigate against too great a sense of dependency. As with a good parent, the adolescent needs to believe that the therapist fosters growth toward independence, while also giving support.

REFERENCES

Arkema, P. H. 1981. The borderline personality and transitional relatedness. *American Journal of Psychiatry* 138(2): 172–77.

Benson, R. M. 1980. Narcissistic guardians: Developmental aspects of transitional objects, imaginary companions, and career fantasies. *Annals of the American Society for Adolescent Psychiatry* 8: 253–64.

Coppolillo, H. P. 1967. Maturational aspects of transitional phenomena. *International Journal of Psycho-Analysis* 48: 237–46.

Dickes, R. 1963. Fetishistic behavior. *Journal of the American Psychoanalytic Association* 11: 303–29.

Ekecrantz, L., and L. Rudhe. 1974. Transitional phenomena: Frequency, forms and functions of specially loved objects. *Acta Psychiatrica Scandinavica* 48(3): 261–73.

Freud, A. 1954. Problems of infantile neurosis. *Psychoanalytic Study of the Child* 9: 26–27.

Galenson, E., R. Miller, H. Roiphe. 1976. The choice of symbols. *Journal of the American Academy of Child Psychiatry* 15: 83–96.

Gassner, Suzanne. 2002. Conversation with author. January 22, Berkeley, California.

Greenacre, P. 1969. The fetish and the transitional object. *Psychoanalytic Study of the Child* 24: 144–63.

Horton, P. C. 1976. The psychological treatment of personality disorder. *American Journal of Psychiatry* 123: 262–65.

Kernberg, O. F. 1974. A psychoanalytic classification of character pathology. *Journal of the American Psychoanalytic Association* 22: 486–511.

Lichtenberg, J. D. 1983. *Psychoanalysis and Infant Research*. Hillside, NJ: Analytic Press.

Litt, C. J. 1981. Children's attachment to transitional objects: A study of two pediatric populations. *American Journal of Orthopsychiatry* 51: 131–39.

Lobel, L. 1981. A study of transitional objects in the early histories of borderline adolescents. *Adolescent Psychiatry* 9: 199–213.

Passman, R. H. 1987. Attachments to inanimate objects: Are children who have security blankets insecure? *Journal of Consulting and Clinical Psychology* 55: 825–30.

Shafii, T. 1986. The prevalence and use of transitional objects: A study of 230 adolescents. *Journal of the American Academy of Child Psychiatry* 25(6): 805–8.

Sperling, M. 1963. Fetishism in children. *Psychoanalytic Quarterly* 32: 374–92.

Stern, D. N. 1985. *The Interpersonal World of the Infant: A View from Psychoanalysis and Developmental Psychology*. New York: Basic Books.

Tabin, J. K. 1985. *On the Way to Self: Ego and Early Oedipal Development*. New York: Columbia University Press.

———. 1992. Transitional objects as objectifiers of the self in toddlers and adolescents. *Bulletin of the Menninger Clinic* 56(2): 209–20.

Tolpin, M. 1972. On the beginnings of a cohesive self: An application of the concept of transmuting internalization to the study of the transitional object and signal anxiety. *Psychoanalytic Study of the Child* 26: 316–52.

Triebenbacher, S. L. 1997. Children's use of transitional objects: Parental attitudes and perceptions. *Child Psychiatry and Human Development* 27(4): 221–30.

Weiss, J. 1993. *How Psychotherapy Works: Process and Technique.* New York: Guilford Press.

Winnicott, D.W. 1953. Transitional objects and transitional phenomena: A study of the first not-me possession. *International Journal of Psycho-Analysis* 34: 85–97.

Wolf, A.W., and B. Lozoff. 1989. Object attachment, thumb-sucking, and the passage to sleep. *Journal of the American Academy of Child and Adolescent Psychiatry* 28: 287–92.

Wulf, M. 1946. Fetishism and object choice in early childhood. *Psychoanalytic Quarterly* 28: 450–71.

·6·

Drama Therapy with Adolescents

Loretta Gallo-Lopez

$\mathcal{A}$s children journey toward adolescence their evolving sense of self propels them forward and back and transforms them into individuals who sometimes even they don't recognize. The complexities of the journey keep adolescents in a state of constant unrest as they search for answers to the lifelong questions: "Who am I? Why am I here? Where do I belong?" Many of the problems and concerns of adolescence seem to stem from the turmoil surrounding this quest for answers. As helping professionals working with adolescents, one of our tasks is to help them navigate this process in a manner that won't cause them irreparable harm.

The first task for therapists is to reach the adolescent, to make that all-important connection. As children move into adolescence, they become more aligned with their peers and more cautious of and distant from the adults in their lives. They build walls of indifference and defiance, leaving us with the task of finding strategies to break through and reach in. Trust is the most important dynamic in the therapeutic relationship because it establishes the foundation for real work to occur. Establishing trust, however, can seem difficult when working with adolescents, who likely put therapists in the same category as parents and teachers—adults who can't be trusted and "just don't get it." But building trust with adolescents is no different than building trust with any other population. It requires honesty, consistency, respect, and acceptance. Confidentiality issues must be clearly spelled out and agreed to by both the parents and the adolescents. The therapist's role should never be to judge, blame, or condemn. Nothing shuts an adolescent down faster than a lecturing therapist. Humor is a great way to break through an adolescent's resistance. Another is to meet adolescents where they are. The parent's primary concern may be their adolescent's defiance, but for the adolescent, the primary concern is likely to be the fight they just had with a boyfriend or their anger about being on restriction. The most effective strategies for reaching adolescents will respect their emerging maturity while tapping into their childlike qualities.

Once the initial connection is made, identifying significant issues becomes the primary focus. Adolescents often struggle with issues from their past while dealing with fears about their future. "Adolescent angst" is the result of these struggles and is a byproduct of the adolescent's search for ways to fit in with their new family—their peer group, while painfully and simultaneously separating from their family of origin.

This process becomes more complicated for adolescents living in situations other than with their biological families. Some of these adolescents may never have bonded with a parent figure; consequently, their intense need to belong leaves them vulnerable to involvement in dangerous and dysfunctional relationships. As adolescence progresses, most adolescents, regardless of their living situation, experience a metamorphosis—of their bodies, their psyches, their overall selves. For some the changes are positive and welcome. For others the changes bring confusion and turmoil.

Though written in 1960, Luisa's monologue from the Jones and Schmidt play *The Fantasticks* aptly communicates the sense of transition, turmoil, and longing that is the emotional life of adolescents regardless of the time period.

> I'm sixteen years old,
> And every day something happens to me
> I don't know what to make of it.
> When I get up in the morning to get dressed,
> I can tell:
> Something's different.
> I like to touch my eyelids
> Because they're never quite the same.
> Oh! Oh! Oh!
> I hug myself till my arms turn blue,
> Then I close my eyes and cry and cry
> Till the tears come down
> And I taste them. Ah!
> I love to taste my tears!
> I am special.
> I am special.
> Please, God, please—
> Don't let me be normal!
>
> —Tom Jones and Harvey Schmidt, *The Fantasticks*

One of the primary functions of adolescence is the formation of an identity, separate and independent from the family of origin. As children make their way into and through adolescence, peers become more important than family, and exploration and experimentation informs the emerging sense of self. The importance of peer relationships in this time of identity formation leads to the need to fit in, to be part of a peer group, to belong. This becomes problematic when adolescents are drawn into dangerous or self-destructive behaviors as a result of their desire to belong, or when adolescents are isolated, excluded, and even ridiculed as a result of their inability to fit in.

Emunah (1995) explains the rebelliousness so often present in adolescence as a "manifestation of the conflicted desire for independence." Through resistance and defiance, adolescents declare their independence from the authority figures in their lives and begin the search for a separate identity. The search for identity leads adolescents to cast off some of their old roles and to try on a variety of new roles. This trying on of roles is a necessary step in the evolution of the adolescents' emerging sense of self. Landy (1986) cites the social psychologist Theodore Sarbin (1954) in characterizing the relationship between self and role. "The self is what a person 'is,' the role is what a person 'does.'"

Discovering the roles we play, or the roles we want to play, is a necessary step in the formation of an identity. Through personal life experiences and by observing others, we gain an understanding of the roles that seem to be available to us. In childhood, we experiment with different roles through play. Adolescents draw on all of their past experiences and continually experiment in order to discover the roles that will be part of who they are.

Stone (1971) espouses the importance of drama and role play to the child's sense of being, indicating that "drama is fundamental for the child's development of a conception of self as an object different from but related to other objects, the development of an identity" (p. 9). Courtney (1968) maintains that dramatic play allows children the opportunity to experiment with new situations by imagining alternatives and solving problems. Oaklander (1969/1988) maintains that drama is a natural means of helping children "find and give expression to lost and hidden parts of themselves, and to build strength and self-hood" (p. 139).

Drama can be both viewed and experienced. By viewing drama, either through theater, film, or TV, we are given the opportunity to identify with new and different roles and to examine the interrelationships between roles. When drama is experienced, it is a means of expanding possibilities, transcending the ordinary, experimenting with the unknown. It allows us to try on new roles. Drama is a natural source of self-discovery (Jennings, 1986; Landy, 1986; Dayton, 1994).

When drama is used therapeutically via drama therapy, adolescents are provided with the opportunity to journey inward and project outward. Drama therapy affords adolescents the opportunity to search for answers and experiment with solutions within a safe and supportive environment. Drama therapists may utilize puppets, masks, props, and costumes, or simple role-play to help adolescent clients to accomplish these tasks. A participant may adopt the role of an imaginary character or may play himself or a family member in an attempt to understand current issues, issues from the past, or concerns about the future. Drama therapy can be utilized in individual, group, or family therapy.

Drama therapy is not about "putting on a play," although in some situations putting on a play may be the end result. Drama therapy is the creative process, not merely the creative product. It is not simply a series of creative games or exercises, although the use of such games and exercises can be an important drama therapy tool. Drama therapy is not an adjunct to more typical forms of psychotherapy, but can be used as a primary treatment modality for adolescents and other populations. When utilized ethically and appropriately, drama therapy can be a very powerful method of doing therapy: one that is capable of effecting real change and positive growth.

Drama therapy is uniquely suited to work with adolescents as it allows them to step outside of their resistance and the often-narrow perspectives of their peer group to discover alternative viewpoints and experiences. When given the opportunity for role-play and creative exploration, children will play out their wishes, fears, fantasies, and realities. The same is true for adolescents; however, adolescents are rarely given such opportunities. Instead, they are asked to think in concrete terms, to restrain their creative selves, to control their desire for excitement, and to keep their emotions well contained. They are advised to decide who and what they want to be and are instructed to follow a rigid path to achieve their goals. This is perhaps the exact opposite of what the natural course of adolescence dictates. Perhaps resistance and rebellion are the natural, necessary defense mechanisms of adolescence.

As in traditional forms of therapy, treatment goals are dependent on the needs of the client. However, in drama therapy an important means of achieving goals and effecting change is to help clients to explore their repertory of roles (Landy, 1993). A full range of roles affords individuals the ability to envision options and to see themselves as capable of changing and moving beyond dysfunctional and harmful situations. A wide reparatory of roles implies options and counters rigidity. For adolescents this translates into an opportunity to use natural means to problem solve, to visualize options, to gain insight and understanding, and to "try on" new and different parts of their developing selves.

DRAMA THERAPY WITH ADOLESCENTS

Drama therapy is an effective modality that can be used to treat a wide range of adolescent problems and concerns. A drama therapy session typically begins with a warm-up, a means of getting ready for the work that will be the main focus of the session. This is not unlike more traditional therapies, where a clinician may provide a warm-up by asking a client about their week or reviewing the events of the previous session. The goals are the same: to help the client focus their attention and begin to identify issues, acclimate themselves to the space, and get prepared for the work to come. Even the act of taking a seat can be a type of warm-up, part of the process of getting prepared to work. In drama therapy, the warm-up can also energize the body, stimulate the imagination, and inspire creativity. The warm-up should also help to reinforce the sense of physical and emotional safety within the session and the space. In individual and family therapy, the warm-up may be used to identify the issue which is the most pressing. In a group setting the warm-up not only prepares the group for the work to come, but may also identify the individuals who will be the focus of the session.

Techniques for warm-up range from theatre games, to movement exercises, to role-playing activities, and can be adapted to meet the needs of a given population. Cooperative or independent drawing activities can be a helpful way to engage resistant adolescents. After attempting several times to get Sam, a thirteen-year-old boy in foster care, to draw a self-portrait, I utilized the one thing that interested him and asked him to draw himself as a wrestler. I asked him to think about what his name would be and what type of costume he would wear. Sam had been in a combination of over twenty foster care and preadopt placements. He was moved from each placement due to violent and/or sexually aggressive behaviors. The idea of drawing himself as a wrestler brought a rare smile to his face and he quickly got to work. He drew a figure which he named "The Puppet Master." Clad in a long cape, the figure's face resembled that of a ventriloquist's dummy and in his hand he held a marionette puppet of a young boy. According to Sam, "The Puppet Master" had the ability to control everyone and everything in his life. This character became the focus of many enactments and became a vehicle for Sam to express his own need for control over his life and to explore his fears about the unpredictability of his future.

A warm-up activity that can be used with groups or families is the Hat Exchange. Each person is instructed to grab a hat from a box. The first person puts on their hat and states "I am _____," identifying their character with a name and a description. Examples might be "Bob the Butcher" or

"Sally the First Grader." That person then passes the hat and the next person adds the first line such as "and I'm having a bad day." This continues until each person has added to the story. The process is repeated with each person's hat, leading to the development of several different characters. One hat character may become the focus of the session or all of the hat characters can be combined together in an enactment.

Jennings (1986) compiles a variety of popular warm-up activities in her book *Creative Drama in Group Work.* These include group cooperation games, name games, group mirroring, and movement activities. One of my favorite warm-up activities is called "Newspaper Stand." I find this especially effective with families. Families or small groups of four to five people are given a large sheet of newspaper and are told to find a way to get everyone's feet on the sheet of newspaper at the same time. After this is accomplished, the sheet of newspaper is torn in half and the participants are again asked to perform the task. This is done once more, requiring participants to work together, problem solve, and tolerate physical closeness. Themes for role-playing often surface as a result of the interaction between group or family members.

The action follows the warm-up in a drama therapy session. The action may involve the development of characters, environment, and conflict, and may be psychodramatic or projective. A psychodramatic approach directly dramatizes scenes involving people and situations from the client's life. A psychodramatic approach provides clients little distance from their issues; however, it is preferred by some clients and may be more appropriate in given situations. On the other hand, many adolescents need the safety of a projective approach to begin to uncover and explore significant issues. Projection allows for varying levels of distance depending on the chosen modality. For example, puppets—which may be worn on or held in the hand—provide a greater level of emotional distance than a mask—which is worn on the face and, therefore, becomes a literal projection of the wearer. Projective techniques include role-playing, improvisation, enactment, and storytelling, as well as the use of masks, make-up, puppets, objects and dolls, and video.

The action will account for most of the session as clients deepen the level of their enactment (Landy, 1986) and creatively explore, experiment, and work toward a greater degree of self-discovery. Whether enactments are projective or psychodramatic, adolescents will utilize images from their own popular culture within these enactments. Ann Cattanach (1994) advises therapists working with children to make themselves aware of the characters from television, movies, and toys that are popular with children of different ages. Therapists who work with adolescents should also be aware of different types of music, video games, and popular heroes that are a part of adolescent culture. Courtney (1981) maintains that "Adolescents emulate heroes." It is therefore essential that adolescent psychotherapists understand the connection between adolescents and their heroes.

Story-starters are helpful in stimulating creativity and imagination in adolescents. Story-starters include things like pictures or postcards that communicate a specific feeling, relationship, or issue (Cattanach, 1994), a series of newspaper headlines glued to index cards (Jennings, 1986), and myths or fairy tales. Cards containing provocative titles such as "The Family Secret," "The Family Crisis," or "The Great Escape," as well as cards identifying a specific character, environment, or emotion, can inspire enactment and role playing.

Scenes and characters can also evolve from techniques such as news reporting or interview shows, where characters are asked questions to enhance their development. Storytelling can also lead to further enactments and character development. The "T.V. Storyboard" technique (Gallo-Lopez, 2001) involves the development of scenes in an imaginary television show. Sheets of paper are divided into six equal parts and a television set is drawn in each of the sections. The adolescent is then asked to create a show, beginning by giving it a title. Words and pictures then tell the story, scene-by-scene, using as many sheets of paper as is necessary. The story can then be enacted using puppets, role-play, or any other projective modality. Sharon, a fourteen-year-old girl, wrote and recorded a theme song entitled "The Sharon Show." The theme song accompanied the videotaping of her T.V. show episode that she enacted using dolls and figures. Videotaping can be used in many different ways with adolescents, as it piques their interest and motivates their involvement. Furman (1990) asserts that video techniques are especially effective with adolescents because of their familiarity with television.

There are many enactment techniques which directly address issues significant in adolescence. Violet Oaklander (1969/1988) describes a role-playing technique that allows adolescents to explore issues related to body image. She asks adolescents to draw a picture of how they think they look and another of how they would like to look. They are then asked to imagine standing in front of a full-length mirror and to engage in a dialogue about their body with their mirrored image.

Tian Dayton (1994) describes a technique that involves clients enacting scenes from their parents' lives in order to increase the understanding of a parent's history and emotional functioning. This is an especially important exercise for adolescents, who often feel they cannot relate to their parents in any way and, as a result, become more and more distanced.

Puppets, masks, and face painting are projective devices that can be used to enact scenes or experiment with different roles. Puppet play is quite reminiscent of childhood play and, therefore, it often engenders resistance in adolescents who see themselves as too old or too cool for such play. With a little enticement, however, adolescents can successfully engage in puppet play. Puppets can be ready-made or created from simple materials such as tongue depressors, paper plates, socks, fabrics, and Styrofoam. Barragar Dunne (1988/1993) identifies four categories of puppets: rod puppets, shadow puppets, hand puppets, and marionette puppets. Most puppets fit into one of these categories. Puppets are wonderful containers for angry, aggressive feelings. They enable adolescents to express these feelings in a playful manner, without the fear of being overwhelmed by them as might occur were they to express these feelings directly. It is not uncommon for children or adolescents with a puppet on each hand to use one puppet to "bop" the other as a safe expression of anger and aggression.

Masks can also be ready-made or created from a variety of different materials. Mask work can be extremely powerful and can often be quite transformational. Masks can be used to explore two sides of an issue, or hidden or unexpressed feelings, qualities, or roles. Adolescents can be asked to create one mask to represent their private selves and a second to represent the face they allow the world to see (Jennings, 1986). Adolescents who have engaged in violent, aggressive, or sexually assaultive behaviors often have difficulty visualizing their sense of personal power in ways that do not involve controlling others. Making masks that represent their sense of internal power can help these adolescents to visualize their power as having a source other than violence and physical prowess.

Face painting is yet another form of mask making, but one that requires the mask to be created directly on the face. Face painting has been used ritualistically in many cultures throughout, and probably before, recorded history. In drama therapy, face painting can be done in conjunction with storytelling (Landy, 1986), or as a prelude to role-playing or other types of enactments. Face painting is most effective when stage make-up is used, as the colors tend to be stronger and more dramatic. Mirrors should be made available so that clients can observe both the process and the product of the make-up application. Face painting allows adolescent clients an opportunity to uncover previously unexplored roles, and becomes a vehicle for a deeper level of self-expression (MacKay, 1987).

Closure in drama therapy, as in traditional therapy, marks the transition between the work of the session and the return to the everyday world (Landy, 1986). It is a time for calming, reflection, and feedback. In drama therapy closure involves de-roling, a means of leaving the role behind and grounding the client in the reality of the present. Closure can be accomplished via simple processing but must include an opportunity for the client to separate from the character or role. It is important that the adolescent does not remain stuck in the role or in the emotion that may have been expressed via the role-playing (Emunah, 1995). Activities such as talking about the character in the third person, writing a postcard or letter to the character, or identifying differences and commonalities between self and role help insure that adequate de-roling takes place. Reflection and feedback should never be a critique of the work, but rather an opportunity for others to communicate how they may have been impacted by the work, or ways they may have identified with the role or situation.

DRAMA THERAPY TOOLS AND MATERIALS

Although drama therapy can be highly effective with no props or materials whatsoever, some tools prove helpful in motivating and inspiring both the therapist and the adolescent client. Adolescents will rarely dive into a costume basket within the first few sessions. They tend to start with smaller props and costume pieces until they have warmed up to the idea. As a result, the therapist may have several different baskets available. One can be filled with pieces of fabric in a wide variety of sizes, textures, and colors that can be used for fashioning costumes or creating environments. Some therapists may prefer not to add typical costume pieces as the fabric pieces provide a greater opportunity for projection and creativity. Most adolescents need a few sessions to warm up to the use of costumes. A hat box can hold hats such as Sunday bonnets, witch and wizard hats, a top hat, glittery crowns, and a police officer's cap, among others. Another basket may be filled with smaller costume pieces such as ties, purses, scarves, gloves, jewelry, badges, and several different types of sunglasses. The last basket can be filled with a variety of props that may be the most popular among adolescents. They can grab one or two items that help to quickly establish character, mood, or setting. The prop basket may contain items such as handcuffs, a feather duster, a stethoscope, pretend money, a genie's lantern, medical equipment, gauze and bandages, a set of eating utensils, a toy microphone, baby bottles, and several telephones.

Two items considered essential are sunglasses and telephones. Sunglasses change us. Watch someone as they put on an especially "cool" pair of sunglasses and you will likely witness a transformation. The change may be subtle, such as a cocking of the head, or it may be more distinct and include a change in body stance and persona. Sunglasses somehow provide a disguise as well as a safety shield. In drama therapy they provide access to a variety of roles and provide distance from issues that might otherwise be too overwhelming. In the movie *Big Daddy*, Julian is the child left on Sonny's (Adam Sandler) doorstep. Whenever Julian is afraid he puts on his sunglasses and becomes "invisible." "Invisibility" helps Julian to conquer new or difficult situations by allowing him to feel safe and less vulnerable. Sunglasses afford adolescents the same benefits.

Telephones are an especially familiar mode of communication for adolescents, who often stay on the phone for hours at a time. Using telephones in therapy is, therefore, comfortable and natural for adolescents. Prop boxes may contain several different types of telephones including cellular and portable phones. Real telephones rather than toy ones are useful because they allow adolescents to move beyond pretending. Telephones are wonderful props. Like sunglasses, they provide easy access to certain characters such as the self-absorbed businessman, the chatty salesperson, or the angry parent. Even the most resistant adolescents seem to feel quite at ease picking up one of the phones and beginning a conversation with an imaginary person on the other end. The telephone affords the sense of freedom that enables one to express thoughts and feelings that otherwise might be left unsaid.

It is not necessary to buy large, expensive puppets. Some of adolescents' favorite puppets can be found at a dollar store. It is also not necessary to have every puppet-character available. It is important to provide both negative and positive themed puppets and to include several with wide mouths. Since puppets become a projection and extension of the self, they must be comfortable on the hand and easy to manipulate.

A mask collection is a valuable resource and may include rubber monster masks, superhero-type half masks, Mardi Gras style masks, and blank white plastic masks that can be drawn on and then cleaned off.

It is helpful to have materials for making masks and puppets. Consider keeping an assortment of materials on hand including: plaster coated gauze, paper plates, tongue depressors, and various art materials.

Most drama therapy tools and materials may be obtained via the bargain table at fabric stores, thrift shops, second-hand stores, and dollar or discount stores. The day after Halloween is a national holiday for drama therapists, as a treasure trove of props and costume pieces become available at bargain prices.

CASE ILLUSTRATION

Amy is an explosive sixteen-year-old brought to therapy by her mother at the request of Amy's school. Amy is extremely bright and has been primarily a straight-A student with no prior history of conduct or behavior problems at school. Approximately one year prior to her referral, Amy's alcoholic father had met another woman and completely abandoned his family. Since that time the frequency and intensity of Amy's anger outbursts had progressively increased. Amy's mother had been the primary target of Amy's anger. Amy would scream at her mother at the top of her lungs, with little provocation, getting right up to her mothers face and on numerous occasions had hit, punched, and kicked her mother. Following her tirades Amy would always apologize, insist that she could not control her temper, and beg her mother's forgiveness.

Until about one month before our first session, Amy's outbursts had been limited to her home environment. Her anger, however, had become less and less within her control and had begun spilling over into her school and social environments. Amy had been defiant and argumentative with her teachers, cursing and yelling at them. She had walked out of class several times and, on one occasion, had thrown a pencil at a teacher, just missing the teacher's eye. Not surprisingly, when Amy came to my office for the first time, she was out of school for her second suspension. Her mother admitted, in front of Amy, that she felt she could not control her daughter and often gave in to Amy's demands in order to avoid a conflict. Amy's mother also expressed concern that Amy was becoming alienated from her friends who had begun to avoid Amy because she regularly instigated arguments and was often verbally aggressive. Amy consistently externalized blame. Nothing was ever her fault.

The first time I met Amy she was slouching way down in a chair in my office waiting room, her hair completely covering her face. I introduced myself and Amy quickly turned her head away. "She says she won't talk to you," her mother said. "She doesn't have to," I responded. Amy then accompanied me to my office and plopped herself down on the sofa with her legs hanging over the arm of the sofa and her face covered with her jacket. I offered her a pillow. She took it, put it over her face, and told me she was only here because her school was making her come. She insisted that she wasn't going to tell me anything. I told her she didn't have to. I didn't ask her about school or her conflicts with her mother or about her anger. After a few moments she began complaining about her mother. She spent the rest of that first session using foul and hateful language to complain about her mother—her words purposefully creating a wall, a shield to contain her pain deep within.

Amy began the second session pretty much the way she started the first, dropping herself onto my sofa, crossing her arms across her chest, and relentlessly complaining—about her mother, her friends, her school. When she paused to take a breath I asked, "How do I get in there?" Amy responded,

"Don't ask me; you're the therapist!" I asked Amy if she would like to be the therapist for a while. Amy quickly sat up, her eyes brightened, her body posture softened, and she indifferently shrugged her shoulders and said "OK." We switched seats. I slouched on the sofa, pulled a pillow in front of me, and took on the role of the angry adolescent. I named myself Tammy. "This is stupid. I'm not telling you anything. It's my mother who's the crazy one, not me!" I angrily stated.

Amy cheerfully took on the role of therapist, mimicking my body posture and voice. She leaned forward and said, "Look if you keep everything locked up inside of you, you'll explode."

"You think you know me but you don't know anything." I responded.

"You just like to be angry," Amy, the therapist, told me.

"That's stupid" I said, "why would I like to be angry?"

Amy replied, "Maybe because it's safer." At that moment Amy broke out of the therapist role. "Man this is a hard job." She said.

During the next session we utilized this same strategy, with me again taking on the role of the angry adolescent while Amy played the role of my mother. We argued about curfew and dating. I begged my "mother" to let go and let me grow up, while at the same time criticizing her for not spending enough time with me. Amy decided the mother needed therapy. I was assigned the role of the mother, and Amy reprised her role of the therapist.

Amy's normal conflict between the roles of child and adolescent was enhanced by her father's disappearance right at the time when Amy's turmoil was at its pinnacle. She needed to know that her mother was still there for her, but also needed to separate and develop a sense of herself as an independent being. This conflict fueled Amy's anger.

As our role-playing continued, Amy's father became a focus for the characters. Amy never chose to have "the disappearing dad" as a character in our role-play. This would likely have been overwhelming for her. Instead, he appeared as a focus of Amy's anger and pain. Via the role-playing, Amy was able to come to terms with the anger she felt toward her father and to understand how she displaced that anger onto her mother—the safer target. She was also able to admit to the enormous pain that she hid beneath her anger, because it was safer to be angry. Anger did not make her feel more vulnerable, but instead gave her a false sense of strength and power.

As our sessions continued, the scenes at times involved friends, teachers, and siblings. Amy began to venture into the props and costume pieces to enhance her characterization and used humor to expose particularly difficult issues. Over time, the intensity and frequency of Amy's anger outbursts decreased and she began to feel a greater sense of control over her emotions.

Amy's mother participated in some of the sessions. At times, Amy assigned her a role. In other sessions Amy cast her mother as an inanimate object such as a tree in a dark forest, or a big, soft, comfy chair. In several sessions I structured the activities. Amy and her mother were instructed to work together to design the plans for their dream house. They were then asked to use the sand tray to create a model of the dream house, and to then use family doll figures to enact a scene between family members in the house.

During one of Amy's final sessions, she and her mother were sent on an adventure to find a hidden treasure. The treasure was actually some gold wrapped chocolates that I had previously hidden in the room. Amy and her mother were given three cards that outlined tasks that had to be accomplished along their journey. Their tasks included crossing a raging river without a boat and building a shelter out of found materials. Each was asked to develop a character and to give their character attributes that might be helpful in accomplishing their tasks. Amy and her mother particularly enjoyed this activity. They playfully joined together to plan their journey, complete the tasks, and discover the treasure.

As the sessions progressed, Amy's relationship with her mother became less confrontational. Amy discovered that she did not have to remain in the role of the angry teen in order to be safe from her emotions. Amy and her mother spent more time engaged in fun, shared activities, and Amy was able to accept affection from her mother again. Although the two continue to argue, Amy's mother has learned to avoid power struggles and has learned to listen and communicate with Amy more effectively. As a result she has begun to enjoy her daughter again.

CONCLUSIONS

Drama therapy is an approach that is well suited to work with adolescents. Drama therapy allows adolescents an opportunity to try out a range of roles and to move away from the peer influenced role restrictiveness that is so common among adolescents. It affords them a safe environment for exploration and experimentation, allowing them to discover sides of themselves that they may not have known existed. Drama therapy respects the developing maturity of the adolescent while giving them permission to be playful and creative.

Therapists wishing to utilize drama therapy techniques with adolescents would be well served to obtain training and supervision before attempting this work with clients. Although acting training is not necessarily a prerequisite, it is essential that therapists are comfortable with role taking and engaging in creative play. Drama therapists must be adequately in touch with their own issues and prejudices in order to avoid censoring or influencing the choice of roles or the progression of an enactment.

Drama therapy is an incredibly powerful modality that can lead to self-discovery and emotional growth and change. This can only occur, however, if the drama therapist provides an emotionally safe therapeutic environment in which containment and expression are balanced.

Adolescence is undoubtedly a time of turmoil and unrest, but it can also be a time of awareness and great discovery. The task for therapists is to find effective ways to engage adolescents, to win their trust, and to offer them opportunities to explore and discover their emerging sense of self.

REFERENCES

Barragar Dunne, P. 1988/1993. *Media in Drama Therapy*. Los Angeles: Drama Therapy Institute of Los Angeles.

Big Daddy. 1999. Columbia Pictures: Culver City, California.

Cattanach, A. 1994. *Play Therapy: Where the Sky Meets the Underworld*. London: Jessica Kingsley Publishers.

Courtney, R. 1968. *Play, Drama and Thought*. New York: Drama Book Specialists.

———. 1981. The universal theatre: Background to drama therapy. In *Drama in Therapy, Volume Two*, ed. G. Schattner and R. Courtney, 1–10. New York: Drama Book Specialists.

Dayton, T. 1994. *The Drama Within*. Deerfield Beech, FL: Health Communications Inc.

Emunah, R. 1995. From adolescent trauma to adolescent drama: Group drama therapy with emotionally disturbed youth. In *Dramatherapy with Children and Adolescents*, ed. S. Jennings, 150–68. London: Routledge.

Furman, L. 1990. Video therapy: An alternative for the treatment of adolescents. *The Arts in Psychotherapy* 17: 165–69.

Gallo-Lopez, L. 2000. A creative play therapy approach to the group treatment of sexually abused children. In *Short-Term Play Therapy for Children*, ed. H. G. Kaduson and C. E. Schaefer, 269–95. New York: The Guilford Press.

———. 2001. TV show storyboard. In *101 More Favorite Play Therapy Techniques*, ed. H.G. Kaduson and C.E. Schaefer, 8–10. Northvale, NJ: Jason Aronson Inc.

Jennings, S. 1986. *Creative Drama in Group Work*. London: Winslow Press.

Jones, T., and H. Schmidt. 1960. *The Fantasticks*. New York: Avon Books.

Landy, R. (1986). *Drama Therapy Concepts and Practices*. Springfield, Ill.: Charles C. Thomas.

———. 1993. *Persona and Performance: The Meaning of Role in Drama, Therapy, and Everyday Life*. New York: The Guilford

MacKay, B. 1987. Uncovering covered roles through face painting and storytelling. *The Arts in Psychotherapy* 14: 201–8.

Oaklander, V. 1969/1988. *Windows to Our Children*. New York: Gestalt Journal Press.

Sarbin, T. 1954. Role theory. In *Handbook of Social Psychology*, vol. I, ed. G. Lindzey. Cambridge: Addison-Wesley.

Stone, G. P. 1971. The play of little children. In *Child's Play*, ed. R. E. Herron and B. Sutton-Smith, 4–14. New York: Wiley.

Adolescent Play Therapy from a Nondirective Stance

Virginia Ryan and Kate Wilson

$\mathcal{T}$his chapter explores the viability and effectiveness of nondirective play therapy as a means of addressing the therapeutic needs of troubled adolescents. The appropriateness of using play therapy with children over the age of twelve with normal intelligence has been questioned by some therapists (e.g., Shelby, 2000), and clinical examples of play therapy with adolescents are seldom documented in the literature. However, nondirective play therapy is a theoretically justifiable approach to working with adolescents. Provided the specific developmental needs of adolescents are kept in mind, and the approach is adapted appropriately to meet these, it is an effective and robust method of working with this age group. Briefly, nondirective play therapy can help adolescents integrate into their developing sense of unique personal identity their earlier childhood experiences, present concerns, and more adult concerns about the future. Because the approach encompasses both play and verbal communication, it is well suited to addressing adolescent concerns, particularly those of early adolescence.

This chapter considers first the model and the theoretical framework of nondirective play therapy and describes the advances made on both sides of the Atlantic in recent years, then sets out general practice principles and some of the age-appropriate adaptations necessary for working with adolescents. A composite case account and illustrative examples of other cases are used to show how traumatic or painful early memories may be reworked on a cognitive, emotional, and motor level using this approach. These cases will demonstrate that the essentially nondirective nature of the method can avoid the feelings of adult overintrusion that may be risked when working with adolescents by a directive or interpretative therapeutic stance.

As other chapters in this book make clear, adolescence is a critical period of development for all individuals, but especially those who have suffered earlier emotional difficulties or trauma. Children and adolescents who have been maltreated have particular difficulties in integrating experiences that have been abusive into an emotionally healthy sense of self. When adolescents' personal mental schemas have been underdeveloped or distorted, they may have difficulty in reworking schemas formed in childhood and adapting them to more emotionally healthy ways of functioning in later adult relationships. They may not only bring into adolescence their often unresolved emotional experiences, but may also lack appropriate adults with whom they can examine troubling current experiences. Difficulties in forming relationships with peers and in becoming integrated into wider adult society may also be present.

It has been suggested that if earlier emotional difficulties go unaddressed, patterns of behavior that become established during this period may be much more resistant to change later in adulthood (Box, 1986). Recent family systems' perspectives on adolescent development have also seen this period as one involving a renegotiation of forms of psychological dependence (Pastore and Ainley, 2000). Therefore, it is important to offer effective therapeutic interventions to emotionally damaged adolescents, so that they may receive help at a time when they are developmentally receptive to it. Part of the challenge for practitioners, however, is that more traditional talk therapies may be resisted by adolescents (Malchiodi, 1999). Malchiodi, an art therapist, has argued that to be effective, therapists need to be flexible and creative in working with adolescents because the "usual approaches to intervention and treatment may not always fit." (p. 14). In addition, their deeply disturbing earlier memories, and current difficult experiences, seem to require a more intensive realignment in therapy than therapeutic approaches based on verbal exchanges alone seem to provide. Nondirective play therapy is a flexible and adaptable method that can take into account the varying responses and needs of adolescents and allows exploration of emotional difficulties in a creative, individually directed way on all levels of mental functioning. Behavioral, perceptual, and motor levels, as well as cognitive and emotional levels, are activated and reworked spontaneously during nondirective play therapy.

NONDIRECTIVE PLAY THERAPY: AN OVERVIEW OF THE APPROACH

Nondirective play therapy was developed in North America by Axline (1946/ 1987) and Dorfman (1952) who adapted Rogerian client-centered therapy with adults to child therapy. The use of play as the principal medium of communication in therapy with children had been introduced by Anna Freud and Melanie Klein (Wolff, 1996), and further established by later practitioners such as Moustakas (1959), Allen (1942), and Ginott (1961). However, as a deliberate riposte to what they considered the inflexible and overly theoretical stance of psychoanalytic approaches on the one hand, and the simplistic and prescriptive tendencies of behavioral approaches on the other, these practitioners eschewed the rigorous development of the theoretical underpinnings of the method. Possibly as a result of this, nondirective play therapy failed to develop into a major school of therapy with carefully formulated techniques and tended to be practiced, particularly in the UK, in a somewhat ad hoc and atheoretical manner and to drift into other methods. More recently, however, both the theory and practice of nondirective play therapy as a method have been developed in North America, most notably by Landreth (1991) and Guerney (1983), and in the UK by the present authors (Wilson, Kendrick, and Ryan, 1992; Ryan and Wilson, 1996/2000).

The distinctive feature of nondirective play therapy—and the one that distinguishes it from other play interventions and play therapies—is its nondirective nature. The choice of issues and the focus of play and actions in the playroom are determined by the child rather than the adult, within certain carefully delineated boundaries. In nondirective play therapy, therapists assume that children and adolescents will instigate changes and gain therapeutic insights themselves. The therapist's role is to develop a close, trusting relationship with them, and to reflect and respond to their thoughts, feelings, and play activities in such a way as to facilitate the resolution of their emotional difficulties at their own pace and in their chosen manner. A core skill, then, is to reflect children and adolescents' feelings during sessions in an accurate but nonthreatening manner. Certain basic limits to behavior in the playroom are set, and the therapist has adult responsibility for physical and emotional safety, for care of the materials and the room, and for time limits. Within these clear and consistent boundaries, the atmosphere in the playroom is intended to be relaxed. The therapist's behavior and communications are designed to promote a sense of trust and safety in which children and adolescents feel free, if they wish, to express and explore issues of emotional saliency. The key characteristics of the therapist's role in nondirective play therapy, then, are:

1. Developing a trusting relationship with children and adolescents by creating a relaxed permissive environment.
2. Enabling children/adolescents to choose the focus of their own activities and topics of interest as the focus of intervention, rather than these being chosen by the therapist.

3. Applying therapeutic limits, including limits of safety, to children and adolescents' actions.

4. Employing his/her own thoughts and feelings congruently in listening, understanding, and reflecting back to children and adolescents the appropriate adult responses to ongoing actions, language, and play.

5. Responding to children and adolescent's expressed feelings, thoughts, and actions by reflecting these back to them in a nonthreatening way.

A THEORETICAL FRAMEWORK FOR NONDIRECTIVE PLAY THERAPY WITH ADOLESCENTS

This volume attests to the increasing recognition that play is developmentally important throughout the life span and that play is therapeutically valuable with adolescents and adults in its own right, instead of being seen as "regressive" or as a means of help confined to young children. Concurrently, the traditional view that adult classification systems for mental disorders and adult-based therapies can be modified for childhood and adolescent problems is being replaced by a developmental psychopathology framework. This framework and the research and treatment resulting from it represents a significant change in thinking. Classifications of psychopathologies and therapies can now be both valued and evaluated for their developmental sensitivity and their suitability to the issues of children and adolescents (Blakemore-Brown, 2001; Ryan and Needham, 2001; Wenar and Kerig, 2000).

The first author's training, thinking, and practice have been based on the primary importance of a developmentally sensitive model of mental processes and therapy. Toward that end a model was proposed with the hope of beginning to explain the power and potential of play in therapy and in everyday life. In this model play, and its role in therapy, is placed within a broader theoretical framework of mental development (Wilson et al., 1992, chapter 2). This model will be introduced below, then concentration will shift to adolescent development and therapy generally, and finally its relevance to one therapeutic method, nondirective play therapy.

The general approach of this model is a broadly Piagetian and organismic one, with the basic assumption that all activity, including mental activity, furthers adaptation of organisms to their environment. This adaptation consists of taking in or assimilating the environment to the organism's ongoing activity and simultaneously adjusting to or accommodating the demands of the environment. Experiences, therefore, are actively internalized into past experiences; and assimilation of other people, objects, and internal mental activities is a more basic and fundamental activity than accommodation. In this context, symbolic play is assumed to be a highly assimilative activity, and similar to dreaming and daydreaming in being a highly spontaneous, self-regulatory mental activity. With symbolic play all events are assimilated into mental activities without conscious attempts to accommodate to the environment. (Intelligent actions, such as planning and problems solving, however, are highly accommodating mental activities and take environmental constraints into consideration in order to be effective.) When children and adults truly play, therefore, feelings of freedom and joyful self-expression emerge for them because environmental constraints can be put aside within a socially and personally acceptable, contained "space."

The second major assumption is the principle of organization; an organism's activity is assumed to always be related to other similar acts in systematic ways. These two principles of organization and adaptation are the two faces of biological activity: underlying internal organization of organisms is externalized as adaptation. Piaget (1951/1962) used the term *schema* to refer to the structures assumed to arise in mental organization of past experiences. Organisms are assumed to often act in the present on the basis of schemas of past experiences, but these frameworks for experiences are also assumed to be nondeterministic. Schemas are viewed as "mobile frames" since organisms must both assimilate new events to past experiences and accommodate themselves to present situations. During development organisms and schemas themselves are assumed to undergo internal differentiation, resulting in increased capacity to discriminate among events within schemas, as well as increased and more complex interconnections among schemas. (We have chosen the commonly used plural *schemas*, rather than the more correct term *schemata* in our writing.) The previous biological concepts are now more familiar because they have been employed extensively since Piaget by attachment theorists and infant development researchers (e.g., Bowlby, 1969; Stern, 1985; Trevarthan, 1980) in particular.

Piaget divided schemas into broadly two types, personal (i.e., those involving people) and objective (i.e., those relating to objects). He further assumed that both types of schemas have affective, cognitive, and motor components. That is, while affective, cognitive, and motor components are not experientially separate, and all three components contribute to each mental state, they can be separated for the purpose of discussing and understanding mental organization. Thus, objective schemas are usually more highly cognitive and personal schemas are more highly affective. With development, as stated previously, schemas become more highly differentiated and more interconnected. For example, more highly developed emotional responses become more highly influenced by higher order cognitive appraisals, as developmental research into emotional understanding (e.g., Harris, 1989) and "theory of mind" attests.

These findings on emotional understanding and "emotional intelligence" are of great interest to therapists, because the findings seem to point to the potential interrelationship and effectiveness of differing kinds of therapeutic interventions. That is, some therapies are more devoted to the "cognitive"; others, including nondirective play therapy, to the "emotional"; and yet others to the "perceptual" and "behavioral" aspects of schemas. In this context, Piaget (1951/1962) assumed that affective schemas do not develop as much generalizability and mobility as cognitive schemas. However, recent developmental research in emotional understanding, emotional intelligence, and neurological processing of procedural ("intuitive") memories and traumas all point to a research trend toward closer examination of the development of personal schemas and their potential capacity for growth and flexibility. Developmentally, children and adolescents develop increasing capacities for cognitive insight into their emotional life and voluntary control over their emotional responses and behavior (i.e., in shorthand, "left-brain" processing).

Yet the processing of events and internal responses experientially (i.e., "right-brain" processing) seems equally important. From a therapeutic viewpoint, therapeutic progress and "insight" for emotionally troubled young children is on the level of experiential, personally assimilative experiences, since this is the primary means young children have for assimilating important events. Concrete cognitive experiences and verbalizing (e.g., structured exercises, etc.) can be utilized by children in middle childhood, along with primarily assimilative experiences of spontaneous play in therapy. By adolescence both types of responses may become increasingly possible. Yet therapeutic insight may be largely on a "half-conscious," experiential level for adolescents and adults too, given the ways in which personally salient experiences are usually processed.

Turning now to consciousness, the mind is consciously active, regardless of our conscious awareness of mental activity. When we are assimilating experiences, we usually are not conscious of our ongoing thought processes; we only become conscious of them when the end results of our mental activities are translated into symbols. Every mental activity, therefore, varies in its possibility for and degree of conscious awareness (Walls, 1972). Because personal schemas are largely assimilative and highly affective, the symbols that are the end results of the activation of these schemas have a higher degree of "half-conscious" and unconscious contents attached to them. Freud (1900/1965) famously recognized this in *The Interpretation of Dreams,* viewing symbols as "ports of entry" to "networks" that are in a "state of excitation," and Jung (1964) later began elaborating his theory of symbols in *Man and His Symbols.*

Symbols can be usefully classified as "referential"—that is an inner or outer event is transformed into an objective symbolic representation to describe facts—and "emotive," in which the feelings about events are given symbolic representation. Our symbolic capacity can also be classified along the dimension of meaningfulness. Every symbol must have personal and unique meanings for each of us, since each of our life experiences differs. Yet equally, symbols have shared meanings because our experiences are never wholly unique. During development, children and adolescents gradually acquire more capacity to express and expand all these symbols on an internal, mental level. Young children require a heavy reliance on external experiences and concrete props (e.g., toys, adult-led verbalization) to become conscious of their mental representations, largely in the form of mental images, rather than of "inner speech." Therapists work at the level of children and adolescents' developmental capacities, with therapists using their own language skills to scaffold and contain difficult experiences. These are the "reflections" of feelings in nondirective practice, which for Rogers (1989) includes the cognitive experiential context of the emotional as well as the emotion itself. Older children and adolescents are more able to use internal means of processing their experiences, using inner verbalization in addition to mental imagery. Thus nondirective play therapy with adolescents, we will argue, that has the potential for both symbolic representations via art, music, role play, alongside verbal communication, seems well adapted to adolescents' mental abilities.

Personally emotive symbols, however, seem to have a lower level of shared meanings and are embedded in more highly affective schemas. Therefore, these are the most difficult experiences to share with others, and present particular difficulties for young children before their mental capacity and symbolic play have developed sufficiently (Ryan, 1999; Ryan and Wilson, 2000). Therapists are needed to help children and adolescents process personally meaningful symbols that have threatening and malevolent emotions bound to them. They may be worked through in the playroom thought-by-thought; thoughts may merge and converge into other symbols, or high anxiety may activate mental coping responses. Play may be interrupted, and children and adolescents may cope by distracting themselves, or denying and distorting their personal experiences, in order to alleviate their emotional distress.

During development these coping strategies are largely nonexistent initially; children begin by expressing their anxiety directly because their mental coping strategies are limited. Their internal strategies seem to gradually develop hand-in-hand with their general level of mental development; adolescent coping strategies, therefore, are often less well developed and entrenched than adults, yet more sophisticated than younger children's. Overall, from early childhood onward, therapists try to help by providing a relaxing environment where children and adolescents can bypass their defenses and give symbolic representation to experiences and thoughts that are largely outside conscious awareness, helping them differentiate and more accurately symbolize these experiences for themselves.

Looking now at play in light of this general framework of mental development, play seems to be an innate capacity that has a mental organizing function during development and is one of the main means children use to develop their understanding of themselves and others, explore conflicts, and rehearse new social and emotional skills (Ablon, 1996; Cohen, 1993; Piaget, 1951/1962; Russ, 1995; Winnicott, 1971/1986). This direct use of symbolic play declines, however, as verbalization and inner thought develop, with play becoming more highly ritualized. Formal games and sports often take precedence over spontaneous play with friends. When spontaneous play is engaged in, it may take on a more limited, socially acceptable, or unacceptable acting out of personal fantasies (e.g., riding "no hands" down the road on a bicycle), or it may fulfill group fantasies in socially acceptable (e.g., a snowball fight) or unacceptable and delinquent ways.

As these examples imply, another strength in activating play during therapy for adolescents, is that play, in addition to activating symbols on a primarily emotive level—rather than a referential level—activates the perceptual and motor level of schemas more thoroughly than other more adult-oriented therapies (e.g., art therapy, counseling). A play activity in which the whole body is utilized has the potential to activate memories and current experiences stored at a primarily bodily level. These experiences may be incompletely processed traumatic memories, such as those involved in physical and sexual abuse (Ryan, 2001; Ryan and Wilson, 2000) or they may be memories of "worst moments," or feelings accompanying bodily impairments arising from accidental injuries (Ryan and Needham, 2001). Play therapy may give adolescents who "act out" their anxieties and frustrations in personally and socially destructive ways a chance to work through their past and current experiences, and their new bodily sensations and feelings, in an active, yet contained manner. This in turn may lead them to develop a more varied and complex means of processing personally meaningful events through mental processing (e.g., daydreaming, fantasizing, dreaming), and through more socially structured means (e.g., music, film, books, verbal dialogues), and through more intimate peer and family relationships. Nondirective play therapy is a way for them to discover their potentials, aspirations, and satisfactions in a fluid, active, and engaged relationship.

Adolescents who need additional help in processing difficult events, in developing more trusting relationships, and in channeling their inner thoughts and outer activities to rework and manage highly charged personal experiences creatively, may be helped by nondirective play therapy sessions. These adolescents, as they grow into adulthood, may then—along with the majority of adolescents who do not need this input—have largely ceased their own spontaneous, symbolic play. But all adults who become parents may recapture their spontaneous symbolic play capacities in enabling their own children to play creatively. (Or they may become play therapists and have the fortunate role of helping children and adolescents by activating their own playfulness daily!)

RECENT ADVANCES IN NONDIRECTIVE PLAY THERAPY

There have been several exciting advances in play therapy generally and non-directive play therapy in particular during the last decade. First, the authors' own work in nondirective play therapy has a developmental emphasis, as the developmental framework for understanding symbolic play given previously shows. The emphasis in Britain is similar to North American play therapists' use of developmental concepts in discussing, for example, play therapy for posttraumatic stress symptoms (Shelby, 2001).

Second, the authors' nondirective play therapy writing, growing from work with statutory referrals, is a systemic approach that delineates ways in which professionals, therapists, caregivers, and birth families need to work in partnership to provide children and adolescents with emotional help and support (Ryan, Wilson, and Fisher, 1995; Ryan and Wilson, 1996/2000). American play therapists are increasingly valuing the seminal model of B. and L. Guerney (Van Fleet, 1994) and the work of Van Fleet (1994) and others in the research and practice of filial play therapy, a systemic way of working closely with children and their caregivers. Gil's family play therapy interventions (Gil, 2001) are innovative and creative ways of involving whole families in play therapy. In addition, Kraft and Landreth (1998) have recently developed their thinking on the role of caregivers and parents in nondirective play therapy. School-based play therapy offers another way of working systemically within children and adolescents' primary environments (Drewe, Carey, and Schaefer, 2001).

Finally, there are accumulating case examples in the play therapy literature of both nondirective and other play therapy practice (e.g., Ryan and Wilson, 1996/2000). Research studies in play therapy, including nondirective play therapy, is expanding primarily in the United States (see Ray, Bratton, Rhine, and Jones, 2001 for an overview), with beginning research efforts in Britain by Wilson and Ryan (2001), Wilson and Ryan (2002), and others (Carroll, 1999/2000; Leverton, 2000). These trends fit in with an emphasis on evidence-based practice generally for child therapy (Ramchandani, Joughin, and Zwi, 2001).

PRACTICE CONSIDERATIONS IN USING
THE NONDIRECTIVE METHOD
WITH ADOLESCENTS

In order to help practitioners in implementing the nondirective approach, this section sets out some of the main practice considerations for its use. Inevitably the discussion is brief, and the reader is referred for more detailed discussion to Landreth (1991) and the two books by the present authors (Wilson et al., 1992; Ryan and Wilson, 1996/2000). In work with adolescents, some important adaptations need to be made to the approach and considered alongside the basic practice techniques.

Careful Preparation and Planning

It is important to ensure that all those involved in the care of children and adolescents who are referred for therapy work together to provide an environment that promotes therapeutic progress (Ryan et al., 1995). This involves both considerations of timing and the availability of ongoing support during therapy. Both issues are likely to be important in all work with families, but become more critical in statutory work. These children and adolescents may be in potentially harmful care environments, or they may have been removed from birth families because of maltreatment. Children and adolescents starting therapy may be put further at risk if they are still living in abusive home environments. Equally, if they are living with relatively unsupportive foster caregivers, then it is unlikely that they will receive the additional emotional support needed to engage in therapy.

Potentially disturbing thoughts, feelings, and behavior may emerge during the course of play therapy and anxieties may be heightened at the outset in developing a relationship with an unfamiliar therapist. Therapeutic assessments will be needed to ensure adolescents' safety and environmental support prior to beginning therapy. (This assessment may recommend concurrent work with parents by another practitioner to address relationship and parenting issues.)

Children and adolescents may begin to change emotionally by making small shifts in their behavior and self-concept at home and school. It is essential that caregivers understand the significance of these changes, and are responsive to small but meaningful gains—for example, the expression of a wish for physical closeness from an adolescent who has hitherto kept adults at arms length. The therapist has a responsibility to help caregivers understand their role, and to make sense if necessary of children and adolescents' behavior. For example, for an adolescent girl living in a residential unit, the therapist emphasized the importance of the girl's residential worker remaining available in the waiting room during therapy sessions, despite the girl's outward offhandedness about this arrangement. The adolescent later remarked that this arrangement had been essential in order for her to engage in therapy sessions initially. Caregivers can provide the therapist with valuable information and insights from their own relationships with adolescents. All adults responsible for the care of adolescents need to be clear about their different roles and tasks (Ryan et al., 1995). This is particularly true of work undertaken in a statutory context, where three or more professionals/adults may be involved: the worker with responsibility for managing the case has the central role of coordination; the therapist is there to help resolve conflicts, create understanding, and lessen fears; and the caregiver (whether foster parent or birth parent) acts as an attachment figure and enables adolescents to establish and maintain a sense of identity and well-being (Koller, 1994).

Introductory and Progress Meetings

As with all therapies with children and adolescents, assessment and preliminary work with caregivers, referrers, and the children and adolescents themselves is vital in order to prepare them for what is involved and help them understand what to expect. Therapists will need to hold introductory meetings with caregivers, key professionals, and adolescents at referral to gain consent and cooperation, to help them understand the aims and practice methods of nondirective play therapy, and to discuss detailed practical arrangements. They will also establish how caregivers may need to be further involved and the timing and purpose of progress meetings. These should be held at agreed intervals, depending on the length of the intervention. For example, in a short intervention of eight sessions, it may be appropriate to hold a meeting with the caregivers after the sixth session to discuss progress and help integrate the adolescent's needs and new responses expressed in therapy into everyday life. Adolescents, unlike younger children, may choose to attend progress meetings themselves. Therapists may offer to discuss beforehand the themes they intend to raise in these meetings and share information openly with adolescents afterward.

Issues of Privacy and Confidentiality

In therapeutic work with both children and adolescents, therapists need to be clear about issues of privacy and confidentiality. However, concerns about these are likely to be more acute for adolescents, and it is essential both to anticipate and discuss these concerns, and the possible limits to confidentiality, at the outset. Many teenagers are self-conscious about others knowing they are having therapy at all, and having "play" therapy in particular. They will only manage to engage freely with the materials in the room if they can feel that the room is private and that they will not be observed or intruded upon.

> Rosie, aged fifteen, asked for the curtains to be drawn when she became aware of the window cleaner outside. "I'd feel stupid if anyone saw me in here with all these kids' things." She moved on to play with a doll, and then set up shop, but was clearly inhibited by sounds of the window cleaner outside, despite having the curtains drawn. (Cited in Wilson et al., 1992, p. 81)

It is, therefore, important to help adolescents think through an appropriately vague explanation to use in order to prevent teasing or labeling. Play therapy sessions can be arranged at times that make absence from school less obvious, for example lunchtimes or after school.

The reverse side of this need for confidentiality is that adolescents who have been maltreated may be particularly sensitive to the suggestion that the therapy sessions are to be kept private, since too much secrecy may be reminiscent of their abusive experiences during which they may have been forbidden to tell what was happening to them. Therefore, therapists need to give a clear message that although they will keep the sessions confidential (within certain limits), adolescents are free to talk about what happens to trusted people.

All therapists working with children and adolescents need to consider issues of confidentiality. This is partly because of their professional obligation to report allegations of abuse, but also because of the importance of involving caregivers, and sometimes schools, in the intervention, so that therapeutic progress is sustained in the adolescent's environment. Added considerations, then, include the kind of information to be shared with the caregivers and school and, when working in a statutory context, what kinds of information should be communicated to the referring agency and the courts (Ryan and Wilson, 2000).

With adolescents, confidentiality is likely to become a much more important issue than it is for younger children, and more complicated—particularly if statutory agencies are involved. Adolescents have the intellectual ability to understand, for example, the implications of the therapist writing about the sessions for a report to the court. Their particular stage of development, with all its concerns about keeping their developing identity separate and, therefore, to some extent concealed from their families, makes confidentiality a critical issue. Adolescents who have been abused may want complete confidentiality for several reasons. For example, the adolescent may have been subjected to different forms of coercion by adults to ensure the secrecy of the abuse. This need for security and exclusivity, then, may be generalized to any adult relationship, including that in therapy.

It is imperative that the therapist clarifies confidentiality issues and recording procedures with adolescents at the beginning of their time together. A failure to do this may mean that adolescents justifiably feel betrayed when the therapist has to report general session themes or specific concerns about abuse or dangerous behavior to others. In some instances it may be possible to find ways of minimizing these difficulties; for example, by citing a less personal or potentially embarrassing example to support the therapist's opinion in a report. However, in others, the therapist may decide, in balancing the possible negative impact on the therapeutic relationship with the long-term needs of an adolescent, that sensitive information needs to be shared.

In one case of work with a fourteen-year-old boy, the therapist discussed with him what she would say in her progress report to the referrers, and explained that she felt it essential to give her opinion that he had been sexually abused and emotionally harmed by his family. In talking this through, the teenager said he was much more worried about the therapist informing his social worker that he had cried in one of the sessions than he was about "the rest of it," clearly feeling anxious that he might appear effeminate. The therapist was able to reassure him that it wasn't necessary to tell the social worker about his tears. She needed to talk to others, as she'd said at the beginning, about child protection concerns, and sometimes about what he needed for his future care. It seemed to be a direct result of this discussion that the fourteen-year-old felt more able to work on his feelings of vulnerability and sexual identity in subsequent sessions.

Realistically, however, the adolescent's more sophisticated understanding of confidentiality may have a restricting effect on the therapy, and may make the relationship more guarded and less effective than it otherwise might have been. On the other hand, adolescents may find it reassuring that an adult is concerned enough to exercise authority and to take responsibility for protecting them. Therefore, it can model a healthy relationship between adults and adolescents.

For example, Patricia, age thirteen, had grown up in a family where adult-child roles were blurred in many areas, including sexual relationships. As a result of ongoing abuse concerns, and her family's failure to protect her, she was place in foster care and referred soon after for therapy. Because her family had so often distorted the truth in what they told her, a key issue for her in her initial sessions was whether the therapist would be a reliable and trustworthy person. She tested the therapist's trustworthiness repeatedly, questioning her about what she told other professionals and her foster parents, and asking her with genuine curiosity about the others who used the therapy room. The therapist stressed that she kept both what she said about Patricia's sessions and others' confidential, as she had said at the outset. She also reiterated that, although she accepted Patricia's genuine interest in others, their privacy was important also. They then had further conversations about the reasons for privacy. Their conversations seemed to help Patricia to focus on her own values and beliefs, and to begin to reflect on how these, and the therapist's values, differed from those of her own family. (For a more complete case discussion and analysis, see Ryan and Wilson, 1996/2000, chapter 6.)

Adapting the Play Therapy Room for Working with Adolescents

As in working with younger children, the therapist needs to select materials that lend themselves to unstructured symbolic play and activities. Materials such as art supplies, clay, puppets, and materials for dressing up and staging should be selected for the highest potential level of adolescent functioning as well as materials which can be used for younger, more regressive play. Some materials seem particularly well-adapted for older children and adolescents: Play-Doh and clay can be manipulated and modeled while talking; soft balls can be kicked around or used in organized games; playing cards can be used for magic tricks or card games with the therapist; puppets and dress-up clothes can be used for staging plays; and paints, chalks, and other drawing materials can be used for symbolic representations.

In organizing the therapy room, it is important to be aware of adolescents' heightened sensitivity and negative reaction to being treated like a child. Adult-size furniture, some structured games, and books should demonstrate to adolescents that the room is used for a range of ages to both sit and talk in and play in. As with younger children, the therapist must enable adolescents to feel a sense of permissiveness in the room that extends to whatever thoughts, activities, inaction, play, talk, and silence they themselves choose. By having available materials suitable for a range of ages, adolescents may be more easily reminded of different stages of their own development. For this reason, it is important to include in the therapy room materials that will allow this to occur, and to include a variety of objects with which both genders may identify—such as dolls, a doll's house, tea set, baby's bottle, bricks, farm animals, small creatures, scary figures, monsters, and masks. Unlike other more directive methods, or those based more exclusively on cognitive or verbal approaches, adolescents can choose materials and activities appropriate to themselves, and at the appropriate time for their use, free from outside pressure or fear of losing face.

Using Key Nondirective Skills in Therapy with Adolescents

While much has been written about basic nondirective skills, particular aspects of these skills need refinement and development when working with adolescents compared with younger children. As discussed earlier, different approaches to therapy often hone in on one major aspect of mental functioning in order to help clients effect positive changes in their lives. Nondirective play therapists emphasize the emotional, rather than the behavioral, or cognitive levels of mental functioning. Clients' feelings are given particular attention and therapists are trained to be highly aware of clients' feeling states, along with their own feelings arising within the therapeutic relationship. Therapists' adaptations of skills, due to the developmental needs of adolescents, therefore, often involve the development of more complex ways to convey feelings.

With adolescents, play therapists will be called on to refine the timing, accuracy, and complexity of their verbal reflections of feelings. Talking often is a primary means of establishing relationships with others for adolescents. Adolescents will generally be more advanced in both their awareness of complex feelings in themselves and others, and in their language development than younger children. Their language in play therapy, therefore, will be used in more varied and advanced ways as both a means of communication with others, and as an internal dialogue within themselves (e.g., "inner speech"). Nondirective play therapists, in turn, will also use their own feelings within therapeutic relationships with adolescents in more complex and varied ways than with younger children. Congruence, in which therapists' inner feelings match their outer expression of feelings and thoughts, will need to be practiced in a more developed way. Therapists will need to use the feelings arising for themselves within their relationships with adolescents genuinely, openly, and sensitively. By expressing their own congruent thoughts and feelings appropriately, therapists will enable adolescents to develop an acceptance of their own inner states and also to experience and increase understanding of appropriate, emotionally healthy adult responses to their own opinions, feelings, and values.

Another core skill, unconditional positive regard may also be more challenging to maintain for therapists. Adolescents may directly confront therapists' own deep-seated values and beliefs in their attempts to find out their own values. Often adolescents reveal to therapists experiences and thoughts that have real consequences in actual behavior, given their greater independence from adult authority and control than younger children. Both of these developmental issues may result in therapists having to increase their efforts at unconditional positive regard with adolescents.

Combining Counseling (Verbal Communication) and Play/ Activities in Working with Adolescents

Adolescents in nondirective play therapy will commonly use both symbolic play and verbal communication in their therapy sessions, and therapists need, therefore, to draw on nondirective counseling skills more intensively with this age group than they would when working with children. The extent to which adolescents use play, other activities, or speech to communicate their concerns will of course vary from young person to young person, and therapists need to develop their skills in responding congruently and appropriately to the adolescent's communications, whether expressed verbally or in symbolic play. The following examples illustrate this process in two very different ways.

In her early sessions, Patricia introduced previously, predominantly spoke about her resentment at being in therapy and feelings of missing her family, with the therapist sharing her thoughts with Patricia congruently where needed. As the sessions progressed, Patricia became increasingly absorbed in activity with her hands, covering them repeatedly with clay, and then allowing the clay to harden before washing it off. The therapist hypothesized (to herself, without interpreting to Patricia, as a psychodynamic therapist might have done) that these actions were a reworking on a motor and affective level of some of the abusive masturbatory experiences she had disclosed during earlier investigative interviews. As Patricia began to concentrate more on her activity, her verbal communications lost prominence in the sessions for a time, until, seemingly, she completed the reworking of these intensive experiences, and began verbalizing her feelings once more.

The case of Thomas, age fourteen, provides further illustration of the different ways adolescents may use both play activities and verbal communications in therapy. Thomas was referred for therapy by his school because despite being of average intelligence, he was showing marked learning and behavioral difficulties. He interacted badly with peers at school, had few friends there, and was becoming involved in increasingly delinquent activities that had brought him into trouble with the police. He was offered eight sessions with a trainee therapist. Two key themes emerged in Thomas's sessions, which he addressed both in play and through direct verbal communication. The first, illustrated here, was his sense of vulnerability and need for protection (which also paradoxically involved risk taking), and the second, not discussed at length, involved issues of mastery and anxieties about failure. (See Wilson and Ryan [2002] for a fuller discussion of this case.)

In his second session, Thomas used puppets and initially mimed being friends, with his monkey behaving lovingly and affectionately to the therapist's zebra. He then attacked the zebra suddenly and viciously, following this soon after with the instruction to the therapist to make friends and then repeating the process while the therapist reflected her feeling of being scared, confused, and vulnerable. The sequence evoked the sense of being bullied—in fact, painfully reminding the therapist of her own playground experiences. (Thomas later described his experiences of school bullies.)

In a later session, Thomas made a scene where trucks took rescue supplies to the Third World, repeatedly going to help protect innocent people from suffering, and looking for guns to use so that he could defend them. This theme was further amplified by reference to current news items about people he saw as victims. In later sessions, he used verbal communication rather than symbolic play to work through his concerns, talking, for example, about a boy who had been hurt at the school and how he wanted to punish the perpetrator. He was proud of his new steel toecaps on his shoes, which he said he needed as protection. Later this developed into explicit expression of his own feelings of vulnerability and victimization, as he described his experience of being bullied and mocked by other boys at school. In the last two sessions, a tricking game developed with a ball of salt dough, in which each had to try and catch the other out. For Thomas, it seemed that life was like that: a game you needed to be skilful at or you got hurt. It was important to be able to practice this in a safe place. The sense of security and acceptance in the playroom seemed essential to Thomas's ability first to enact and then to articulate these fears. In the final session he played a tape of his favorite group, singing the words to the therapist about "being safe with you." He knew he was not going to "get it wrong" within the therapy room, whereas outside he never quite knew the rules of the game and could never confidently fulfill the expectations of his teachers, his classmates, or his parents.

The play materials available in the play therapy room allowed Thomas to move easily between play activities and verbal communications. He used symbolic play, such as the exchange with the monkey and the zebra, to enact experiences that had saliency for him. The balls of dough enabled him to try out physical dexterity, and to play games in a setting where he felt secure and unthreatened. He enacted sequences of activities which communicated at intense emotional levels both to himself and to his therapist, but also verbalized his feelings as well, with the therapist combining nondirective counseling skills with play therapy skills to reflect her understanding of what he was communicating to her.

WORKING WITH ADOLESCENTS
WHO DISSOCIATE IN NONDIRECTIVE
PLAY THERAPY

This section will illustrate in more detail the work of nondirective play therapists with adolescents who dissociate. Dissociation is viewed as an automatic mental coping response to traumatic personal experiences; it becomes less normal and more pathological, according to the Diagnostic and Statistical Manual of Mental Disorders IV, when it involves a serious disruption in the "usually integrated functions of consciousness, memory, identity or perception of the environment" (American Psychiatric Association, 1994, p. 447). Extreme and habitual forms of dissociative responding may alter complex neurophysiologic processes; experiential information does not seem to be stored or processed to have its usual associations with other personally significant events when this occurs (Van der Kolk, 1994; Putnam, 1997).

The following example utilizes the first author's experiences in clinical practice as a nondirective play therapist with adolescents who dissociate by using a compilation of several of her cases that have strong clinical similarities to one another. A compilation of cases, rather than an individual case, will be used for two reasons. First, it bypasses issues of confidentiality arising for adolescents when asked by therapists to have their intimate clinical material used more publicly. Second, a compilation illustrates several aspects of nondirective play therapy simultaneously. The illustration will demonstrate: the therapist's use of a developmental framework to aid her responses and understanding; her use of key nondirective practice skills of empathy, congruence and unconditional regard; and a few ways in which other structured therapeutic techniques can be incorporated within an overall nondirective stance.

An Illustrative Example

Jane, a fourteen-year-old, was the second eldest of five children. She had been in her foster placement for a year along with one of her younger sisters when her play therapy began. A care order by the court had been made on the grounds that she and her siblings had been seriously neglected and unprotected from harm by their alcohol-addicted parents. There was a poor prognosis for recovery of their parents, and Jane and her sister were to remain in their foster placement long-term. Jane's younger sister had recently alleged sexual abuse by their maternal grandfather. Jane, too, had begun to talk to her foster caregivers about severe sexual abuse over an extended period of time by her maternal grandfather, but had remained silent during the investigative interview that had been carried out.

For Jane, her allegations seemed to be the first demonstration of deeper intimacy and trust in her foster caregivers' commitment to and concern for her. Jane generally was withdrawn and lacking in confidence, both around her caregivers and around other teenagers. Her physical maturity and overweight body seemed to create more self-consciousness in her and seemed literally a burden for her to carry around. While Jane took part in everyday family activities when requested by her caregivers, and was now more confident of both family and school rules and expectations, she often seemed to drift into her own internal world when not externally directed. Jane was frequently found by her caregivers to be staring blankly at the television screen, or spending long hours staring into space either in her bedroom or in the bathroom. Jane's school was concerned about her "blanking out" and "daydreaming" during lessons, as well as her lack of friends.

With Jane's agreement and with the agreement of the local authority, longer-term play therapy began after an initial therapeutic assessment period. Her assessment play sessions and initial further sessions began with Jane wanting the therapist to direct her activities; she seemed unable to play or talk spontaneously. Jane progressed toward choosing activities for herself, focusing on school-related activities, such as completing homework assignments and designing art projects. After a while Jane was drawn toward using the paints and Play-Doh on a nearby section of the table to complete her art work, and then began to busy herself with making shapes resembling food and drink for part of their sessions. More symbolic play emerged and, after several more sessions, Jane began to devise brief role-plays using puppets centered on domestic themes such as cooking and eating. These role-plays were suddenly transformed on a few occasions into highly emotionally charged scenes, with the therapist and Jane herself taking major acting roles. Jane's role would begin as the tormenter and the therapist as the victim, but then it would fragment into a distressing scene of Jane as the victim. Jane would become immobilized and drifted into her internal world.

During these dissociative episodes the therapist tried to be available to Jane by talking gently to her, but she was unreachable. However, Jane would suddenly become vigilant when the therapist arose and moved about the room to help Jane to end their sessions. After a few dissociative experiences in the presence of the therapist, Jane was able to hear the therapist's voice when she slowly emerged from her dissociative states, and seemed to realize the therapist had been trying to maintain emotional contact with her. The therapist was able to use her nondirective skills more actively at this point, verbally reflecting on Jane's state in an empathic way: "You seem all alone; it must be a frightening place to be" and "You seemed far away from me, thinking about things all by yourself."

The therapist had strong feelings of powerlessness, fears for Jane's mental state, and horror over the extent to which Jane must have been abused, based on her empathic understanding of Jane's feelings. However, she respected Jane's need for this way of coping with her overwhelming feelings and experiences, and managed her own reactions internally (and took them to invaluable, supportive consultation/supervisions). She strived to remain emotionally available to Jane during these episodes, without attempting to direct Jane's responses. By managing her own thoughts and feelings, the therapist was then able to express her feelings in a genuine and congruent way to Jane: "Seeing you turned off like that, and knowing you like to come here and be with me. . . . I feel sad about that for you" and "I'm glad I can be with you, so you're not alone now."

At the same time, the therapist seemed able to help Jane reconnect her internal feelings with her bodily state during these dissociative episodes. After the therapist repeatedly had expressed her emotional availability and understanding, Jane gradually began to spontaneously talk about her abusive memories. She started finding ways within the playroom of reconnecting her bodily states and feelings after these episodes, beginning to move around the room, and later to use musical instruments, dancing, and singing to express herself. Other structured techniques for bodily relaxation were initiated within the playroom and elaborated on at home. Jane was able to listen to the therapist's voice helping her body to relax: "You seem to need a very deep breath now . . . and another one" and "Your legs seem so cramped and stiff . . . they haven't moved for so long . . . needing a gentle stretch." And the therapist began to help her to reconnect herself with the world around her by reflecting: "You seem far away, if only you could reach out and touch something nearby, to know you're here."

These processes were gradually assimilated by Jane, as she began to become less threatened by her inner world, and much more consciously aware of her feelings, bodily states, and thoughts, with both the therapist's and her foster parents' understanding and help. Jane increasingly became able to be attuned to her physical and mental states when beginning to dissociate, able to verbalize feeling the tremors in her limbs, and seeing flashbacks of her abusive experiences. Using her increasingly close relationship to Jane, the therapist was able to metaphorically "hold onto" Jane and reassure her. As Jane developed her own self-awareness and feelings of emotional connection with the therapist, she grew less frightened. Gradually she became able to prevent herself dissociating, first in the playroom and then at home and at school.

Discussion of the Illustrative Example

This composite example showed that the way in which a nondirective play therapist works with adolescents with dissociative problems is one in which adolescents are helped to develop age appropriate control over their own bodily states, memories, and feelings. This self-direction is embedded within a nonthreatening relationship with the therapist. The therapist attempts to express her own feelings and thoughts genuinely and congruently within the relationship, going at the pace directed by adolescents, and refraining from interpretation and confrontation of the adolescents' dissociative strategy.

As discussed, developmentally adolescents need greater independence from adult control, often acted out by abused adolescents as being at the extreme of being "out of control" or of being "controlled by others." Adolescents increasingly make use of peer relationships for intimacy and shared values, yet also require close and intimate family relationships to help them support this development. For adolescents like Jane, neither peers nor family relationships supported her in her emotional development; a highly corrective and intensive relationship with a therapist was needed, alongside the skilled and caring therapeutic environment provided by her foster parents.

Nondirective therapists work within the whole presentation of adolescents and work with the clinical material they choose to share, rather than choosing a particular area of functioning to address with them. In Jane's case working with her dissociative episodes was only one part of her therapy and occurred when Jane herself chose to address them. Indeed, integrating these cut-off experiences is one of the goals of treatment for adolescents who dissociate. In play therapy this integration can occur on a bodily and perceptual level, as well as an emotional and cognitive one.

In some cases, however, the reworking of the bodily experiences alone in play and within a supportive therapeutic environment may be sufficient for integration to be achieved. Patricia, previously referenced, seemed to have strong ambivalence towards her hands, both grooming them carefully and yet sometimes finding them disgusting at a basic bodily level. During dreamlike states in her play therapy sessions, Patricia was observed:

> layering her hands with one bright color after another, until her hands became coated again, with the colors merging into a sticky turgid brown sludge . . . [her] body moving in a swaying, sensual motion . . . she was enjoying it so much. . . . As the paint thickened . . . Patricia kept going on, losing the nice colors . . . but didn't seem able to stop. Then I reflected her disgust with her sticky, messy, muddy-looking hands . . . and how quickly she had to scrub until all the paint was gone. . . . I always spoke briefly . . . almost to myself, but with feeling. [I]n her next sessions, she began to relax somewhat, her hand motions becoming less frantic and less prolonged. . . . She was uncharacteristically silent, yet her movements continued without self-consciousness or restraint. (Ryan and Wilson, 1996/2000, p. 169)

The use of nondirective skills, the need in particular for the therapist to use verbal responses with sensitivity and empathy, and to genuinely express her own congruent feelings arising within her relationships with adolescents are highlighted in the examples used.

CONCLUSION

In this chapter, it was argued that nondirective play therapy is an effective method of intervention with adolescents, provided that the approach is adapted to address some of the particular age-related issues which arise in working with adolescents. Therapists, in reflecting adolescents' feelings with sufficient accuracy, can communicate to them a sense of being understood and valued as individuals, without the feeling of overintrusion risked by a directive or interpretative stance. More specifically, this chapter has shown the value of symbolic play in enabling adolescents to rework traumatic memories on a bodily and emotional, as well as a cognitive level. The examples have illustrated how nondirective play therapists can help adolescents reintegrate their dissociative responses by reflecting and articulating sensations and feelings during this process.

The nondirective nature of the approach ensures that adolescents are left free to address concerns when they choose to do so, rather than at the instigation of the therapist. This has both the advantage of respecting adolescents' emerging adult identities, and also, as in the case of Jane, of leaving defenses against intrusive memories intact. Cognitive processing and conscious acknowledgement may (or may not) occur at a later date or in another context. Finally, clinical examples were used throughout to show how this highly individualized, flexible, and integrated therapeutic approach enables adolescents to develop complex, individual—and hopefully more manageable—relationships with significant adults and peers at a crucial developmental period in their lives.

REFERENCES

Ablon, S. L. 1996. The therapeutic action of play. *Journal of the American Academy of Child and Adolescent Psychiatry* 35(4): 545–47.

Allen, F. H. 1942. *Psychotherapy with Children*. New York: Norton.

American Psychiatric Association. 1994. *Diagnostic and Statistical Manual of Mental Disorders*. 4th ed. Washington, DC: American Psychological Association.

Axline, V. 1987. *Play Therapy*. Rev ed. New York: Ballantine Books. First edition published in 1946.

Blakemore-Brown, L. 2001. *Reweaving the Autistic Tapestry*. London: Jessica Kingsley.

Bowlby, J. 1969. *Attachment and Loss, Vol. 1: Attachment*. London: Pimlico.

Box, S. 1986. Some thoughts about therapeutic change in families at adolescence (a psychoanalytic approach). *Journal of Adolescence* 9: 187–98.

Carroll, J. 1999/2000. Children's experiences of play: The missing voice. *The World of Children* 5: 6–21.

Cohen, D. 1993. *The Development of Play*. London: Routledge.

Dorfman, E. 1952. Play therapy. In *Client-Centered Therapy: Its Current Practice, Implications and Theory*, ed. C. Rogers, 235–77. London: Constable.

Drewe, A. A., L. J. Carey, and C. E. Schaefer. 2001. *School-Based Play Therapy*. Chichester, England: Wiley.

Freud, S. 1900/1965. *The Interpretation of Dreams*. New York: Hearst.

Gil, E. 2001. Engaging families in therapeutic play. Keynote address, Eighteenth Annual Association for Play Therapy International Conference, Portland, Oregon.

Ginott, H. 1961. *Group Psychotherapy with Children: The Theory and Practice of Play Therapy*. New York: McGraw-Hill.

Guerney, L. F. 1983. Client-centered (nondirective) play therapy. In *Handbook of Play Therapy*, ed. K. J. O'Connor and C. E. Schaefer, 21–64. Chichester, England: Wiley.

Harris, P. L. 1989. *Children and Emotion*. Oxford: Blackwell.

Jung, C. G., ed. 1964. *Man and His Symbols*. New York: Dell.

Koller, T. J. 1994. Adolescent theraplay. In *Handbook of Play Therapy. Vol. II*, ed. K. J. O'Connor and C. E. Scheafer, 159–88. Chichester, England: Wiley.

Kraft, A., and G. L. Landreth. 1998. *Parents as Therapeutic Partners: Listening to Your Child's Play*. New York: Aronson.

Landreth, G. L. 1991. *Play Therapy: The Art of the Relationship*. Muncie, IN: Accelerated Development Inc.

Leverton, B. 2000. Critical moments in play therapy with sexually abused young children. Paper presented at the 2000 BASPCAN Conference, University of York.

Malchiodi, C. A. 1999. Foreward in S. Riley (1999), *Contemporary Art Therapy with Adolescents*, 11–15. London: Jessica Kingsley.

Moustakas, C. 1959. *Psychotherapy with Children: The Living Relationship.* McGraw-Hill, New York.

Pastore, T., and M. Ainley. 2000. Appraisal processes in adolescent–mother conflict. *Journal of Adolescence* 23(2): 175–88.

Piaget, J. 1951/1962. *Play, Dreams and Imitation in Childhood.* NewYork: Norton.

Putnam, F. 1997. *Dissociation in Children and Adolescents: A Developmental Perspective.* London: Guilford.

Ramchandani, P., C. Joughin, and M. Zwi. 2001. Evidence-based child and adolescent mental health services: Oxymoron or brave new dawn? *Child Psychology and Psychiatry Review* 6(2): 59–64.

Ray, D., S. Bratton, T. Rhine, and L. Jones. 2001. The effectiveness of play therapy: Responding to the critics. *International Journal of Play Therapy* 10(1): 85–108.

Rogers, C. 1989. The therapeutic relationship. In *The Carl Rogers Reader*, ed. H. Kirschembaum and V. L. Henderson, 61–152. London: Constable.

Russ, S. W. 1995. Play psychotherapy research: State of the science. *Advances in Clinical Child Psychology* 17: 365–91.

Ryan, V. 1999. Developmental delay, symbolic play and nondirective play therapy. *Clinical Child Psychology and Psychiatry* 4(2): 167–85.

———. 2001. Nondirective play therapy with abused children and adolescents. In *The Child Protection Handbook*, 2nd ed., ed. K. Wilson and A. James, 423–41, London: Bailliere Tindall.

Ryan, V., and C. Needham. 2001. Nondirective play therapy with children experiencing psychic trauma. *Clinical Child Psychology and Psychiatry* 6(3): 437–53.

Ryan, V., and K. Wilson. 1996/2000. *Case Studies in Nondirective Play Therapy.* London: Jessica Kingsley.

———. 2000. Conducting child assessments for court proceedings: The use of nondirective play therapy. *Clinical Child Psychology and Psychiatry* 5(2): 267–79.

Ryan, V., K. Wilson, and T. Fisher. 1995. Developing partnerships in therapeutic work with children. *Journal of Social Work Practise* 9(2):131–40.

Shelby, J. 2000. Brief therapy with traumatized children: A developmental perspective. In *Short-Term Play Therapy for Children*, ed. H. G. Kaduson and C. E. Schaefer, 69–104. London: Guilford.

———. 2001. Developmentally sensitive post-traumatic play therapy. Preconference Workshop, Eighteenth Annual Association for Play Therapy International Conference, Portland, Oregon.

Stern, D. N. 1985. *The Interpersonal World of the Infant.* New York: Basic Books.

Trevarthan, C. 1980. The foundation of intersubjectivity: Development of interpersonal and cooperative understanding in infants. In *The Social Foundation of Language and Thought: Essays in Honor of Jerome Bruner*, ed. D. R. Olson, 80–96. New York: Norton.

Van der Kolk, B. 1994. The body keeps score: Memory and the evolving psychobiology of post-traumatic stress. *Harvard Review of Psychiatry* 1: 253–65.

Van Fleet, R. 1994. Filial therapy for adoptive children and parents. In *Handbook of Play*

Therapy, Vol. II, ed. K. J. O'Connor and C. E. Schaefer, 371–86. Chichester, England: Wiley.

Walls, V. 1972. A theoretical study of daydreaming activity. University of Texas at Austin, unpublished.

Wenar, C., and P. Kerig. 2000. *Developmental Psychopathology: From Infancy through Adolescence*. London: McGraw Hill.

Wilson, K., and V. Ryan. 2001. Helping parents by working with their children in individual child therapy. *Child and Family Social Work* 6: 209–17.

———. 2002. Play therapy with emotionally damaged adolescents *Journal of Emotional and Behavioural Difficulties* 7(3): 178(92.

Wilson, K., P. Kendrick, and V. Ryan. 1992. *Play Therapy: A Nondirective Approach for Children and Adolescents*. London: Bailliere Tindall.

Winnicott, D. W. 1971/1986. *Playing and Reality*. London: Pelican.

Wolff, S. 1996. Child psychotherapy. In *An Introduction to the Psychotherapies*, 3rd ed., ed. S. Bloch, 261–93. Oxford: Oxford Medical Publications.

· 8 ·

Play Therapy Techniques
to Engage Adolescents

Scott Riviere

This chapter will explore some basic assumptions about working with adolescents and expand on typical treatment approaches to include creative based interventions. Adolescents tend to be one of the most misunderstood clinical populations to treat. Society as a whole and many parents tend to have a negative outlook toward this population. Comments like "I never acted that way" or "I always listened to my parents" are common. With this attitude toward the age group, it is no wonder that parents become defensive upon the first signs of puberty and the psychological process of separation and individuation. The multiple insecurities that this developmental stage brings, compounded with parental fears of drug usage, depression, suicide, and teen pregnancy, can create a challenging dilemma for the most seasoned therapist. Most clinicians will agree that this population is in desperate need of capable and willing helpers to guide them through some of the most unpredictable years of their life.

Adolescence is an awkward stage and finding effective treatment methods involving creative therapies can be challenging. The interventions typically associated with children can appear too immature while interventions usually associated with adults can rely heavily on personal motivation to change. All too often the adolescent comes into the therapy office with multiple defenses and may have been coerced into treatment by parents. However, upon understanding some key concepts with this population, working with adolescents can become an enjoyable and productive endeavor.

I have always preferred a "nuts and bolts" approach to understanding complex developmental issues. Therefore, I began developing simplistic models to explain key psychological concepts in behavioral language. The following model describes the development of communication, with a focus on

121

the emotional stage that is most common during adolescence. Although this approach is simplistic in nature, it has been found to be very effective in helping parents and others understand "typical" developmental behaviors and appropriate interventions for each age. This chapter will present this model and focus on how play therapy can be an effective modality for adolescents in any phase of treatment.

THE DEVELOPMENT OF COMMUNICATION

To help parents and professionals understand how to develop the basics of communication, the development of communication is broken down into three distinct phases. Age ranges are included for each stage; however, the numbers provide a "typical" range and are not meant to be absolute. The first stage of communication is called *Mechanical*. This stage ranges from birth to five years old. The primary characteristic of this stage is that the child begins to communicate needs primarily through behavior and vocal cues. Common examples are the cries of a hungry baby, or the child who just takes something he wants without asking. Obviously children begin to use words to communicate before age five, but often the words they use are based on the adult's pairing of the word with the object, rather than the object having an absolute meaning in and of itself. Common childhood nicknames are usually invented during this stage as well. For example, a young child who can't say "brother" may say "bubba" instead, and the name may stick well into adulthood.

The next stage in the development of communication is the *Verbal* stage. This stage usually spans ages five through eleven. It is characterized by a rapid growth in the child's vocabulary and an increased use of words to communicate the child's wants, needs, and emotions. This is a good age to begin to have "talks" with the child and to help him expand his vocabulary so he can better communicate.

The final stage in the development of communication precedes adolescence and tends to be fulfilled by age twenty-two. This stage is called the *Emotional* stage of communication and is characterized by extreme and often-unregulated expressions of emotion. The positive side of this stage is that pleasant emotions tend to be experienced at a euphoric level; however, the downside is that negative emotions are also experienced at a deep level. Most of us can remember the intensity of love at age thirteen, or the extremes of excitement and happiness. These manic-like emotions can be just the thing to balance out the deep pain caused by rejection, confusion, and anger that are all too common during adolescence. A common situation is when a parent and adolescent are arguing and the parent says "Stop yelling!" and the adolescent screams, "I'm not yelling!" This occurs because the adolescent believes that he is simply communicating the intensity of the emotion, rather than intentionally yelling. Other common examples of the extremely emotionally charged nature of this age include the adolescent who makes statements such as, "That's not fair, *everyone* is going to the party! I hate you!" and then ten minutes later asks if he can drive the car to a friends house. The key to, and possibly most difficult part of, this stage is modeling regulation of emotions when dealing with the adolescent. This role modeling along with emotional maturity will go a long way in developing a solid relationship with an adolescent.

The successful completion of all three stages of this developmental model should result in a functional communicator. As adults, our mechanical communication is called body language, our verbal communication is the words that we use, and our emotional communication is the affect or tone of the words. Hopefully this model will help you understand the developmental process in simple terms as well as give you insight into the emotional stage that is characteristic of most adolescents. The next section will focus on some basic skills to consider in preparing to engage the adolescent in the healing process.

THE BASICS

A majority of adolescents come into treatment at the suggestion of a parent, teacher, or probation officer. This can be problematic as their motivation for treatment is primarily external, and they may be looking for an opportunity to resist engagement in the therapy process. Some of the suggestions that follow may be contrary to how many therapists are trained. It may, therefore, be necessary for professionals to examine their own views about these interventions when considering whether to incorporate them into their practice. The first foundation basic is the scheduling of the assessment appointments. Some therapists rarely see the parents prior to meeting the adolescent. If they do, however, the therapist may instruct the parents not to tell the adolescent about the consultation. The reason for this strategy is related to the main need of this population—to establish a relationship. Consider what adolescents left in the lobby are thinking while their parents are brought into the therapist's office for fifteen to thirty minutes. Most adolescents think the parent is informing the therapist about all of the "bad" things they have done over the past few months, which may or may not be true. This is an unintentional set up for the adolescent, allowing them to become resistant or defensive upon entering the first session. The parent's perspective about the presenting problem is very valuable. This information can be obtained by ask-ing the parents to fill out a detailed intake form prior to the first session. This helps the parents to feel that their opinions are valued while reducing possible barriers to the adolescent's participation. The assessment takes a total of three hours; the first appointment is for one hour with the adolescent, the second and third appointments are half-hour appointments with the adolescent, and the final appointment is one hour with the parents. This allows the therapist three different opportunities to begin to build a relationship, obtain necessary information, and engage the adolescent in the therapy process.

CLOTHING

Clothing choice's can have a significant psychological influence, as well as the ability to communicate a variety of things about an individual. The clothing a therapist wears will often influence how adolescents perceive them. The same is often true of the clothes that adolescents wear. The adolescent's style can communicate information about self-image, peer group identification, and basic values and beliefs. The therapist should examine his or her goals regarding the adolescent's first impression. Does the therapist want the ado-lescent to feel intimidated? Comfortable? Threatened? Relaxed? Submissive? Engaged? In many clinical settings it is customary for a male to wear a tie and a female to wear a business suit or similar attire. Adolescents may view the formally dressed therapist as "one of them" (alias for "adult," "people who possibly couldn't understand," "main reason why I am miserable" etc.) and are often uptight and talking "to" the therapist rather than "with" the therapist. It is often a challenge to find a happy medium. Therapists are faced with the dilemma of wanting to look "professional" and "competent" to the parents, but may feel the need not to intimidate the patient. (I have settled for com-fortable pants with a dress shirt, and without reservation have decided to not wear a tie.) Women may want to consider wearing a more comfortable outfit rather than a business suit and heels. This tends to project professional com-petency combined with a relaxed appearance. The important word here is "relaxed." Anyone spending time with adolescents quickly learns that they do not particularly enjoy "nice, quiet, peaceful talks" about their feelings or other "horrible things" they have experienced. Therapists should carefully choose the clothes that they wear when working with adolescents because it can influence the way that adolescents initially interact with and perceive the therapist.

THERAPY ENVIRONMENT

The environment of the therapy space can have tremendous initial impact on the adolescent's opinion of what the therapy experience will be like. The type of furniture and general layout communicates a variety of things to the adolescent. This author's office is very casual in appearance. There is no desk or other typical business supplies. The office has a couch, loveseat, and chair with a coffee table covered with "fiddle toys" and a television set. The "fiddle toys" are simple objects that the adolescent can play with while talking to help reduce anxiety or offer a distraction. Most adolescents will comment, "You don't have a desk?" or "Can I play with that?" Adolescents seem much less inhibited and more relaxed when the therapist sits with them, rather than behind a desk or in a high-back chair. This is another way to convey to them a willingness to see things from their perspective and meet them in their place. It is important for the adolescent to know that the therapist is willing to enter into his world and is interested in developing a helping relationship.

LANGUAGE

The next foundation belief is centered on the use of language. The slang words that adolescents use change rapidly, and therapists often wonder what a word means when a new word comes up. Understanding slang words used by adolescents helps the therapist to better understand other kids who will come in and to feel more comfortable when talking with them. Another issue is the use of curse words. This author typically will use mild curse words in the initial sessions in an attempt to engage some adolescents and to not appear "like every other adult." This usually shocks the resistant adolescent and helps to lower defenses. The frequency of these words decreases as the sessions progress. Some adolescents use cursing as a defense to shield their fear of vulnerability. As the therapist gradually uses other words to communicate intense emotions, the adolescent also begins to explore alternative ways to express the intensity of his emotions.

SELF-DISCLOSURE

Disclosing personal information in the therapy setting can be a tricky and confusing dilemma for therapists. Typical graduate programs discourage self-disclosure for a variety of reasons such as getting the therapist's own needs met, blurring of boundaries, and appearing incompetent and unprofessional.

With adolescents, however, it can be a powerful tool in developing a relationship and creating a therapeutic alliance. One way to utilize self-disclosure is by participating in an activity along with the adolescent. This is an important aspect of working with this population because many adolescents think that they are "too cool" or "too old" to engage in creative interventions. By participating in the activity, the therapist can role model appropriate risk-taking, validate emotions and experiences, encourage emotional reciprocity, and build a trusting and emotionally safe environment. This does not mean that the therapist should work out his or her own issues when in session with an adolescent. On the other hand, the therapist can give examples of similar struggles from her teenage years in an attempt to demonstrate empathy. It is important for professionals to have effectively dealt with their own issues before working with this population. The story that used to illustrate this point involves two people who are drowning. Both have a keen insight into how the other is feeling, but because of their panic, neither one sees the person on the shore throwing them a life preserver. Therapists can be more effective guides if they can relate to what the adolescent is experiencing, especially if they have found ways to overcome similar difficulties. Therapists should explore their own adolescent years and spend time examining their own adolescent struggles. After dealing with past experiences in a healthy manner, the therapist should get ready because "when the teacher is ready, the students will come."

MAKING CONTACT

The ultimate goal of these basic skills is to engage the adolescent in the process of healing. It is useless to obtain an abundance of information during the first session about an adolescent who is then unwilling to come back. Initially establishing a relationship with an adolescent cannot be stressed enough. This is a fundamental need of this age. Adolescents will do amazing (and sometimes destructive) things for the people in their life to whom they feel connected. Therapists can help adolescents to establish a safe, trusting, and healthy therapeutic relationship, and can use the power of this relationship to help adolescents believe in their own self-worth and personal power to change. Trust is a vital element in any healthy relationship. Trust is something therapists must be willing to earn; however, gaining the trust of some adolescents will not be quick or easy. Due to their involvement in dating relationships as well as peer friendships, some adolescents have experienced their share of betrayal and rejection by the time they come into your office. Although rejection and betrayal is "typical" in adolescence, previous experiences of parental abandonment, abuse, neglect, and other losses can compound it. Some may have been through multiple therapists and have had their fill of the stereotypical "psychobabble." For these adolescents, especially, it is very important that the therapist remain consistent, trustworthy, and predictable. Although adolescents may struggle with trust and attachment, the therapist must show that they care anyway.

The theoretical basis for establishing relationships with adolescents have been examined, and now, armed with these basic skills and a pure desire to engage with this population, this chapter will examine some play therapy techniques that will build on the developmental strengths of adolescents.

INTERVIEW AND DIAGNOSTIC STAGE

Charles Schaefer (1993) has outlined several therapeutic powers of play including overcoming resistance, communication, and relationship enhancement. The techniques that follow are designed to help engage the adolescent in the therapeutic process, lower defenses, help the adolescent begin to communicate the struggles he is experiencing, and empower him to take control of the direction of counseling.

The Rules

To begin this activity, the therapist should inform the adolescent, "Since we both have to follow the rules, then we both should be able to make them up." The therapist can begin or can offer the adolescent the opportunity to go first. The therapist's rules should center on meeting basic safety needs both physically and emotionally. Typical rules to include are: (1) Nobody gets hurt (physical safety), (2) No laughing or making fun of serious things (emotional safety), (3) We can talk about anything (emotional risk-taking), and (4) Tell the truth. Adolescents will typically suggest rules that include: "Don't tell anybody what we talk about (the therapist will have to explain the limits of confidentiality), We don't have to talk if we don't want to, Don't talk about me behind my back, and Don't judge me." Adolescents will often propose rules that offer clues about what they are missing in their relationships with others. After both the therapist and adolescent decide on their "rules" and write them down, both individuals sign the bottom of the paper, indicating that they agree to follow the rules when in session. When the initial session is almost over, the parents are called into the session and the adolescent reads the rules to them, and the therapist explains each one. When finished, the adolescent then asks the parents if they agree to the rules and has them sign their name on the paper as well. (In over ten years of using this intervention, I have never had a parent refuse to sign and the adolescent usually leaves the session feeling empowered and in control.)

Behavioral True False Inventory

Neil Cabe (1998) developed the Behavioral True False Inventory (BTFI) (appendix 8.1), and it has been adapted in this chapter to function as an invaluable tool to help the adolescent communicate common behavioral, emotional, relational, and cognitive concerns. After completing "The Rules," adolescents are asked to fill out this BTFI form as a way for the therapist to obtain basic information without being intrusive. (I have found that adolescents are more honest on a checklist than if the therapist asks them to answer out loud.) After the adolescent has completed the checklist, the therapist asks him to add up the number of items to which he answered "true." Next, the therapist asks permission to read the statements that were given "true" responses and to complete a "time line" with these items. The therapist should then read the true statements out loud and ask, "How long has this been true?" writing the response next to the question. This helps the therapist to understand the adolescent's perception of how long he has struggled with the various issues as well as identifying patterns that help gain insight.

An example of this is a seventeen-year-old male whose father had died seven months prior to our first visit. He was a typical seventeen-year-old who did not want to be in my office and definitely did not like talking about his father's death, indicating, "It doesn't bother me anymore." He checked several items on the BTFI as true and when completing the time line maintained that each had been true for "six months." When asked if he saw any patterns in the numbers, he smiled and said "six months." I then processed with him by asking if he knew of any event or events in the past six months that made these items "true." He responded," I guess my dad's death did affect me." The BTFI and Time Line activity helped this adolescent to communicate the effects of the death of his father while allowing him to develop insight into his grief.

Heart Felt Feelings

The *Heart Felt Feelings* activity (appendix 8.2) is a modification of O'Conner's (1983) *Color-Your-Life Technique*. This technique gives the adolescent an opportunity to quantify his emotions and introduces creative art as a means of self-expression. The set up is very simple and only requires a piece of paper and crayons or color pencils. The therapist draws a heart on a sheet of paper and asks the adolescent to choose colors to represent various feelings. (I usually include the words happy, sad, angry, scared or nervous, and embarrassed.) The therapist writes the feelings alongside the heart with a box to the left of each emotion. As the adolescent picks a color for each emotion, the therapist colors in the box to show that one is never too old (or too cool) to color. The adolescent is then asked to color the amount of each feeling he has in his heart using the corresponding color. The entire heart should be filled with color when completed. When finished, time is spent processing each color. It is important to follow the adolescent's lead and to back off if there is resistance. Remember to go at the adolescent's pace.

Draw a Person

This tried and true projective technique has been adapted to open the adolescent's world of abstract thinking. The instructions are very straightforward and supplies are minimal. Provide a piece of paper and a pencil and request that the adolescent "Draw a picture of a person; make it the best person you can draw and make sure it is a picture of the whole body." If there are any questions, the therapist should indicate that only the instructions may be repeated. After the drawing is completed, the therapist should use a book that includes common interpretations of children's artwork to process with the adolescent what the various items could mean. After identifying which items might be significant according to the author of that book, ask the adolescent, "Does that sound like you?" Follow the adolescent's lead as some items will not apply and some items may stir up defensiveness. (I have found that most adolescents respond "No way! That is so cool!")

Draw Your Family

Draw Your Family is another simple creative art activity in which the adolescent can explore current perceptions about her family and establish a vision of how she would like her family to be. To set up the activity, the adolescent is given a large sheet of paper and is asked to make a drawing of how her family really is on one side and how she would like her family to be on the opposite side. The drawing can be realistic in nature or abstract using various symbols, objects, or colors. Stock the room with crayons, pastels, or magic markers, as well as several large sheets of paper and give the adolescent as much time as needed (typically this exercise takes approximately fifteen minutes). Due to the insecurity that some adolescents feel about their artistic ability, it may be helpful to remind them that it is not art class and what is important is their ability to explain what they create. The adolescent is then given the opportunity to talk about both pictures and to identify obstacles that prevent her family from being the vision of what she wants her family to be.

WORKING STAGE

Continuing with Schaefer's (1993) therapeutic powers of play, the functions of creative thinking, metaphoric teaching, visualization, and abreaction will be explored in the working stage. These interventions are designed to help the adolescent understand the usefulness of gaining insight, reprocessing events, and reliving experiences to gain mastery and competence, and develop a vision of what could be. These activities will be most effective if the therapist has engaged the adolescent in the therapeutic process and has an ongoing, trusting relationship with the client. If not, these activities may produce resistance due to the emotional vulnerability which they represent.

Empty the Bottle

The *Empty the Bottle* activity has been particularly useful in helping the adolescent to visualize how experiencing traumatic events can effect and even change us if they are not dealt with. The supplies include an empty water bottle, a small amount of brown paint, and a pitcher of water. To begin this activity, squeeze a small amount of brown paint into the water bottle and fill it up with water. Explain that the brown paint represents the traumatic event (or events) that the adolescent has experienced, and the clear water represents the pleasant events of his life prior to the traumatic event. After shaking up the bottle and mixing the paint and water, process with the adolescent how the traumatic event (the paint) clouded the majority of pleasant memories. Next, explain the value of reprocessing and reexperiencing the event. Pour half of the brown water out and discuss with the adolescent what would happen if he talked about "some" of the memories but didn't "empty the bottle." Then, refill the bottle with clean water and process what happens. The clean water is polluted by the remaining brown water. This leads into a discussion of the importance of "getting out" all of the unpleasant emotions, memories, and effects of the traumatic experience so that when he begins to "fill" his life back up with pleasant memories, it will not get clouded by the effects of the past. This activity usually ends with the question "So, if you really want to feel better what do you have to do?" Most adolescents will respond, "Empty it all out!"

Pile of Clay

Pile of Clay is another visual activity to help the adolescent understand how a traumatic experience impacts the way he views himself and others. It is very important to complete the assessment and know the various events that the child has experienced prior to attempting this activity. The supplies needed include several large and small balls of clay. Instruct the adolescent to pick a ball of clay to represent himself and to put it on the floor. The therapist then proceeds to list the various events that the adolescent has gone through and allows him to pick a ball of clay to represent each event. Typical events include parental divorce, abandonment, physical and/or sexual abuse, neglect, drug and alcohol use, sexual promiscuity, death of friends or family, and so forth. As the adolescent's history is discussed, pieces of clay are placed on and around the piece that represents the adolescent until it is covered. The therapist processes the activity by asking, "Where is the real you?" Most will respond, "You can't see it." This is a good springboard activity to help the adolescent understand that in order to feel like the "real" person he is, he will have to remove the negative effects of the things he has experienced. I have also found it helpful to process the adolescent's method of dealing with the various events by removing the balls of clay one at a time and offering potential interventions such as doing a gravesite visit to explore unresolved grief issues. In processing the activity in this way, dealing with the events is much less overwhelming for the adolescent and leaves him feeling empowered.

Best Thing and Worst Thing About . . .

This simple creative art activity is effective in the working stage of therapy because it challenges the adolescent to identify the negative effects of a traumatic event while exploring potentially positive changes that have taken place within him due to experiencing the event. First, using paper and crayons or clay, the adolescent is asked to either draw or create "the best thing about _____ and then on another sheet either draw or create "the worst thing about _____." The focus of the drawing can change depending on the direction of therapy, but common examples are parents' divorce, mother's illness, breakup of relationship, being a teenager, and so forth. The therapist should spend some time allowing the adolescent to process the drawing and offering encouragement. If the adolescent is especially guarded or resistant, the therapist can complete the activity with him and explain his own drawing first to role model risk-taking and trust. It may also be helpful for the therapist to choose a life event that is somewhat parallel, so that the adolescent can better identify with the activity. Be sure, however, to follow the guidelines set forth in the previous *Self Disclosure* section.

The Song That Describes You Best

Most adolescents love listening to music and frequently identify with either the style of music or the lyrics. A good first assignment for tapping into this creative means of self-expression is for the adolescent to bring in a song that "describes you best." Assure the adolescent that she can bring in any type of song and whatever style of music he wishes as long as the song describes her best. (By not censoring the type of music that is acceptable, I have found that the songs selected have interesting and powerful lyrics to explore.) The only thing necessary for this activity is a portable stereo with CD and cassette capabilities. The adolescent is asked to bring in the song jacket and lyrics along with the music because it helps the therapist to listen more attentively. After the song is played, time is spent processing the lyrics. The therapist may offer insight and/or feedback about what was heard in the song. Another interesting modification of this technique is to ask the adolescent to bring in a song that "best describes how you would like to be."

Animal Phototherapy

This intervention presented by Terri Kottman (1996) has been invaluable in helping with the exploration and expression of feelings, identifying defense mechanisms, and describing relationship dynamics. The materials needed are many photographs gathered from magazines, depicting animals either alone or in groups. Photographs should include a selection of different types of animals: wild, domestic, aggressive, gentle, and so forth. The adolescent is then asked to choose a picture based on a topic that the therapist introduces. Common topics for exploration include:

- Pick the picture that best describes how you act around your friends.
- Pick the picture that best describes how you act around your family.
- Pick the picture that best describes how you feel about your father/ mother (not how you act around him/her).
- Pick the picture that best describes how you really feel about yourself.
- Pick the picture that best describes your relationship with . . .
- Pick the picture that best describes how you would like that relationship to be.

Using this activity in individual therapy provides an opportunity to offer self-disclosure by participating in the game (see *Self-Disclosure* section). This intervention has also been used very effectively in family settings or as a relationship enhancement tool with the adolescent and his parents.

Life Experience Questions

Some adolescents have difficulty initiating conversations or knowing how to talk about the things that they have experienced. *Life Experience Questions* (appendix 8.3) is a simple activity which offers a structured set of insight-oriented questions used to facilitate communication between the adolescent and therapist. The questions are organized into various sections such as childhood and family or personality. The therapist can have the adolescent begin by asking a question of the therapist who follows by asking the adolescent a question. Once again, please refer to *Self-Disclosure* section. Begin by asking the adolescent one of the easier questions to help build his confidence and reinforce the effort. After processing the answers, the therapist and adolescent develop a game plan to deal with whatever issues arose.

Therapeutic Letter Writing

Therapeutic Letter Writing can be a powerful tool for helping the adolescent get in touch with and express feelings. This method offers a private, nonverbal alternative to confrontation and enables the adolescent to experience a level of "safety" that is not always present in verbal communication. It also offers the adolescent "proof" that she has expressed the feelings in an appropriate manner. A good starter activity is to complete the feelings synonym sheet (appendix 8.4) so that the adolescent can have a "cheat sheet" to identify various emotions. The two types of letters, Structured and Unstructured, are listed below with guidelines to help the therapist choose which one would be best for each individual.
Structured:

- Better for "beginners" or resistant adolescents
- Guaranteed coverage of a variety of feelings
- Can structure letter to deal with a variety of topics
- There is a clear beginning and end
- Can be "filled in" for those who cannot write

Unstructured:

- Better for a person with higher intellectual functioning
- Preferred by most older adolescents
- Appropriate for someone motivated for treatment
- Better for someone with good writing skills and vocabulary
- Allows for more freedom of expression

The *Love Letter* (appendix 8.5) is an excellent format for the structured letter and can be used for a variety of issues. Therapists may want to add or delete sentence stems as warranted (love, understanding, and forgiveness may not be an appropriate section for an adolescent dealing with rape).

After the letter has been finished, ask the adolescent to read it aloud. If the adolescent refuses, the therapist should hold the letter on file and give a compassionate response such as: "It probably is difficult to talk about some of your feelings. I'll hold the letter in your chart and we can read it later, when you feel more comfortable." If the adolescent agrees to read the letter, listen empathically and give feedback concerning the content and emotional tone as well as the adolescent's courage in agreeing to read the letter. The feedback section is very important because most adolescents feel very vulnerable after reading this type of letter, and the therapist's supportive feedback is an opportunity to help them adjust their self-image to a more positive framework. (A common bit of feedback that I give is how brave or courageous they are for completing this letter and reading it. Most feel very scared and intimidated by the issues they are confronting and they need to hear these words to counteract their own perceptions and rebuild their confidence.)

The therapist may want to offer a "closure" activity if the adolescent wants to "move on" after the letter was processed. An effective closure activity following a letter dealing with a traumatic event is to burn the letter and ask the adolescent to think of a metaphor that the burning might symbolize. After the letter is burned, the ashes can be put into a cup of dirt along with some seeds. The metaphor is that "something good can come out of something bad." Another example of a good activity: Following a grief resolution letter, do a gravesite visit and have the adolescent read the letter aloud. The letter can then be taped to several helium balloons and released after saying "goodbye."

CLOSURE

Due to the amount of emotional investment that both the therapist and adolescent have put into counseling, the closing sessions are vital. Incorporating termination activities can address the remaining therapeutic powers of play identified by Schaefer (1993). These include competence, mastering developmental fears, and positive emotions. Openly and directly addressing the issues of termination with the adolescent has multiple therapeutic benefits. Some of these benefits include acknowledgement of the therapeutic relationship, role modeling healthy grieving, identifying therapeutic progress and goal attainment, as well as celebrating the achievements that have been accomplished. Although it may not always be possible to complete a closure session, it is important to incorporate some type of closing ritual or ceremony to honor the work that has been accomplished. The following closing activities can help address these issues.

Your Own Celebration

Most adolescents enjoy celebrations and food is usually a central theme. The *Your Own Celebration* intervention takes advantage of this typical adolescent ritual, incorporating it into the closure process. Adolescents are given the opportunity to celebrate reaching their therapeutic goals by having a party. They pick the "menu" that typically includes food (pizza!), drinks (Coke), a small guest list (most often it includes parents, siblings, and possibly a best friend), and a closure activity that involves everyone. The therapist explains that the celebration is a way of expressing thanks to the adolescent for trusting the therapist with personal issues and is a means of communicating that the therapist is proud of the work the adolescent has done. The atmosphere is very casual, and the adolescent is encouraged to be the "host" by serving the food and drinks to the invited guests.

Goodbye Game

Through the use of the *Goodbye Game* the adolescent is given the opportunity to invite to the closing session family members or friends who have supported him through his struggle. After sharing a snack, each person, including the therapist, is given the opportunity to relate to the adolescent changes they have observed since counseling began. When each person is finished the adolescent is only to say "Thank you." The adolescent is then given an opportunity to tell each person how he or she has helped him to make these changes. Each person responds, "Thank you." This structured approach helps to reduce the anxiety related to termination while allowing freedom of expression. Prior to the session, parents should be coached to keep the tone of the meeting positive and to focus on the strengths of the adolescent rather than on unmet goals. The therapist may want to use this as an opportunity to address the positive changes that the parents have made as well.

Transitional Objects

Although this activity may seem unconventional, the message it sends can be very powerful. Prior to the final session, the therapist should inform the adolescent that they will each make a handmade gift to give to the other at the closing of therapy. The gift serves as a means of remembering each other. This sends the message that the adolescent is a valuable individual with many gifts that can be shared to benefit the lives of others. It also lets the adolescent know that she will be missed and that the relationship that was established is valued. The gift the therapist gives should involve some type of visual reminder of the progress that has been made. Common gifts include friendship bands, motivational stories or poems, personal letters or cards, or pictures that the therapist has drawn. Common gifts received include notes, cards, hand-painted items, and pictures of the adolescent. (A ten-year-old patient I worked with painted a picture of a sun and gave it to me during our closing session. I hung the painting in my office. That patient reentered counseling years later and seeing her picture on the wall stated, "I can't believe you really kept that! That's awesome.") Transitional objects are easy to make, inexpensive, and are very effective in building a bridge for the adolescent to transition from the supportive environment that counseling offers to relying on their own inner strength to deal with the struggles of life.

CASE STUDY

A seventeen-year-old male was referred for counseling after the death of his father. The patient had initially seen a psychiatrist and attended one session with a counselor. The patient, however, refused to take medication and did not attend the second session of counseling. The mother was concerned over his sudden drop in academic performance, poor sleep patterns, frequent irritability, and a refusal to visit the gravesite or talk about the loss.

The mother was in the lobby for the initial appointment and indicated that her son "refused to get out of the car." I spoke briefly with the mother regarding her concerns and asked about her son's favorite soft drink. She indicated that he liked Dr. Pepper, so I grabbed one from the refrigerator and asked her to go to the bathroom for a few minutes so that her son did not have to walk past her in the lobby. This was to help reduce his defenses since he already "promised" her he was not going inside. I then went out to the parking lot and tapped on the window with the drink. The patient took the drink and said, "Thanks." We talked causally for a couple of minutes and made an agreement that if he didn't like the first session then he didn't have to return. He agreed and we went into the office, but he was very guarded. We completed "The Rules" and that helped to lower his defenses. The only rule that he offered was "I don't have to come back if I don't want to." I included his rule and we both signed our name indicated our agreement with the rules. He then filled out the *Behavioral True False Inventory* indicating "true" to sixteen items. I then asked him to go through each item and write down how long each item had been true. He answered "six months" to all of the true items. Upon processing the time line, he answered," I guess my dad's death did affect me."

The patient agreed to return to the next session but did not want to talk about the previous session. I followed his lead and we spent the rest of the time talking about everyday events from school to social life. He returned for a third session and agreed to complete a therapeutic writing assignment. When giving him the options between a structured or unstructured letter, he chose the structured format. I gave him privacy while writing the letter, and after two sessions, he completed the letter. He was given the choice of what to do with the letter and decided to complete a gravesite visit. We met at the gravesite for the next session and he was fifteen minutes late. However, he was able to go to the gravesite and read aloud the emotional letter to his father. After the letter was read, he chose to keep it as a reminder of the experience. At his sixth and final session, we celebrated his closing with his mother and uncle. After eating pizza and acknowledging his achievements, I gave him a friendship band and he gave me a picture of him and his father. Although all cases don't go this smoothly, it was incredible to witness the therapeutic power of creative interventions.

CONCLUSION

I hope that these suggestions have given therapists the encouragement and inspiration to jump into the world of adolescence and embrace all of the wonderful things that this stage offers. Although a good therapeutic relationship does not guarantee a successful outcome, it is *the* most important component of working with this population. If the relationship is sacrificed for the sake of control, or to gain compliance, an unpleasant experience awaits for both the therapist and the adolescent, and this will only confirm the adolescent's belief that the therapist is "just like every other adult." Working with adolescents will be challenging and even frustrating at times. If, however, the adolescent is allowed to show the therapist his world as they walk together through this turbulent stage of development, both will be wiser as a result.

REFERENCES

Cabe, N. 1998. Play Therapy for anger management. Workshop presented at Association for Play Therapy International Conference, Phoenix, Arizona.

Kottman, T. 1996. Animal Phototherapy. Workshop presented at Association for Play Therapy International Conference, Chicago, Illinois.

O'Connor, K. J. 1983. The Color Your Life Technique. In *Handbook of Play Therapy*, ed. C. Schaefer and K. J. O'Connor, 251–58. New York: John Wiley and Sons.

Schaefer, C., ed. 1993. *The Therapeutic Powers of Play*. Northvale, NJ: Jason Aronson.

APPENDIX 8.1
Behavioral True/False Inventory

NAME: _____ TODAY'S DATE: _____

This is a TRUE/FALSE set of questions about some basic feelings in your life. Please be honest. There is no passing or failing, only better understanding.

1. ___ I have a hard time trusting other people.
2. ___ My self-esteem is lower than I would like it to be.
3. ___ I often feel down in the dumps or depressed.
4. ___ Sometimes I'm down or depressed and I don't know why.
5. ___ I have had problems in my relationships.
6. ___ Sometimes I overeat to get over feeling bad.
7. ___ When I am upset, I don't eat at all.
8. ___ I have had problems with using alcohol.
9. ___ I use or have used recreational drugs.
10. ___ I feel a deep need for relief from pain and an empty feeling inside.
11. ___ Shopping makes me feel better.
12. ___ I go to church/synagogue more than my friends.
13. ___ I am lonely a lot of the time.
14. ___ I feel like something is "wrong" almost all of the time.
15. ___ I sometimes think touching equals pain; touching others or being touched by them actually bothers me a little.
16. ___ Having deep feelings and emotions usually means you're going to get hurt.
17. ___ I feel like I have always been an adult.
18. ___ I was robbed of my childhood.
19. ___ My family life was inconsistent and unpredictable.
20. ___ People always seem to expect more from me than I am able to give.
21. ___ I feel like I never had a childhood.
22. ___ As a child, I felt alone and isolated.
23. ___ Loud, sharp noises bother me badly.
24. ___ I am a little afraid of letting people get too close to me emotionally.
25. ___ I avoid feeling things because it hurts.
26. ___ I have a lot of unexpressed anger inside of me.
27. ___ I am very careful when I meet people, because you never really know what they want from you. Everyone seems to be after something.

28. ___ I usually do not push for what I want or need.
29. ___ I see things in black and white terms: all or nothing; a lot or not at all.
30. ___ I usually expect the worst in other people.
31. ___ I am very sensitive to being rejected.
32. ___ I hold my anger in rather than expressing it.
33. ___ I have chosen friends or partners who were abusive to me.
34. ___ I often feel like life is hopeless.
35. ___ I feel helpless a lot of the time.
36. ___ I am actually hungry for human contact; I want to be close to someone.
37. ___ I have, on purpose or not on purpose, sabotaged relationships in my life.
38. ___ I feel like I need to be close to people all of the time.
39. ___ I often "test" others in my relationships.
40. ___ I feel detached from my surroundings sometimes, like I don't fit or I'm not me.
41. ___ I feel emotionally numb most of the time, as if nothing can touch me emotionally.
42. ___ I have thought seriously about suicide.
43. ___ I sometimes feel like I am outside myself and split off.
44. ___ There is a little boy/girl inside me that no one ever sees.
45. ___ Part of my personality is always trying to be in control of my surroundings.
46. ___ It is hard for me to just let go and play.
47. ___ I do not like large groups of people, like parties.
48. ___ For me, acceptance requires performance. I have to be doing something for people before they will like me.
49. ___ I have very high standards for myself and others.
50. ___ I was physically, emotionally, mentally, or sexually abused as a child

Cabe, Neil. (1992). *The Behavioral True-False Inventory*. Northfield, OH: Cabe, Inc.

APPENDIX 8.2
Heart Felt Feelings Activity

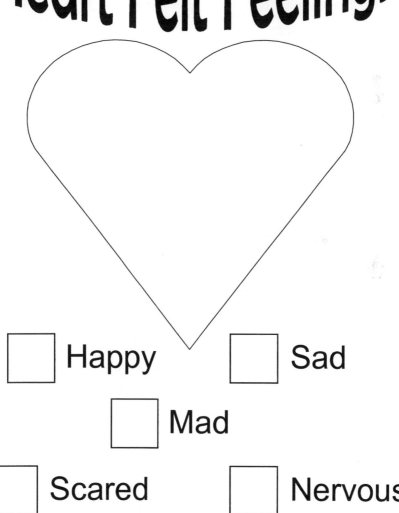

APPENDIX 8.3
Life Experience Questionnaire

CHILDHOOD AND FAMILY

1. What characteristics did you have as a child that have remained?
2. What characteristics have you lost or changed upon reaching adulthood?
3. What event or circumstances of your childhood do you think had the most impact on who you are right now?
4. Have you ever deliberately lied about a serious matter to either parent?
5. What were you most punished or criticized for when you were a child?

EXPERIENCES AND PHILOSOPHY

1. What experience of accomplishment has brought you the greatest amount of pride?
2. How do you feel about couples living together without being married?
3. Are females equal, inferior, or superior to males?
4. Have you ever been tempted to kill yourself?
5. How do you feel about crying in the presence of others?
6. Do you think there are times when cheating is justified?
7. How important is money to you?
8. Have you ever had a spiritual experience?
9. Have you ever been arrested or fined for violating any law?

PERSONALITY

1. Is there anything you sometimes pretend to be that you're not?
2. How loving of a person are you? Give an example of something that you think shows how loving you are. (How would you rate yourself [loving wise] on a scale of 1–10, 10 being the most loving, 1 being the least loving?)
3. Have you ever disliked anyone to the extent of plotting things against them? (Explain the situation or circumstances.)
4. How honest are you? Rate yourself and give an example.
5. How attractive do you think you are? Rate yourself and give an example.

6. What are you most emotional about?
7. What do you regard as your chief fault in your personality?
8. What emotions do you find most difficult to control?

FINISH THE SENTENCE

1. When I think about the future, I see myself . . .
2. When I am feeling anxious in a new situation, I usually . . .
3. When I am rejected, I usually . . .
4. Breaking rules that seem unimportant makes me feel . . .
5. I feel most affectionate when . . .
6. When I am alone I usually . . .
7. I am rebellious when . . .
8. The emotion I find most difficult to control is . . .
9. I am afraid of . . .
10. I am most ashamed of . . .
11. One thing I'd like to improve in the way I start conversations is . . .
12. My biggest fear in meeting people is . . .
13. Would you help me with . . . ?
14. One thing I want you to know about me is . . .

FEEDBACK

1. Name something you think I have to do.
2. If you had just one word to describe me, what would it be?
3. What about me do you like the most?
4. What about me would you like to change?

TIME

1. If you had just one year to live, and no financial restrictions, how would you like to spend the year?
2. If you had just one hour to live, starting right now, what would you want to do?
3. If you had just one minute to live, what would you like to say to me?

APPENDIX 8.4
Words for Unpleasant and Pleasant Feelings

Words for Unpleasant Feelings	Words for Pleasant Feelings
afraid	accepted
angry	appreciated
annoyed	brave
bad	capable
bored	comfortable
confused	compassionate
defeated	determined
disappointe	encouraged
discouraged	excited
disgusted	glad
embarrassed	good
frustrated	grateful
guilty	important
hurt	interested
indifferent	loved
insignificant	pleased
irritated	proud
put down	relaxed
rejected	relieved
sad	satisfied
shocked	sure of
uncertain	surprised
uncomfortable	sympathetic
unfairly	trusted
unloved	wonderful
other:	other:

APPENDIX 8.5
Structured Letter Format

ANGER AND BLAME
I don't like it when . . .
I resent . . .
I hate it when . . .
I'm fed up with . . .
I'm tired of . . .
I want . . .

FEAR AND INSECURITY
I feel afraid . . .
I feel scared because . . .
I feel afraid that . . .
I don't understand . . .
I want . . .

GUILT AND RESPONSIBILITY
I'm sorry that . . .
I'm sorry for . . .
Please forgive me for . . .
I didn't mean to . . .
I want . . .

HURT AND SADNESS
I feel sad when . . .
I feel hurt about . . .
I feel awful when . . .
I feel disappointed when . . .
I want . . .

LOVE, FORGIVENESS, AND UNDERSTANDING
I love you because . . .
I love you when . . .
Thank you for . . .
I understand that . . .
I forgive you for . . .
I want . . .
I am willing to . . .

The Use of Poetry in Play Therapy with Adolescents

Andrew Taylor and Steven C. Abell

$\mathcal{T}$he use of play as a therapeutic medium with children has its history in the psychoanalytic model through the work of Anna Freud and Melanie Klein (Segal, 1972). Anna Freud used the process of play as a means of developing a therapeutic alliance. She would use games and toys to increase the child's interest in therapy, and then gradually begin to concentrate more on analyzing the child's dreams and daydreams (Mishne, 1986). In contrast, Klein recognized the use of play as a medium of expression for children. Klein treated the child's play as free associations and would begin interpreting the child's play immediately (Segal, 1972).

As Klein began writing more about the use of play therapeutically, its use became more widespread among clinicians. Specifically, Levy (1938) developed a technique called "release therapy" to treat children who had experienced a traumatic event. With this technique, Levy would provide the child with specific play materials aimed at helping the child recreate through play the traumatic event, until he or she could assimilate its associated negative thoughts and feelings.

In addition, Solomon (1938) developed a technique called "active play therapy" designed for impulsive/acting-out children. This technique was meant to help the child express rage and fear through the medium of play. In doing so, the child would then be able to redirect the energy previously used for acting-out (fighting, damaging property) to more socially appropriate play behaviors.

The use of play therapy was further refined by Virginia Axline (1947), who modified the client-centered approach of Carl Rogers into a play technique. Axline's technique aimed at resolving the imbalance between the child and his or her environment so as to facilitate natural, self-improving growth.

This was accomplished by developing a warm relationship with the child, in which the therapist reflects back the child's feelings. Axline believed her almost completely nondirective approach would allow the child to gain insight, and permit the child to solve his or her own problems and make changes as he or she desires. Axline took this stance because of her unequivocal support for the notion developed by Rogers (1942) and other humanistic theorists, that every individual, including every child, had an innate drive for self-actualization and the creation of a nuclear destiny. In keeping with this belief, Axline sought to create a play environment for children that was free from pressure, frustration, insecurity, and restraints. Because she viewed play as being the natural medium for self-expression, she would utilize play materials that the children could choose and play with in any way that they wanted. Then, as the child's true self began to emerge, she would reinforce this through an atmosphere of total acceptance and understanding.

ADOLESCENT PLAY

As new scholarship emerged focusing on the application of therapeutic techniques to children, an additional focus also emerged on the period between childhood and adulthood—adolescence. Much like the origins of play therapy, the early interest in adolescence had some of its origins in the writings of Anna Freud who, in her seminal paper in 1958, described adolescence as a unique and specific period of late childhood, characterized by normative upheaval and turmoil. As Anna Freud continued to gain clinical experience with adolescents, she further characterized this group as difficult to work with using the classic analytic technique, given the adolescents' rapid shifts in emotional position and tendency toward abrupt termination of therapy (Mishne, 1986). The treatment difficulties inherent with this population as discovered by A. Freud have also been cited by other researchers (Bowman and Halfacre, 1994; O'Connor, 1991). Specifically, the period of adolescence is a time of separation and individuation, as well as identity formation (Erikson, 1950). At this age youngsters are attempting to depart from their previous identity as a child and, instead, to appear adult-like. This is further supported by Blos (1979), who points out that as the child enters puberty, the pubertal drive intensification involves regulations along the body-mind continuum resembling the child's infantile training period. As with this early developmental period, adolescence marks a new assertion of power by the teenager in taking over control of his or her growing body. In doing so, it becomes the task of the adolescent at this stage to abandon the gratifications of early childhood as he or she prepares to move into adulthood. As a result, adolescents may strongly rebel against the use of conventional play materials in an effort not to appear as a "kid." While the self-conscious nature of the adolescent makes traditional play therapy difficult, this same self-consciousness, as well as a tendency toward regression to earlier developmental stages, also makes a more typical adult-oriented therapy session difficult (O'Connor, 1991). Despite the difficulties inherent in the use of play therapy with adolescents, one should not assume that adolescents do not play and that the function that play serves for children does not apply to adolescents. As outlined by Malmquist (1985), theories on the nature of play have included:

1. The child has a need to discharge excessive energy.
2. Play is a form of practice for activities children will later require as adults.
3. Play is a form of relaxation or an escape from emotional fatigue.
4. Play is a recapitulation of past stages the human species has lived through.
5. Play is a means of discharging affect.
6. Play is seeking an outlet for childhood desires since ways accessible to adults are often prohibited. (p. 843)

Adolescents also share a need to engage in activities that perform all of these different types of functions. This can be seen in the adolescents' tendency to engage in obscene play through pranks, mocking, pretend fighting, and sexualized play. This need leads the clinician to utilize techniques that will allow the adolescent a safe avenue to express his or her feelings, and also prevent the adolescent from resisting the interventions due to their child-like nature.

POETRY THERAPY

As many clinicians began to see the benefits of play therapy and expanded its use throughout the twentieth century, clinicians also began to see the therapeutic benefits of poetry and, like play therapy, its practice developed during this time. Although the use of poetry in a therapeutic setting was popularized in the twentieth century, the recognition of the benefits of the arts came long before. The earliest recorded recognition of the use of the arts therapeutically came from Aristotle in 330 B.C., who believed that the arts aroused emotions within a person in such a way as to have beneficial effects (Abrams, 1978). The use of poetry as a therapeutic technique did not begin until much later when, in the nineteenth century, Benjamin Rush used poetry with mental patients in conjunction with his attempt to change the treatment of the mentally ill. In addition, one of the forerunners of poetry therapy—bibliotherapy—was born when, in 1904, McLean Hospital was opened as one of the first hospitals for the mentally ill and marked the recognition of an affinity between psychiatry and the therapeutic use of literature (Abrams, 1978). As the use of bibliotherapy grew, it became the foundation for the technique of poetry therapy. The validity of this technique as a therapeutic intervention was assisted in 1959 by Eli Greifer, Samuel Spector, and Jack Leedy, who started the first psychiatric hospital poetry therapy group at New York's Cumberland Hospital (Leedy, 1969). The use of poetry in psychotherapy continued to be refined throughout the 1960s, culminating in its widespread use in the 1970s (Abrams, 1978; Lerner, 1973; Rothenberg, 1972). The use of poetry therapeutically continues to be regarded as a useful therapeutic technique and the current research points to its effectiveness with an adolescent population ranging from emotionally troubled adolescents and children (Abell, 1997; Mazza, 1981; Meiffren, 1993), to adolescents in an in-patient hospital setting (Atlas, Smith, and Sessoms, 1992), and even to adolescents who are suicidal (Alexander, 1990; Bowman and Halfacre, 1994).

THERAPEUTIC RATIONALE

Much of the therapeutic use of poetry with adolescents revolves around the need to overcome superficial interactions, so that one can build a deeper and more honest type of communication with the troubled young person. To facilitate this, the use of play and poetry can often be synthesized, because both may serve as a powerful opening to previously closed portions of the adolescent's inner world. In this manner, play has long been recognized as a form of creativity, in which children use their imagination to try out and practice older roles, experience power and control, and express emotions that are otherwise too difficult to verbalize. Play for children represents a means of communicating and interacting with their environment that gives them a sense of freedom and safety that is otherwise not afforded to them. As a result, the use of play as a therapeutic medium is a very effective way of engaging a child in the treatment process. With adolescents, however, the process is made much more difficult. Under normal conditions, adolescents must go through a process of disengagement from family situations, while simultaneously seeking transformation of the parent/child relationships they once knew (Larsen et al., 1996). It can feel quite unnatural for adolescents to become attached to a psychotherapist when their normal tendency is to break away from and reinvent their former relationship patterns with adults. It is ironic that the most emotionally troubled adolescents who desperately need treatment often have the most difficulty forming a therapeutic alliance due to the developmental conflicts they are having with normal separation. These adolescents will resist treatment since the process of individuation is already more difficult for them. A psychotherapist, therefore, must use great creativity and flexibility in attempting to reach adolescent clients. Play techniques, as well as the reading and writing of poetry, can be used flexibly with traditional forms of talk therapy for the clinician who wishes to increase his or her chances of success with adolescent clients.

Poetry and play often go well together because they are both significant forms of creative expression. The act of creativity has been repeatedly viewed as being highly significant to the individual personality (Alexander, 1990; Mazza, 1981; Meiffren, 1993). In the act of creativity, the person uses their imagination to express sentiments that are particularly salient to them. As a result, the poem that the adolescent creates invariably represents unconscious dynamics as free association does for an adult. This belief in the power of creativity to represent unconscious processes was spoken about by Sigmund Freud, who saw a great similarity between neurosis and creativity, as he believed they both originated in conflicts that sprung from fundamental biological drives (Arieti, 1976). Freud postulated that works of art, such as poetry, represented a sublimation in which the person's wishes or sexual energy could be satisfied. In this sense, Sigmund Freud found much similarity between the process of creativity and the process of play in children, in which the child engages in fantasy play as a means of wish-fulfillment. Regardless of how one feels about the assertion that creativity is linked to sexual energy, the relationship between creative expression and unconscious feelings is clear.

This belief in the processes underlying creativity was also supported in the writings of Jung (Philipson, 1963). He believed that the creative process occurs in two modes: the psychological and the visionary. In the psychological mode, Jung believed that the content of the creative product is drawn from human consciousness. In the visionary mode, Jung believed the content of the creative product originates from the collective unconscious. As a result, he believed the creative process consists of an unconscious animation of an archetype. Much like Freud, we might question aspects of Jung's view of creativity, particularly the belief in the creative work being a reactivation of an archetype as opposed to a novel expression. We are, nonetheless, struck by the relation between creative expression and conscious or unconscious processes.

The sublimatory use of poetry can be a twofold process whereby the patient produces a piece of art that is a part of them representing their feelings, fears, and desires, and is accepted by the therapist, thus demonstrating the innate value of the patient and the validity of the patient's experience.

Based on this assertion, the theory of self psychology developed by Kohut (1977) is also applicable. The production, acceptance, and experience of poetry can serve a mirroring self-object function for the adolescent, as the artistic expression can serve as a means of validation for their thoughts and feelings, as well as their personal worth. As a result of the symbolic nature of poetry, its use with adolescents can be an effective way for the therapist, and at times the parents, to gain insight into the adolescent's inner emotional world while providing the adolescent a comfortable atmosphere in which the therapeutic process can take place. In addition, as the therapist is forming an alliance with a more resistant adolescent, the poetic medium can be a less threatening arena for the initial therapist interventions to occur.

In conjunction with the production of poetry, the reading of published poetry in the therapy session can also be beneficial. Reading established poems can reassure the adolescent by familiarizing them with other people who have had experiences similar to their own, as well as cause them to be motivated to think about the conflicts within themselves and perhaps discuss them in treatment sessions. Finally, as stated earlier, the writing of poetry may also act as a means of free association in which the adolescent's poetic expression of his or her thoughts and feelings may stimulate additional thoughts and insights.

IMPLEMENTATION

Poetry therapy is very powerful when used as part of the therapeutic process. It provides the adolescent with a means of self-expression while affording the therapist a better understanding of the patient and a source of clinical material for discussion. Specifically, the therapist can utilize poetry in two different ways: introducing poetry into the therapy, and having the client write poetry in the therapy.

One of the earliest poetry therapy techniques is the introduction of poems into the therapeutic milieu (Leedy, 1969). This intervention involves more than simply reading poetry, however. For poems to be beneficial their use must have a purpose, and the reactions of both the adolescent and the therapist should be explored. One way to introduce poetry into the treatment involves the therapist carefully selecting a poem, series of poems, or even certain passages to be read by the therapist or the adolescent during the session. The content of the poem should be related to the therapeutic material being focused on, and can serve several different purposes. First, the selected poem can be used as a means of support for the adolescent as they relate to others who have had experiences similar to their own. For example, depressed adolescents with negative beliefs about themselves, others, and the future can gain solace from seeing the similarities between their experience and that of Shakespeare's Macbeth:

> Tomorrow and tomorrow and tomorrow,
> Creeps in this petty pace from day to day,
> To the last syllable of recorded time;
> And all our yesterdays have lighted fools
> The way to dusty death. Out, out, brief candle!
> Life's but a walking shadow; a poor player
> That struts and frets his hour upon the stage,
> And then is heard no more: it is a tale
> Told by an idiot, full of sound and fury,
> Signifying nothing. (Act V, Scene V, 25)

In addition, the use of poetry can aid the adolescent in creating a feeling of hope toward the future as demonstrated in the poem "Today" by Thomas Carlyle:

> So here hath been dawning
> Another blue day.
> Think, wilt thou let it
> Slip useless away?
>
> Out of eternity
> This new day is born;
> Into eternity,
> At night, will return.
>
> Behold it aforetime
> No eye ever did;
> So soon it forever
> From all eyes is hid.
>
> Here hath been dawning
> Another blue day;
> Think, wilt thou let it
> Slip useless away?

The reflection on poems as a whole, or even certain lines, can provide the clinician with valuable material for understanding the major issues facing the client, as well as the client's world and self-view. This reflection can also help provide the adolescent with self-understanding, and can be used as a tool to help the adolescent gain insight into the difficulties that they are facing (Mazza, 1999). As a word of caution, clinicians may want to avoid giving to very fragile patients the work of poets whose lives ended tragically. For example, Anne Sexton's work might be inappropriate for an acutely suicidal patient who has poor reality contact and may have trouble differentiating poet and self. A healthier adolescent, however, might feel empathic resonance with some of Sexton's poems. The potential difficulties inherent in the selection of poetry is a good example of why effective therapy cannot be accomplished in a cookbook or programmed fashion. Clinicians must use all of their diagnostic skills and their best sense of professional timing when deciding whether to suggest a particular poem to any patient at a given point in the treatment process.

If clinicians have doubts about how a poem will be received by an adolescent patient, it is best to begin the session with the poem's introduction. This will give the patient adequate time to explore their reaction to the poem in the therapist's presence, and will allow the therapist to respond to any unforeseen negative feelings that a particular poem may elicit. A poem's introduction can be handled quite differently with an adolescent in long-term treatment, with whom the clinician feels a great deal of familiarity. If there is more certainty about an adolescent's stability and probable emotional reaction, outpatient psychotherapists may at times give an adolescent a poem to take home to provide food for thought for subsequent sessions. For adolescents who have trouble tolerating a temporary separation from their psychotherapist, a poem can be taken home to function as a type of transitional object or phenomenon that was so eloquently described by the British psychoanalyst, D. W. Winnicott (1971). Winnicott spoke of how the transitional object was a thing or phenomenon that facilitated our ability to maintain a significant emotional relationship with a caretaker in the caretaker's absence. So in the same way that a young child in daycare may receive great comfort from a favorite stuffed animal or blanket that is brought from home, a poem may connect a more disturbed patient to his or her psychotherapist. The psychotherapist who possesses a working knowledge of literature is likely to discover many ways in which great poems can be shared with adolescents.

While the use of conventional poetry can be very successful, some adolescents may also benefit from utilizing current song or rap lyrics, or by writing their own lyrics. Using this medium can be very helpful as it allows the therapist to learn which artists and subsequent images the adolescent identifies with and permits exploration of the benefits or problems the adolescent receives from this identification. When working with adolescents who regard traditional poetry as too "soft" or "uncool," using song or rap lyrics can be a more acceptable means of self-expression. Due to the self-conscious nature of adolescence, it would be best to allow the adolescent to choose rap or song lyrics that they find meaningful since current trends in adolescent music may make it difficult for most psychotherapists to ascertain which lyrics would be viewed as acceptable by their client.

While reading and reflecting on poetry can be beneficial in the course of treatment, the production of poetry in the course of therapy with adolescents has also been shown to be therapeutic (Abell, 1997; Alexander, 1990; Mazza, 1981; Meiffren, 1993). Creating poetry can be accomplished in a number of ways. The first is the technique of creative writing. In this model, the adolescent engages in free writing about any topic in any form they choose. The therapist can also have the adolescent engage in a more structured form, based on the work of Koch (1970) in his book *Wishes, Lies and Dreams: Teaching Children to Write Poetry*. The therapist can have the adolescent write a poem in which every line begins with "I wish . . ." or use contrasting themes by alternating lines such as "I used to be . . . /But now . . ." The therapist can join in the creative process by alternately writing lines of poetry with the adolescent. In doing so, the therapist can intervene therapeutically as the adolescent creatively expresses the difficulties and concerns (Mazza, 1999). For further resources, the reader is also directed to Koch's (1973) *Rose, Where Did You Get That Red? Teaching Great Poetry to Children*.

In conjunction with this technique, the therapist can have the patient write about specific topics such as childhood, relationships, the future, or fantasies, wishes, and dreams. This is illustrated in the following poem, reported by Morrison (1969), which was written by a female adolescent who, due to her depression, had completely removed herself from society:

Perhaps if I tried to communicate
To someone I don't know
Who wouldn't care
And wouldn't think of me
And would carry nothing of me away—
Or to something not committed to listen
Some object, some state of being
That couldn't feel . . .

I've only negative expressions
Emptiness
You would be listening only to the sound of no sound

In "you" or "I" there is nothing real
What is there in front of my eyes
Besides objects? (p. 93)

An additional technique involves having the adolescent free associate images related to a certain word, and then use the images to form a poem. This technique can be modified to include the use of metaphor. Combs and Freedman (1990) provide several ways to elicit metaphors for emotional states and attitudes:

1. List a dozen emotional states or attitudes (such as confidence, relaxation, indignation, and compassion) that might be useful in therapy.
2. Take the first item on your list and ask yourself, "If that state or attitude was a picture or image, what would it be a picture or image of?"
3. Wait for an image to occur to you. When an image has presented itself, make note of it on a separate piece of paper.
4. Then go back to the first item on your list. Ask yourself, "If that state or attitude were a physical posture or action, what posture or action would it be?" Make a note of the answer that you find.
5. Ask yourself, "If the state or attitude was a sound, what sound would it be?" List your answer beside your previous answers for this particular state or attitude.
6. Go through the same process with each of the other states or attitudes on your list. Each image, posture, and sound that you discover could be used as a symbol for the state or attitude.
7. Feel free to add other categories to the three listed, such as, "If this attitude was a movie star, which movie star would it be?" These also could be used as symbols. (pp. 90–91)

As a final point, since control is a major issue with many teenage clients, it is best to give them a choice about what they will be writing or reading, in order to maximize the difficult task of establishing rapport and open emotional communication. Clinicians should also remember that matters of spelling and grammar, which might be quite important in an academic setting, are of very little consequence in the therapeutic enterprise.

CASE ILLUSTRATION

The case of Charlotte K. can serve as a useful example of the multitude of ways in which poetry and play can enhance the treatment of a seriously disturbed adolescent client. When Charlotte was first brought to the attention of mental health professionals, she was a fifteen-year-old teenager living in the suburbs of a large metropolitan area in the western half of the United States. Charlotte lived at home with both her parents and considered herself to be "a psychological only child," even though her father had two other children from a previous marriage. These children were older adolescents when Charlotte was born, however, and she indicated that her contact with them had been rather infrequent and superficial. Charlotte's father was a lawyer, and her mother was an interior decorator, though her mother had been a stay-at-home parent for six years after Charlotte's birth, and had then worked part-time while Charlotte was in elementary school. In addition, both parents described themselves as evangelical Christians and attended church regularly. During Charlotte's initial appointments, her mother, Mrs. K., indicated that she had always considered her daughter to be something of a personal miracle. Charlotte was born after her mother had been through a series of bitterly disappointing miscarriages, and at a time when Mr. and Mrs. K. were struggling to reconcile themselves to the fact that they were perhaps becoming too old to have or adopt a child. For these reasons, Mrs. K. indicated that Charlotte's successful birth had been the highlight of her life, and that she found Charlotte to be an "almost perfect" baby. Mrs. K. claimed that Charlotte had rarely cried as an infant, and had achieved nearly all of her early developmental milestones in a precocious fashion. Charlotte had always done well in school and had been an eager participant in ballet lessons and other activities.

At the time of her intake appointment, Charlotte was attending a prestigious church-sponsored school in the relatively affluent suburban area where she lived. Charlotte continued to do well academically, though she had dropped out of dance lessons several years earlier, and complained that her academic work, which she had once enjoyed, now seemed utterly pointless to her. Charlotte complained, "I only keep my grades up to please my parents—school seems like such a stupid waste of time to me." During the year before her intake, Charlotte had also gone from being an outgoing young person to being quite socially isolated. After school, Charlotte only maintained contact with two long-term friends, both of whom were also in mental health treatment; her only contacts were a young man who was reportedly very confused about his sexual orientation and a teenage girl who was recently hospitalized for anorexia. Charlotte indicated that for a number of months she had felt deeply unhappy and lethargic, and that she spent much of her free time at home alone, listening to music or isolating herself in some other way.

Charlotte's parents suggested that she obtain mental health treatment, due to their concerns over what appeared to be their daughter's deepening depression. Charlotte readily agreed to this, though she expressed some concern during her initial session over the presence of toys and art supplies in her psychotherapist's office. Charlotte stated rather pointedly that she was far too old "for such childish things" and needed to talk to someone who would understand what she perceived to be her more adult concerns.

Charlotte seemed relieved when the therapist explained that no one was ever required to use the toys or art supplies, and that he would try to understand Charlotte on her own terms. Charlotte became quite open about discussing her current sadness, which seemed to be fueled by a relentless perfectionism. Charlotte indicated that she had been told for years by educators and her parents that she was intellectually gifted, and that now even getting a B + in school would be utterly unacceptable. Charlotte was paralyzed by her perfectionism, to the point where she had left many activities for fear that she would be unable to perform them in a flawless fashion.

Charlotte also expressed her belief that her mother's life was rather empty and meaningless, and that Charlotte was personally responsible for her mother's feelings and general level of happiness. Charlotte actually stated that she and her mother were "so close, it hurts." Her father, on the other hand, Charlotte found to be so emotionally distant and detached from the family that she derisively referred to him as "the emotion clam." Based on Charlotte's level of emotional distress, an agreement was reached with Charlotte and her parents that the therapist would see her twice a week for individual sessions. Charlotte was also referred to a child/adolescent psychiatrist who prescribed an antidepressant medication for her.

Initially, the therapist had noticed that Charlotte seemed to be quite thin, but her weight still seemed to be within normal limits for her age. Unfortunately, Charlotte's mother made a very distressed phone call to the therapist approximately three weeks into the treatment to tell the therapist that Charlotte had apparently been lying for some time about the amount of food she was eating. During her next session, Charlotte admitted that this was the case. Charlotte said that she was beginning to learn elaborate ways to push the food around on her plate and make it appear that she was eating. Charlotte began to talk openly about how it was becoming increasingly difficult for her to eat over one thousand calories a day. At the therapist's suggestion, Mr. and Mrs. K. took Charlotte to a pediatrician who had experience with eating disorders, and she also began to work with a dietician who had experience in this area.

Though Charlotte acknowledged her problems with food, she began to restrict her intake more and more. As is often the case with eating disorders, her situation got significantly worse before it got better. Her weight dropped during the next three months to the point where it became medically unsafe for her to be treated as an outpatient. The situation was complicated by the lack of appropriate inpatient programs in her area. Psychiatric programs refused to take her because of the precarious nature of her medical condition. Charlotte was admitted to a pediatric unit, and arrangements were made for the therapist to have sessions with her several times a week during her hospitalization.

While Charlotte went willingly to the hospital, she found the experience dull and humiliating. She complained bitterly of boredom. It was at this time that the therapist suggested that Charlotte write poetry to help fill the long hours in her hospital room. She took to this task eagerly, and regularly began to present the therapist with short poems. One of her first pieces was reportedly about her hospital room:

The Perfect Pattern

I'd like to be this room
I lie in—
Clean,
Pristine,
Perfect and white.
I'd like to be the light
That shines in—
Bright
And clear.
I am the stain here
Not the room.
I only serve to break
The perfect pattern.

As Charlotte discussed this poem, she was quickly able to see that it was more about her own need for perfection and purity than about the hospital room. A painful, yet productive discussion of the "stain" lead Charlotte to describe for the first time her experience of the onset of menses and her sexual development. Charlotte confessed that she found menstruation to be "disgusting and messy" rather than a normal and healthy experience. Writing poetry also allowed her to talk more freely about how her developing sexuality made her feel out of control, and the ways in which her anorexia was an attempt to deny and control her physical existence.

As she became more open about her inner struggles, several other interesting changes in Charlotte occurred as well. Charlotte became receptive to suggestions from the psychotherapist about the work of particular poets that she might like to read. Instead of focusing so heavily on the work of female poets who ultimately committed suicide, Charlotte began to read widely from contemporary poetry and began to enjoy poets who were more life affirming. With her strong intellectual abilities, she was drawn to the work of such diverse writers as Lawrence Ferlinghetti, Anne Waldman, and Sharon Olds.

After her discharge from the hospital, Charlotte's behavior also began to change during her psychotherapy sessions. She surprised the therapist by slowly beginning to finger the toys in his office, discuss the memories she associated with them, and occasionally arrange the furniture in the dollhouse as she was talking.

Charlotte was able to remain within a few pounds of her target weight after she left the hospital, and became more assertive in a number of areas of her life. She rejected her mother's classical taste in décor, and redid her bedroom in psychedelic colors. Charlotte's parents contributed to her recovery by making some efforts to support Charlotte's growing independence, and by entering marriage counseling to work on their relationship with each other. Mrs. K. began to see how she had avoided her marital problems and personal unhappiness by focusing excessively on Charlotte, and Mr. K. began to question his detachment from the family.

One year after her discharge from the hospital, Charlotte still felt somewhat alienated from her peers, but she had made several new friends. She was working part-time and learning to play the guitar. She was gradually beginning to realize that she was no longer responsible for all of her mother's emotions. Charlotte was beginning to learn to trust her own emotional reactions. Her age-appropriate quest for identity seemed well-conveyed by these lines from a poem she wrote about ballet dancers:

> The little ballerinas in the line
> Must someday learn to dance
> To rap and more, must learn to dance
> To music never heard before.
> Will grace appear from music
> Never heard before?
> Will steps come from within?

While Charlotte's complete recovery was far from certain, she did make significant gains during her roughly two years of intensive treatment. The use of poetry and play materials seemed to facilitate honest emotional communication in her psychotherapy, allowing the therapist to gain a more complete and empathic understanding of her situation.

CONCLUSION

Play represents a means for children to express their feelings and anxieties, as well as to live out fantasies and experience power and control. This process makes its therapeutic use very beneficial for treating children. However, this can also be beneficial with an adolescent population. Adolescents, like children, also need a medium through which they can express their feelings, fears, and doubts, yet still leave them able to separate from their previous child-like image. Given the similarities between play and poetry, with their use of imagination and basis in the unconscious, the flexible combination of these modalities can be quite useful when working with an adolescent population.

REFERENCES

Abell, S. C. 1997. The use of poetry in play therapy: A logical integration. *The Arts in Psychotherapy* 24: 1–5.

Abrams, A. S. 1978. Poetry therapy in the psychiatric hospital. In *Poetry in the Therapeutic Experience*, ed. A. Lerner, 64–72. St. Louis, MO: MMB Music, Inc.

Alexander, K. C. 1990. Communicating with potential adolescent suicides through poetry. *The Arts in Psychotherapy* 17(2): 125–30.

Arieti, S. 1976. *Creativity: The Magic Synthesis*. New York: Basic Books, Inc.

Atlas, J. A., P. Smith, and L. Sessoms. 1992. Art and poetry in brief therapy of hospitalized adolescents. *The Arts in Psychotherapy* 19: 279–83.

Axline, V. M. 1947. *Play Therapy*. New York: Ballentine Books.

Blos, P. 1979. *The Adolescent Passage: Developmental Issues*. New York: International Universities Press, Inc.

Bowman, D. O., and D. L. Halfacre. 1994. Poetry therapy with the sexually abused adolescent: A case study. *The Arts in Psychotherapy* 21: 11–16.

Combs, G., and J. Freedman. 1990. *Symbol, Story, and Ceremony: Using Metaphor in Individual and Family Therapy*. New York: Norton.

Erikson, E. H. 1950. *Childhood and Society*. New York: Norton.

Koch, K. 1970. *Wishes, Lies, and Dreams: Teaching Children to Write Poetry*. New York: Harper and Row.

———. 1973. *Rose, Where Did You Get That Red? Teaching Great Poetry to Children*. New York: Random House.

Kohut, H. 1977. *The Restoration of the Self*. New York: International University Press.

Larsen, R. W., M. H. Richards, G. Moneta, G. Hombeck, and E. Duckett. 1996. Changes in adolescents' daily interactions with their families from ages ten to eighteen: Disengagement and transformation. *Developmental Psychology* 32: 744–54.

Leedy, J. J. 1969. Introduction. In *Poetry Therapy*, ed. J. J. Leedy, 11–13. Philadelphia: Lippincott.

Lerner, A. 1973. Poetry therapy. *American Journal of Nursing* 73: 1336–38.

Levy, D. 1938. Release therapy for young children. *Psychiatry* 1: 387–89.

Malmquist, C. P. 1985. *Handbook of Adolescence: Psychopathology, Antisocial Development, Psychotherapy*. New York: Jason Aronson, Inc.

Mazza, N. 1981. The use of poetry in treating the troubled adolescent. *Adolescence* 16: 403–8.

———. 1999. *Poetry Therapy: Interface of the Arts and Psychology.* New York: CRC Press LLC.

Meiffren, M. 1993. The use of poetry and ritual with troubled adolescents. *Journal of Humanistic Psychology* 33: 24–44.

Mishne, J. M. 1986. *Clinical Work with Adolescents.* New York: The Free Press.

Morrison, M. R. 1969. Poetry therapy with disturbed adolescents. In *Poetry Therapy,* ed. J. J. Leedy, 88–104. Philadelphia: J. B. Lippincott Company.

O'Connor, K. J. 1991. *The Play Therapy Primer: An Integration of Theories and Techniques.* New York: John Wiley and Sons, Inc.

Philipson, M. 1963. *Outline of Jungian Aesthetics.* Evanston, IL: Northwestern University Press.

Rogers, C. R. 1942. *Counseling and Psychotherapy.* Boston: Houghton Mifflin Company.

Rothenberg, A. 1972. Poetic process and psychotherapy. *Psychiatry* 35: 228–54.

Segal, H. 1972. Melanie Klein's technique of child analysis. In *Handbook of Child Psychoanalysis: Research, Theory, and Practice,* ed. B. B. Wolman, 401–14. New York: Litton Educational Publishing, Inc.

Solomon, J. 1938. Active play therapy. *American Journal of Orthopsychiatry* 8: 479–98.

Winnicott, D.W. 1971. *Playing and Reality.* New York: Basic Books.

Metaphorical Thinking with Adolescents
Dorothy Breen

The Crocker Bowl spills over with the pink sunrise as it calls to me:
"Over here, notice me, I'm on fire with the dawn of a new day." The
Crocker Bowl is part of Crocker Mountain in the Western Maine
Mountains and I have the pleasure of experiencing this beautiful sun-
rise on many mornings. I feel myself filling with awe as I begin each
new day.

Adolescents spill over with the pink sunrise as they call to me:
"Over here, notice me, I'm on fire with the dawn of a new day." I
work with adolescents, and I have the pleasure of experiencing their
beauty on many occasions. I feel myself filling with awe as I see an
adolescent begin a new day.

The energy of the Crocker Bowl sunrise flows into my day and
my life is plentiful.

$\mathcal{R}$ecognizing the many metaphors around me helps me explore life's experiences and express my thoughts. Metaphors allow me to fill with exciting feelings and ideas. Metaphors help me communicate.

Adolescents often struggle with being able to look at the world from
perspectives other than their own. This limited view can interfere with functioning in school, social, and family relationships. Developing metaphorical
thinking (Davis, 1986) serves as a stimulus for creativity and problem solving.
Fostering creativity, enhancing creativity, and exploring the creative process
can help adolescents with problem solving, building relationships, and living
the life of an adolescent.

Metaphors provide indirect, nonthreatening ways to explore. A metaphor is "a figure of speech in which one object is likened to another by speaking of it as if it were that other" (*Webster's Dictionary*, 1992). Metaphors assist
adolescents in developing insight and understanding their roles in family and

groups. Through the use of metaphors adolescents may express concerns, fears, and other feelings. In their metaphors adolescents explore alternative modes of thinking that may help them find solutions, ways of coping, and possibilities for changing circumstances.

Adolescents have developed abstract thinking and are able to understand metaphorical thinking. I like to help adolescents discover the metaphors in their lives in order to develop the process of metaphorical thinking. That means that I need to be attuned to the metaphors in my life. Sometimes it is simply a matter of seeing the metaphor as it already exists. For example, when adolescents read their journals during a counseling session, I look for the metaphors. They are surprised as we pluck the metaphors out of their writing and challenged as we work to change some of their metaphors.

The literature provides examples of working with metaphors in play therapy. Margaret Lowenfeld (1993) uses sand with children and calls it "The World Technique." Children create their world in the sand tray with various toy figures. Allan and Berry (1987) discuss the stages of the sand play: chaos, struggle, and resolution. Children transfer the chaos and struggle in their lives to the sand tray. The sand tray becomes the metaphor for their lives and a manageable environment for working out a resolution.

Oaklander (1989) uses sand play with all ages and describes cases in which adolescents develop insights based on the metaphorical representation of their world in the sand. Oaklander encourages children and adolescents to create their representation of their worlds on paper as well, encouraging them to not draw anything that is recognizable, but to simply express themselves by drawing lines and shapes of various colors. She may then ask them to "be" the line or shape as they process the drawing.

Working with metaphors in stories provides emotional distance and is a safe way to address trauma-related issues (Miller, 1990; Stiles and Kottman, 1990). Miles (1993) writes about songwriting as a type of storytelling and a means of expression, understanding, and generating alternatives and change. Miles provides a case example in which he describes a process of writing songs with a child, changing the song lyrics as they explore and bring resolution to the problem. Woytowich (1994) discusses the power of writing poetry and how it is as important in counseling as it is in the classroom. This chapter will give examples of ways to use metaphors with adolescents.

WHAT IFS

It is helpful to talk about metaphorical thinking before expecting adolescents to engage in it, since it may not come naturally. Metaphorical thinking is a process of transferring ideas from one context to another context. The following are exercises that encourage adolescents to stretch their thinking and ways of expressing themselves.

"What Ifs" are prompts that encourage creative thinking. Engaging in "What If" discussions can help cultivate awareness of and sensitivity to the things in life that go unnoticed. Sometimes we need to work with adolescents for them to be open to their surroundings, to others, and to themselves in an effort to better understand these many influences on their development. "What Ifs" help adolescents take notice of what is going on in the world around them. For example, you can ask adolescents to tell you what it would be like if they were the size of ants and were walking down a country road. Follow with prompts such as: what would you see, what would you smell, how would you feel? "What Ifs" can be tailored to the adolescents' environment.

Begin with "What Ifs" that make an adolescent look at the world in a different way and stimulate awareness of senses.

- What if you walked on your hands rather than your feet?
- What if you had an eye in the back of your head?
- What if your nose was on your thumb?
- What if you were a newspaper in a newspaper stand in New York City?
- What if you were a spot of ketchup on the wall in the local country restaurant?

Then offer "What Ifs" that are phrased as metaphors in order to give examples of metaphorical thinking.

- What if peace was the feel of ocean spray on your face as the waves lick the shore?
- What if criticism was a blizzard of wind and snow slapping your face?
- What if your beauty was an evening primrose?
- What if your strength was the ocean tide?
- What if life's challenges were like finding an English setter hiding in the birches during a snowstorm?
- What if you were the dawn filling the Crocker Bowl?

Example

Adolescents like to develop their own "What If" metaphors. For example, John was a bright teenager who liked to write stories, and he had confidence in his writing abilities. When it came to sports that required him to use athletic skills in front of a crowd, his lack of confidence prohibited him from carrying through. His skills were sharp, but he worried what others were thinking about him. He liked to participate in sports, and he demonstrated good skills during practices; however, he doubted himself while on the playing field.

We worked on tapping John's creativity in terms of "What If" metaphors in an effort to help him transfer his confidence in creative writing to confidence in athletic situations. I began with some easy prompts: what if the baseball had eyes, what if the bat could speak, and what if the bases had little feet?

After having fun with some simple "What Ifs," I asked John to help me "throw out" some "What Ifs" so we could "field" metaphorical thinking. We tossed around some of these: What if you were the baseball approaching the bat? What if you were a bat swinging toward a pitch? What if you were the baseball sailing out of the stadium, what if the bases could scream as you stepped on them while rounding the bases after hitting a home run? John began to realize that he could help himself to focus on his athletic skills and keep his mind from wandering to the crowd by applying some of his creative thinking to his sport.

METAPHORICAL CARTOONS

Looking at a problem in a different way can be risky. Adolescents are more likely to explore another perspective in a playful or pretend situation. Metaphorical cartoons are a fun and creative means to stretch thinking and expression. Gary Davis (1986) writes about using metaphorical cartoons to foster creativity and problem solving. He describes the development of metaphorical cartoons as the process of combining a character or idea with an unrelated event or situation. Davis suggests creating a cartoon by selecting one of the characters or ideas from the first list and combining it with one of the situations or events from the second list to develop the metaphor.

Original Scenario—Source of Characters and Ideas

> Alice in Wonderland (Queen of Hearts, Mad Hatter, March Hare, mushroom that makes you grow)
> Snow White (seven dwarfs, Prince Charming, Wicked Queen with "Mirror, Mirror on the Wall," poisoned apple)
> Cinderella (ugly step-sisters, wicked step-mother, magic coach)
> Goldilocks and the Three Bears

Three Little Pigs and the Wolf (straw, wood, and brick houses)
Sleeping Beauty (awakened by kiss from handsome prince)
Rapunzel (let down hair for prince to climb)
Little Red Riding Hood (the Wolf, basket of goodies, Grandmother)
Kissing a frog who turns into a prince
Tom Tom the Piper's Son, Stole a Pig and Away He Run
Robin Hood (steals from the rich to give to the poor)
Star Wars Characters (Luke Skywalker, Princess Leia, Darth Vader, Ben
    Kenobi, Yoda, Ewoks, walking machines)
E.T. (an alien who wants to phone home and go home)
Sasquatch (Yeti, Big Foot); Loch Ness Monster (Nessie)
A McDonald's commercial (Ronald McDonald, the Hamburglar)
Coca-Cola commercial
Weather forecast, with weather map showing storms, sunny skies

Situations in Which to Use Characters and Ideas

Star Wars space defense system
Summit talks between U.S. president and Russian leader
China becoming more capitalistic, less communistic
Political revolutions in Central American country (pick one)
Revisions in federal income tax that still favor the rich
Local school board
Growing drug abuse problem
News about fertility pills leading to multiple births
News about unsafe automobiles
News about federal spending or the growing national debt
News about Japanese car imports
Other current news event (pp. 124–25).

Begin the process of making metaphorical cartoons by talking about metaphorical thinking. Use metaphorical "What Ifs" to provide examples. Show the adolescents some examples of metaphorical cartoons from the newspaper.

Provide the adolescents with paper, markers, and crayons, and two lists—one of characters and ideas, the other of situations and events. Modify individual lists so each is appropriate for the adolescent you are working with, given the issues at hand. The lists of characters and ideas might include people they know and communicate with on a daily basis or figures from politics, music, stories, sports, or movies. The list of situations and events might focus on political issues in the national or local news, or they might address school, family, or peer concerns.

Show the lists to the adolescents and give them the opportunity to add to either list. Then ask them to choose one from each list and draw a cartoon combining the two in some fashion. They can write captions under the cartoons or use bubbles for conversation among the characters. Afterwards give them a chance to present their cartoons to the group or to you if you are working with an individual. This technique can be taken further asking the adolescents to tell a story about their cartoons and to develop other cartoons as their stories and problem solutions develop.

Example

A classroom of fifteen students made metaphorical cartoons. I divided the students into three groups of five, each group making a metaphorical cartoon. I showed them some examples of cartoons from current local newspapers and gave them a list of characters and ideas and a list of situations and events.

They had the option of choosing from this list or coming up with their own ideas. At first, this seemed like a difficult task and they took some time to decide what they would draw. Allow plenty of time for this project, not only for the students to plan the metaphor, but also for them to complete the cartoon and process it afterwards. You'll hear interesting working conversations as they discuss the issues. They will engage in decision making about which issue they want to focus on, and then more decision making about how to combine characters and situations to develop the metaphor. They may even exercise conflict resolution skills. There are many group dynamics to watch as this process unfolds. Be sure to pay attention to the dynamics and use them for processing afterwards.

One group decided to work on reduction of social services benefits as an issue and combined it with *The Little Old Woman Who Lived in a Shoe* to look at it from creative metaphorical perspective. The cartoon portrayed the Little Old Woman and all her children. They were camped out on the street next to the shoe because they were evicted for not having enough money to make the rent payments. The shoe, with a new coat of paint and surrounded by beautiful gardens, had new inhabitants: The government.

The processing is important within each group and between the groups. To begin, each group needs to process as a group. How did they decide on the issue the cartoon would represent? How did they decide what to draw in order to represent the issue? How did each group member contribute to the development of the metaphorical representation?

Next, each group needs the opportunity to show and describe their cartoon to the other groups. The students generally are very excited to show their cartoons. Usually the group will choose one person to represent them to describe their metaphorical cartoon to the others. This person can talk about how and why the group made the decision to choose the issue and what was involved in their discussion about the issue as they developed the metaphorical cartoon.

Finally, each cartoon can generate large group discussions regarding the issues represented by the metaphors. How did these metaphors help portray the issues? How do these metaphors apply to their lives? What can they take from these metaphors to their situations? What are some possibilities for solutions?

DRAMA

By engaging in drama, adolescents choose the characters and combine them with events or situations, just as they do with the metaphorical cartoons. However, rather than drawing the characters, they become the characters. The dramas are enactments of current events in the news. Current events are chosen from headlines in school or local newspapers. The adolescents take the roles of the characters in the news article and act out the event. This is powerful because with drama adolescents become the metaphorical representation of the event. They experience the action, feelings, and responses of the characters. This can be powerful, so consider directing adolescents to choose humorous headlines to try out as their first drama. Be sure to have enough time for processing their actions, feelings, and responses, especially if adolescents are enacting an emotionally laden issue.

Example

I handed the group two newspapers and asked them to divide into two groups to work on two dramas. I instructed them to choose humorous articles in the news for these dramas because it was a Friday afternoon and it was a good time to have some fun while working on creativity.

One group played out a news story about theft in a small town. Four flower boxes had been stolen from a neighbor's garden, and the neighbor offered a pizza with one topping as a reward. While this was a serious complaint—and not at all humorous to the neighbor who planted and tended the flower boxes—it turned out to be a very funny drama. There were five adolescents in this group, and all participated. Even the shyest had a role, which was that of the thief, disguised by a sweatshirt with a hood keeping her face completely out of view of the audience.

Example

When you want to help adolescents develop a perspective on something that is hard to understand, you might want them to choose a news article that is about a serious event. One group chose to enact a news story about the bombing of the Federal Building in Okalahoma City. This particular news story was about a police officer who was part of the response team the day of the bombing. The drama group was large, and there were several roles including the police officer, victims, and family members of victims. It was a powerful enactment and required careful processing. The members of the drama group who took the victim roles actually felt like they were part of the bombing. Others could feel what it would be like to lose a family member in a disaster. The one who took the role of the police officer developed an appreciation for the work response personnel do. We processed what it was like to have these perspectives and how they impact their lives now.

Example

Metaphor can be used to enhance learning. I asked students in one Play Therapy class to apply their learning by engaging a drama that was a metaphor for something they learned in class in combination with a newspaper story.

One drama group chose a newspaper story about a political figure's adolescent daughters. They had been arrested because they were caught drinking alcohol, and they were under the age of twenty-one. Both were required to have counseling. In their deliberations, the drama group decided the siblings could benefit from play therapy provided by several different play therapists. To make it interesting, their grandfather, also a political figure, attended the sessions with them. The drama group very creatively enacted several play therapy sessions, each session with a different play therapist. We laughed with amusement as we watched the exaggerated styles of the play therapists. This humorous enactment sealed the learnings of the play therapy theories and techniques as the drama group members metaphorically became a different play therapist for each session.

GROUP DRAWING

The group drawing serves many purposes: expression of self, expression of group, validation of self and others, cooperation, problem solving, and conflict resolution. The drawing starts out as a metaphor for the individual and becomes a metaphor for the group. Begin with a group of about seven adolescents standing around a table covered with newsprint paper. Have a pile of colored markers and crayons in the middle of the table. Ask adolescents to draw something on the paper that is a metaphor for something in their lives. Using varied time intervals, ask them to stop drawing and take one step to the right and continue drawing. Continue this process until they are back to their original place at the table.

The amount of time it takes can vary depending on how many adolescents are in the group, how much time they are allowed to draw at each space, and how much time it takes to process. Consider varying the amount of time at each space, watch the participants and observe how they were engaged in the process. This activity can last thirty minutes by giving the participants about fifteen minutes for the drawing and the remainder for processing. Be sure to allow enough time for processing. Depending on what is happening during the drawing, more time may be needed for processing.

Processing questions will vary depending on what is happening in the group. The therapist may bring out feelings, help group members resolve conflicts, or help group members give supportive comments to each other. Some processing questions are:

> What was it like to come back to your drawing and see how it changed?
> How did it change?
> How did it stay the same or expand?
> What was it like to have to move to the next space and not be able to continue with the drawing you were working on?
> What are the themes you see in your drawing and the big picture?
> How does it feel to have someone comment on the drawing you began?
> What is it like to have a part in this entire picture?
> What does this picture say about you?
> What does this picture say about this group?

Example

The following is an example of a group drawing that is a bit different from the process described previously. Seven young women were asked to stand around a table covered with newsprint paper. There was a pile of different colored markers and crayons in the middle of the table. I directed each to draw something on the paper in front of them that was a metaphor for something about herself. I gave them as much time as they needed to complete their metaphors. When they told me they were finished, I asked each to take a turn to describe her metaphorical representation to the group. Next, I directed them to draw lines between and among the drawings as they saw metaphorical connections. The group discussed these connections in light of their representations of themselves. The discussion brought out many similarities and differences. The processing was positive and each young woman felt validated for her individuality and connection.

One of the group members was from a different cultural background than the others. She pointed out that many of the drawings around the table had something that fit with the metaphorical representation of her, which was influenced by her culture. The fact that she saw these connections helped her feel validated. She was able to express openly some of her cultural values, and the other group members developed a deeper understanding. The group continued with a discussion and an exploration of cultural influences in all of their lives. One group member continued to draw as the discussion ensued, and they had yet one more metaphorical representation of their group.

INDIVIDUAL DRAWING

Some adolescents are comfortable with drawing and are quite talented in expressing themselves through their drawings. Others are not and need to feel an acceptance for whatever they draw before they can engage in metaphorical thinking. My office is equipped to work with children as well as adolescents and all my play materials are visible. Sometimes adolescents feel safe enough to play with the children's toys, and they will get out the coloring books and crayons. Others will go to the chalkboard and draw pictures. This is a start. I think these activities help their confidence and the feeling of acceptance strengthens enough to risk exploring their stored up thoughts and feelings.

Example

Randy, an older adolescent, came to counseling because he had depression. Randy spent much of his free time in his bed. After school he would go home and get in bed. He claimed he would spend most of Saturday and Sunday in bed. While in bed he might listen to music, do homework, watch television, or call a friend. He claimed he could do everything from his bed and he felt a sad, melancholy, coziness in bed.

After several sessions of talking, Randy got up from the chair in my office and looked over the toys on the shelves. He took the stack of coloring books with large, child-size pictures and sat on the floor with them and a basket of crayons. He began to color one of the pictures in one of the coloring books, looking at me to see my reaction. I acknowledged he was coloring: "It looks like you're coloring that picture." He nodded silently. I gave him an accepting environment to engage in that activity and he seemed to feel safe. He continued to color the picture and looked to me for acknowledgment. In a nondirective way, I noted what he was doing: "you used a red crayon to color the boy's shirt and a blue crayon to color his pants." I continued to use a nondirective approach as he colored pictures for the remainder of the session.

In the next session, because Randy seemed to like using the crayons, I asked him to draw a picture. As you might expect, he said: "I can't draw." I asked him to draw a metaphorical representation of his room on a large piece of newsprint paper. I explained that I was not looking for an exact replication, but his sense of his room.

Randy's representation of his room was dark and dingy. His bed was a major focus, and there were no windows. From his drawing, it looked like he was spending much of his time in a dark space. I asked him to describe his drawing, and he explained that he arranged his furniture so he could reach everything without having to get out of bed. In an effort to be able reach his music, books, television, and telephone, he created a dark cubby for himself. As we talked about his representation, I discovered that his bed was in a part of the room that was blocked from the windows. He had two windows, yet from his bed, he could not see them because a large armoire and bookcase partitioned his bed from the rest of his room. He had no light coming from the windows, and he could not see the view out of the windows.

We talked about his sense of his space and he described it as being a place he could not change. It seemed to have a kind of dreary comfort to him. I was thinking about the Crocker Bowl spilling with the pink sunrise and wished he could experience some of that feeling. I asked Randy to think about a different feel to his space. I asked: "What would it be like to have a lighter space?" "What if the daylight were to join you in your space?" "How would it feel to have the rays of sunshine peek into your room and dance on your bed?" He began to join in the metaphor and smiled a bit with the fun of a new way of thinking. I asked him to draw a picture of what his room might look like if the sun could dance on his bed. He did and in the next session he told me how he rearranged his room so he had daylight on his bed.

With this experience Randy began to realize he could change other parts of his life as well. For example, he was able to tap his creativity, and he joined the drama group at school. He stills struggles with depression, but he works on finding creative ways to feel positive.

SAND PLAY

Using sand play with adolescents can be a freeing experience for them. Sand seems to foster risk taking in expressing and exploring metaphors because the sand can be quickly and easily restructured to change the metaphor. Adolescents know they can change the metaphor and experiment with a new metaphor without having to keep it for very long. If they don't like it or if it is too threatening, they can run their hands through it and it is gone.

Example

Tony was a young adolescent who came to counseling because he was getting in trouble at school, so much so that it was interfering with his schoolwork and interrupting the class. He had no friends. It appeared he instigated fights among his peers in order to prove he was right. His parents were very critical and were quite vocal with their complaints. In fact, I learned that the family regularly engaged in arguments to the point of verbal aggression at home. It seemed to me that there was a lot of conflict in Tony's life. You might say his world was a battlefield, fighting at school and fighting at home.

Tony wanted to use the sand tray and, not surprisingly, after looking over the shelves holding the sand tray figures, he chose the army figures. I was already seeing the metaphor developing. He set up a battle in the sand with a definitive line between sides. All the troops were in place, with figures on each side strategically placed behind bunkers, in tanks, and behind trees. Then the battle began and it was powerful, including fierce verbal attacks along with the gunfire. It was soon over. All the troops were killed with the exception of one. One lonely figure remained on a lofty sand hill.

We processed the sand play. When I asked him if he was part of this battle, Tony saw himself as the figure that was left on his lofty perch. He won his fight, but the consequence was that he was alone with no friends, just as the figure in the sand tray. We discussed the metaphorical sand representation of his life as a battlefield where winning the battle was taking priority over having friends.

I asked Tony if he wanted to change the metaphor. It was not easy. He tried out several sand trays in which he replayed the battle. Each battle became less fierce and each battle ended with more and more troops surviving along with him. At the end of that session Tony removed the figures and put his hands in the sand tray. As he picked up the sand and let each handful slowly pass through his fingers, he looked at me with a knowing smile, letting me know that he understood the significance of what had just occurred.

SONG WRITING AND POETRY

Many adolescents enjoy writing songs and poetry. They might have song lyrics and poetry running through their heads like water flowing down a stream. Sometimes, however, the water in the stream is iced over, and though we can hear the stream, we miss the beauty of the flow. If we engage in metaphorical thinking with adolescents, the warm acceptance we convey may help melt through the ice. The beauty of adolescents' metaphors will bubble and swirl around and over the rocks.

Example

Often adolescents are singing the "blues." Karen sings on a regular basis. It is a habit. She is not even aware of what she sings much of the time. During one session while we were talking about making a behavioral plan to get her schoolwork done, she began singing in a blues tune under her breath. It went something like: "She's lazy, she's a procrastinator . . . a prooooooocraaaaaaasti-naaaaaatooooor, she's molasses . . . moooolaaaaasees . . . molasses dripping off a spoon . . . driiiiiiip . . . driiiiiiiip." At first I thought Karen was singing in order to take attention from the work we were trying to do. I decided to attend to the lyrics of her blues tune, the lyrics she thought were distracting us from our work. She was surprised when I brought our focus to her lyrics and picked out the metaphor she was expressing. We processed her metaphor and she was proud of herself for developing a metaphor. She could not deny her creativity. I asked her to sing a new song with a different metaphor, one that would help her with a plan for her behavioral changes. She sang: "This lazy old girl is busy, not lazy anymore. No more prooooooooocraaaaaaaasti-naaaaaaatin." She is a firecracker . . . fiiiiiiiiirecraaaaaaaaker."

Example

Thoughts of growing up and leaving home can be roadblocks to pursuing work or college after completion of high school. Mary is an only child, raised by her mother. They grew very close to each other as the two of them made the best of their lives with few resources. Mary was finding it difficult to talk about her relationship with her mother and what it would be like to venture off to college. Mary expressed her thoughts about leaving her mother with this poem.

Our Life

The bond of a mother and a daughter
becomes the tightest that can be found.
Mommy's always there to pick me up,
whenever I fall to the ground.

She's my best friend,
through everything I do.
We change and grow together,
with every new experience.

We laughed together
when I got my first kiss.
And we giggled at Thanksgiving,
when I took my first sip of wine.

She would make our clothes.
And sometimes she would make
matching outfits for us.
When we wore them together
I was proud as a lion.

Now things have changed.
I want to be as different as I can.
As I pursue other relationships,
we begin to have conflicts and draw apart.

Yet I have found that as I mature,
I begin to share many of her traits.
Our expressions and habits and many
characteristics are similar to one another.

Then there will come the time,
when I must leave to start my own life.
This will be the time when we realize our worth.
We'll experience our first real pain,
and rivers of salty water will flow
down our blushed cheeks.

We'll hold on to every last strand
of hair and savor every last scent.

Even when we're parted,
our hearts will be as close as our hands,
when our fingers were clasped together and
we carelessly frolicked from place to place.

I'll still be mommy's little baby,
but mommy won't be there to pick me up.

Mary expresses her joys and anticipated sorrows with many metaphors. The metaphor "rivers of salty water will flow down our blushed cheeks" is powerful. Mary cried and seemed relieved to acknowledge these feelings and realize that these emotions will be present when they part. She began to accept that it might be possible to experience this parting as it became clear to Mary that she and her mother have a heart-to-heart bond that is tightly clasped, never to come apart.

CONCLUSIONS

On some mornings I'll snowshoe to the Crocker Bowl before dawn. I like to watch, giving the dawn its time, so I can experience the privilege of witnessing the Crocker Bowl fill with the fiery dawn of a new day. Give adolescents their time. Experience the privilege of witnessing adolescents fill with the dawn of a new day.

One afternoon as the sun peeked through the clouds, I was snowshoeing with Winston, my English setter. We went to see the Crocker Bowl toward the end of this afternoon. The Crocker Bowl was blanketed with the comforting shadow of the ending of the day. Dusk was descending such that I could barely see Winston hiding in the birches. As I turned to go back home and looked across to the mountains on the other side, my eyes were drawn to the sunset spreading its peaceful glow across the Burnt Mountain. Ah, there's another metaphor.

The Crocker Bowl was hidden this morning, nestled in a snowstorm. I'm ready to capture the beauty of the fire spewing out of the storm, filling the Crocker Bowl on the next new dawn. Prepare yourself. You may see it too.

REFERENCES

Allan, J., and P. Berry. 1987. Sandplay. *Elementary School Guidance and Counseling* 22: 300–306.

Davis, G. A. 1986. *Creativity Is Forever*. Dubuque, Iowa: Kendall/Hunt.

Lowenfeld, M. 1993. *Understanding Children's Sandplay: Lowenfeld's World Technique*. London: Margaret Lowenfeld Trust, Brudenell House.

Miles, R. 1993. I've got a song to sing. *Elementary School Guidance and Counseling* 28: 71–75.

Miller, C. 1990. Tears into diamonds: Transformation of child psychic trauma through sandplay and storytelling. *The Arts in Psychotherapy* 17: 247–57.

Oaklander, V. 1989. *Windows to Our Children*. Highland, New York: Gestalt Journal.

Stiles, K., and T. Kottman. 1990. Mutual storytelling: An intervention for depressed and suicidal children. *The School Counselor* 37: 337–42.

Webster's Dictionary. 1992. Chicago: J. G. Ferguson Publishing Company.

Woytowich, J. M. 1994. Power of a poem in the counseling office. *The School Counselor* 42: 78–80.

II

SPECIAL POPULATIONS

Adolescents in Foster Care: Grounded Play Therapy

Neil Cabe

$\mathscr{T}$he boy squirmed in the barber's chair. His hair lay in matted curls over his forehead and ears, flipped almost defiantly up at the rear. "A crew cut," he said, "I want a crew cut!" In an effort to foster normalcy and adolescent identity formation, he was allowed in his current placement to get his hair cut however he liked. In the staff secure residential center for adolescent boys, it was not a problem. The barber made quick work of the curls, and expertly leveled the hair on the thirteen-year-old's head. There were no sideburns to trim, as Tyler (Note: All names are fictitious) was regressed physically, as well as emotionally and developmentally.

The next time I saw him, he asked me how he looked. I put my hand under his chin, turning his head from side to side. "You'd make a good Marine!" I told him. Then I noticed the scars.

Above the boy's left eye, and just above the hairline, were two scars, perhaps one inch long, and less than one-half inch apart. At first he said his dog had done it, until I reminded him he had been in out of home placement facilities since he was about six years old. He laughed then, and said his father had done it.

Tyler had been "helping" his father hang dry wall, when the boy was four years old. Tyler kicked over a can of something, and his father hit him with the first available weapon: the claw end of a hammer. The child had been in one of approximately fourteen placements ever since. He told me later that his father used an entire arsenal of weapons on him, including the hammer, beer bottles, a belt, and, on one occasion, barbed wire across his legs. His mother had never interfered.

Most mental health problems, except those that are clearly organic, are caused by a breakdown—a disconnection—in relationship: with self, with

177

others, or with some power greater than ourselves. In the lives of clients, reconnection represents the avenue to recovery, but the losses themselves necessarily lead to an emotionally and psychologically barren state.

In Tyler's case, and in the case of most, if not all, foster children, broken connections abound. There was a broken bond between Tyler and his father due to the very severe physical abuse the child suffered. The maternal bond was broken and fueled by her lack of intervention, love, or care. Tyler was raped by a family acquaintance on numerous occasions when he sought connections outside of his family. Later, the medical staff took him for HIV testing at the request of a grandmother who had reentered his life, after it was learned that the perpetrator had AIDS. As Tyler came closer to puberty, he sexually assaulted his younger brother and sister, and engaged in sexual activity with a large number of boys in several placements.

At about the age of five, his parents enlisted him as a courier, delivering cocaine and crack cocaine on his bicycle. Frequently, Tyler sampled the products. In addition, he was encouraged to "finish" adult drinks and cans of beer when he was made to clean up after parties. At some of these parties, he was made to dance naked on a table for the perverse pleasure of the adults, some of whom later sexually assaulted him in exchange for even more cocaine. His back and legs were scarred from beatings. He avoided some foods and hoarded others. Often Tyler had to be forced to bathe, and he did not know how to brush his teeth until he was in placement. He required physical restraint almost daily.

It was my duty to complete the initial clinical assessment and diagnosis for this adolescent. The psychosocial symptoms with which Tyler presented were numerous. They included clusters of behaviors such as disruptions in relationships (buried feelings, lack of trust, rage), territorial behaviors (withdrawal, aggression, exaggerated fight/flight behaviors), damaging habits (alcohol and drug abuse, compulsive masturbation, self-mutilation), reactional problems (nightmares, suicidal and homicidal ideation, hopelessness, shame), and physiological symptoms (enuresis, rashes, problems with food). In all, the initial clinical assessment identified at least forty-eight behaviors or symptoms of clinical importance.

Sorting through this almost overwhelming list of behaviors in order to determine diagnosis was a difficult task. For the sake of illustration, based on both history and observation, I surveyed the DSM-IV for what might have been *potential* diagnoses for this boy. He was in residential care at the time I met him, but had been in several foster homes, none of which could meet his enormous needs. I was able to identify over thirty diagnoses for this child, ranging from several of the Adjustment Disorders, through Pedophilia, Substance Abuse diagnoses, Bipolar Disorder, Oppositional Defiant Disorder, Conduct Disorder, and Reactive Attachment Disorder of Early Childhood.

It is important at this point in this chapter to note that the child described in the preceding pages is a very real human being. At the time of this writing, he is fourteen-years-old and still in residential placement where he is likely to remain until adulthood when he "ages out of the system." He will then be on his own and attempting to live in a community. It is also important to note that among foster children generally, he is perhaps more a *typical* than an *atypical* client. Neither his history nor his symptoms are at all unusual in foster children who present for counseling.

THE COUNSELING NEEDS
OF FOSTER CHILDREN

According to Fine (1985), problems among foster children may include grief, anxiety, agitation, depression, withdrawal, failure to thrive, an inability to love, retarded development, aggression, oppositional and defiant behaviors, repetition compulsion, head banging, bed rocking, and fecal hoarding. Other behaviors may include food gorging, elective vomiting, enuresis, encopresis, separation terrors, tantrums, fire setting, self-mutilation, and sexual problems. Holman (1973) found that foster children have a low frustration tolerance, lack normal guilt about aggression, have impulse control problems, are cruel to animals, fight, attack other children, openly defy adults, have temper tantrums and screaming fits, are deliberately destructive, are verbally aggressive, and are persistent and profound liars.

Fanshel and Shinn (1978) completed a longitudinal study of children in foster care. Using a battery of psychological tests, they saw evidence of internal conflict, low self-confidence, poor social relationships, and regression. Behavior difficulty increased with age and time spent in foster care. Over time, the foster children became less agreeable, more defiant, less likeable, and more emotional and tense as time in foster care increased. Indeed, many of the children were worse after five years in care. Fanshel, Finch, and Grundy (1990) found the symptoms most often reported concerning foster children were moodiness and depression, stealing, running away, problematic sexual behaviors, destruction of property, drug use, and some gang involvement.

In a 1997 qualitative exploration of the counseling needs of foster children, Cabe (1997) found that behaviors reported by foster parents as being troubling enough to require therapeutic intervention fell into four orders of severity based on a behavioral true/false inventory (table 11.1). The inventory itself is reproduced in Appendix 8.1.

Table 11.1   Results of the Childhood Behavioral Checklist Used in a Study of the Counseling Needs of Foster Children

Order	Description
Most Critical Behaviors	Hiding or hoarding food Trouble sleeping Inappropriate touching of others, often sexual in nature Overeating Anger Aggression Stealing Inability to trust Makes situations where punishment is necessary
Second Order Behaviors	Child seems almost unable to love or care Refuses to clean his or her room Too affectionate with adults Talks to imaginary friends or hears voices Touches self sexually in inappropriate situations Will not obey foster parents Gets in many fights School problems
Third Order Behaviors	Self-injury Withdrawn Mentions or attempts suicide Complains of being treated unfairly Depression Constipation or diarrhea Nightmares Cultural issues
Areas of Concern	Keeps feelings buried Isolated or alone a lot Sets fires Jumps whenever anyone touches him or her

Note. See Appendix 8.1 for a copy of the Childhood Behavioral Checklist used in this study.

In an unpublished doctoral dissertation (Cabe, 2002) using the Personality Inventory for Children (Lacher, 1990) and the Randolph Attachment Disorder Questionnaire (Randolph, 2000) and triangulating them with interviews of foster parents and a focus group interview with foster care professionals, Cabe (2002) found a long list of issues and behaviors in foster children severe enough to require therapeutic intervention (table 11.2). While the behaviors and issues discovered are not significantly different from some previous studies, the qualitative nature of the study provides a graphic representation through the voice of primary care givers, and the RADQ successfully differentiates attachment disordered children from oppositional defiant and conduct disordered adolescents. Indeed, Randolph contends that there is a material difference between attachment disordered, or character disordered, children and those who may technically be diagnosed as having the Reactive Attachment Disorder of Early Childhood or Adolescence (313.89, DSM-IV-TR). Table 11.2 presents a summary of the behaviors and issues potentially in need of therapeutic intervention based on the responses to standardized interview protocols and the results of both the Personality Inventory for Children and the Randolph Attachment Questionnaire used in the Cabe (2002) study.

Almost half of the children entering foster care are placed for protective reasons (Tatara, 1993), including the poor emotional or physical condition of the parents, delinquent offenses, the child's own handicap, the relinquishment of parental rights, unwed motherhood, deinstitutionalization, or family interaction problems. Alcohol and drug abuse are factors in the placement of more than 75 percent of the children who enter foster care (U.S. Government Accounting Office, 1994). According to one study, 39 percent of the foster care population in the United States is over the age of sixteen (Aldgate et al., 1989). Trend data from the Children's Defense Fund suggests that the foster care population in the United States will continue to grow and that foster care caseloads in five of the largest states more than doubled from 1984 to 1994 (George et al., 1994). The population in care in 1995 was estimated at 500,000. Perhaps half of those children are adolescents.

THE DIAGNOSTIC DILEMMA

DSM-IV-TR states that an emotional or mental disorder should be "conceptualized as a clinically significant behavioral or psychological syndrome or pattern that occurs in a person and that is associated with a present distress (a painful symptom) or disability (impairment in one or more important areas of functioning) or with a significantly increased risk of suffering death, pain, disability, or an important loss of freedom. . . . Whatever its original cause, it must currently be considered a *manifestation* [emphasis added] of behavioral, psychological or biological dysfunction in the person" (DSM-IV-TR, p. x). Diagnosis itself represents the initial step in a more comprehensive evaluation in order to plan treatment and predict outcome. The multiaxial system proposed in DSM-IV-TR is the accepted standard in clinical practice, existing as a biopsychosocial descriptive assessment of a single client.

In light of Tyler's symptoms and the potential diagnoses listed pre-viously—even with the privilege of multiple diagnoses on Axes I and II—which are appropriate? In light of the symptoms verified by research and listed in table 11.2, what diagnosis might best be assigned to a "typical" adolescent foster child?

Referring again to Tyler's case, he meets all thirteen of the Category A requirements for Conduct Disorder, Severe, Solitary Aggressive Type (312.00). Conduct Disorder, Oppositional Defiant Disorder (313.81), and the frequent addition of Attention Deficit Hyperactivity Disorder (314.00) are in my own private practice most often the preexisting diagnoses with which foster children present. In over twenty years of practice, never has this author had an adolescent foster child whose preexisting diagnosis *as an adolescent* was Attachment Disorder.

Indeed, for many years, using the various editions of the Diagnostic and Statistical Manual as diagnostic, treatment planning, and prognostic guides, therapists may have been trying to treat the wrong things! Attempts at behavior modification and cognitive behavioral therapies with Oppositional Defiant Disorder and Conduct Disorder adolescents have been notorious failures. New understandings of the use of human touch, attachment issues, and advances in brain chemistry may help to improve our treatment strategies with these troubled teens.

ATTACHMENT ISSUES

In an oversimplification, attachment has to do with the way human beings form enduring and meaningful connections with other human beings. Bowlby (1982) viewed attachment as instinctive behavior, when human instinct was understood to include four main characteristics:

1. It follows a recognizably similar and predictable pattern in almost all members of a species, or all members of one sex.
2. It is not a simple response to a single stimulus, but a sequence of behavior that usually runs a predictable course.
3. Certain of its usual consequences are of obvious value in contributing to the preservation of an individual or the continuity of a species.
4. Many examples of it develop even when the ordinary opportunities for learning it are inadequate or absent. (Bowlby, 1982)

On some level, organisms adapt to suit an ecological niche, an environment to which such an organism is particularly suited. This adaptation is focused on survival. Further, children seek proximity and a secure base. These, too, are survival-based mechanisms. Proximity keeps the child close to an attachment figure, so that if danger arises, the attachment figure may defend the child or remove him or her from danger. The secure base is the place from which the child's proximate behaviors extend, and to which he or she returns when necessary.

Children who have early experiences involving rejection of the their proximity seeking behaviors, including protection, support, and caring, develop disrupted attachment patterns. They develop a sense of being alone and unwanted. The child internalizes a model of others as rejecting and untrustworthy. In fact, the proximity seeking behaviors of these children become disengaged. This lack of attachment seeking behavior was conjectured by Bowlby (1982) to lead to delinquency and antisocial behaviors.

Richards and Sullivan (1996), in discussing psychotherapy with delinquents, note that the treatment of delinquency in adolescence has an abysmal failure rate. Most of the delinquent population may be classified to one degree or another as nonattached. One of the essential components in their article is the transgenerational perpetuation of disruption and maladaptation in such youth. Citing Farrington (1990), the authors noted that in a longitudinal study of 411 males over a period of twenty-four years, the typical offender tended to perpetuate the same sorts of dysfunctional family for his own family that the adolescent himself experienced. Farrington's suggestion is that effective treatment of such youth could lead to a reduction in alcohol abuse, drunk driving, drug abuse, sexual promiscuity, and family violence, and probably school failure, unemployment, marital disharmony, and divorce. The authors conducted a study of forty-five boys and two girls seen in psychotherapy between 1990 and 1994. Treatment results seem to indicate that subjects who stayed in therapy longer developed a stronger alliance, had done the most therapeutic work, and showed better outcome. The quality of the therapeutic alliance appeared to be of primary importance. The model used by the authors included a secure base (consistency, regularity, responsiveness, and reliability), exploration (talking, relevance of detail and reflection), affect (processing of emotions), and termination (contracting and offering the possibility of reengagement). The clients in their study generally improved. It seems then that the secure base is a necessity in dealing with nonattached youngsters, and Bowlby's concern about nonattachment leading to delinquency may be supported.

Pearce and Pezzot-Pearce (1994) affirmed that abused and neglected children were less likely to develop secure attachments. The authors stated, however, that with the exception of gross parental deprivation, the deficiencies of early childhood appeared capable of modification by a series of experiences and especially in subsequent interpersonal relationships. Significantly, in a discussion of foster children, the authors stated, "We cannot assume that an abused child's psychological functioning will automatically improve if we remove the child from an abusive environment and then provide him or her with what we regard as positive and supportive care taking" (p. 428). Since our young clients tend to recreate their own abusive histories, they will have to undergo multiple experiences of favorable and positive experiences "in order for their developmental pathway to move in a more positive direction" (p. 428).

The process of therapy for these children, according to Pearce and Pezzot Pearce, involves a sense of safety in the child, clear, simple, and honest communication, the exploration and clarification of fantasies, consistency, reliability, constancy, predictability, and the establishment of a secure base. *The therapist may actually assume the role of secure attachment figure.* Again, the concepts that Bowlby and others propose concerning the enduring effects of insecure attachment are clear: the need for a secure base arises as perhaps primary, and the importance of consistency, constancy, dependability, predictability, responsiveness and reflection are critical.

Dr. Elizabeth Randolph is a pioneer in the study of children with attachment disorder. She compared attachment disordered children to mistreated children who have no symptoms of attachment disorder, to children with no history of attachment disorder or maltreatment who exhibit disruptive behavior, and to depressed and anxious children. She found that attachment disorder is a very different diagnosis than Reactive Attachment Disorder or Conduct Disorder. Her hypothesis is that attachment disordered youth must meet the criteria for both Reactive Attachment Disorder and either Oppositional Defiant Disorder or Conduct Disorder. The Randolph Attachment Disorder Questionnaire (Randolph, 2000) successfully differentiates the two categories, and may very well become an extremely useful and meaningful tool for clinicians working with adolescent foster children.

Dr. Tim Harlan, cited in Randolph, conducted a study of severely abused children in an effort to determine why some of these children developed Attachment Disorder and others did not. Among two groups of maltreated children, he found that those diagnosed as Attachment Disordered were more intelligent (with a mean difference between groups of fifteen points on the WISC-III full-scale IQ score), had less interest in other people, believed others would not care for their needs, and had "distinctly different personality traits." His conclusion was that some children are at greater risk for developing attachment disorder but other children with more durable personality traits were more at risk for the development of Post-traumatic Stress disorder, depression, and atypical psychosis.

ATTACHMENT AND THE HUMAN BRAIN

In light of Bowlby's definition, attachment is an instinctual behavior. It operates in a similar fashion pan-culturally, and its function is the same in all cultures: self-preservation and species perpetuation. Appropriate attachment keeps the child safe, while the secure base provides the source of proximate behaviors, in addition to allowing the development of loving and reciprocal relationships. In appropriate situations, that secure base and the capability for loving and reciprocal relationships are then passed from one generation to the next.

Attachment itself is based on family roles, environmental stimulation, and brain chemistry. Human infants require much longer periods of nurturance and protection than do other species. Clinging, sucking, smiling, gazing, and touching develop within this context of prolonged helplessness and dependency. However, the child also requires environmental stimulation for biologically based processes to develop. For example, contact comfort and feeding provoke strong responses in both babies and their caregivers. In cases of severe abuse and neglect, attachment is interrupted, and this disruption is then transgenerationally communicated. In current family situations, with divorce rates soaring and traditional male/female roles often confused or altered due to economic necessity, "the function of the family as an environment for safety, security, healthy social learning, and positive emotional attachment is now questionable" (Levy, 1996).

The human brain is best seen as triune: made up of three parts, which evolved at different times and for different purposes. The brain stem, called by some the "Reptilian Brain" is the oldest part, and was the first to evolve. It regulates the basic life functions of digestion, breathing, reproduction, and metabolism, and is responsible for the human traits of sexuality, territoriality, and survival instincts. The second part of the brain to evolve was the Limbic System, which developed with the first mammals. The Limbic System provided the ability to experience emotions, it refined the capabilities for learning and memory, and created the immune system. In the Limbic System are lodged the source of all relationship bonds and attachment behaviors. The Neocortex, the third and final part of the triune system, controls thinking, reasoning, creativity, and symbolic language. The Neocortex enables humans to observe their own emotions, and allows the possibility of choice in response to those emotions.

The brain stem and the mid-brain control much of our behavior. If we think of this as the "old brain," higher intellect is really not involved. The old brain governs maternal instinct, attachment behavior, self-preservation, and stress-related responses. When threat or danger is sensed, a part of the mid-brain—the amygdala—triggers the release of norepinephrine, which increases the brain's overall reactivity, making the senses more alert. Dopamine readies the body for "fight or flight," increasing heart rate and blood pressure, and rivets attention on the source of the fear.

In children who have experienced abuse, neglect, and multiple life disruptions, a deficit in attachment occurs. Trauma, fear, anxiety, and painful emotions are lodged in the most primitive portions of their brains (the old brain). Consequently, as previously noted by others, cognitive behavioral approaches with these children simply will not work. Cognitive behavioral, and many other modern therapies, are directed at the neocortex, the home of cognition, language, and thought, and this intellectual approach simply cannot provide access to the more primitive parts of the brain necessary for healing and positive change. Play therapy, on the other hand, using tactile activity and social cues, may allow access to the "old brain" and promote healing.

Dr. Bessell Van der Kolk, speaking at an ATTACh conference in Omaha, Nebraska (1998) discussed the effects of trauma on the human brain. In that address, summarized in two articles in the Attachment Center at Evergreen newsletter, he noted that traditional approaches to therapy simply do not work for severely traumatized children because they fail to reach the areas of the brain that suffered the greatest impact as a result of the trauma. In part, he stated that, "Therapy that goes over the trauma again and again without changing the outcome of the traumatic events reinforces the trauma and prevents healing." What is required is an approach to therapy that takes the child through the trauma, and then helps him or her find a different outcome. In addition, traditional therapies focus on talking about or playing out the conflicts and trauma, which addresses the left hemisphere of the brain, while traumatic memories are more likely stored in the right hemisphere. Trauma resolution, including the amelioration of attachment difficulty, must occur through the limbic system and the tissue memories that may exist therein. Van der Kolk noted that for therapy to work, high arousal for the client is necessary, since the traumatic memories and attachment disruption are stored in conditions of high arousal. The reduction of arousal in therapy with attachment and trauma clients is contraindicated.

In addition to the information Dr. Van der Kolk provided in the ACE articles, he has considered endogenous opiates in the lives of traumatized children. Endogenous opiates are those body chemicals released in times of great stress or in moments of intense pain; they are the painkillers of the body. Because so many foster children have endured such massive trauma, are in states of constant hyperarousal, and have experienced regular doses of the endogenous opiates, one might question whether or not these children on some level become addicted to their own behaviors. They can escalate even minor situations, due to their hyperarousal, into a major catastrophe, and thereby experience the flood of relief that accompanies the body's release of the endogenous opiates (Van der Kolk, 1989).

Van der Kolk believes that once the right side of the brain has been triggered to produce traumatic memory or the powerful emotions involved in disrupted attachment, a shift to the left side must occur. At this point, the therapist may use language (a left hemisphere function) to help resolve the trauma. While well-meaning therapists often try to help children avoid intense feeling, this does not help the child resolve the trauma.

In the second summary of Dr. Van der Kolk's address, he noted that the tasks of normal infancy and childhood are to learn to attach to and trust others, to learn how to play and share with others, to have conflicts and learn ways to resolve them, to learn to dream and to imagine, to learn to have empathy for oneself and others, to learn how to settle oneself down when upset, and to learn how to regulate one's level of arousal. Serious, chronic trauma—including the multitude of events leading to attachment disorder—interferes with each of these tasks. The trauma experiences induce a devastating loneliness in the child, as well as a sense of isolation.

Healthy attachment cannot take place when a child's mid-brain—the limbic system—is in a state of constant arousal, and subjected to floods of stress hormones. Consequently, these children never learn how to play, relax, and develop empathy or compassion. Significantly for therapists, Van der Kolk says that the moment these children are required to trust someone, they feel as though the defenses they have learned are ineffective, and they respond to what feels like an attack by others by attacking those who desire their trust. In part, they have learned to self-soothe and self-stimulate. While these children may go to anyone for care, they resist truly close relationships, as those may interfere with the self-soothing behaviors that have stood them in good stead since early childhood.

Dr. Van der Kolk suggested that chronic trauma affects the development of the brain, the immune system, the threat response systems, and the memory systems of children. The midbrain comes to expect that most life events will be traumatic, and operates in a state of constant hyperarousal. This causes these children to be over active, often responding far beyond any necessary stimulus. Often these children are diagnosed as ADHD or as having Bi-polar Disorder, when in fact their problem is actually one of hyperarousal. Even minor stimulation may result in hyperarousal. In response, many will dissociate.

INCUBATED IN TERROR

Dr. Bruce Perry (1995) discusses brain structure and its relationship to violence. He states that "The child and the adult reflect the world they are raised in. Literally, incubated in terror" (p. 3). This perhaps best describes the abuse, neglect, and disrupted attachment suffered by foster children. Perry's aim in this article is to describe the effect of this pervasive violence in the developing child.

He states succinctly that "[e]arly life experience determines core neurobiology" (p. 3). That is, the environments and attachments, or lack of attachments, within which the child is raised determine the very structure of the brain in a developing child. Violence, however, may be physical, emotional, or both. Emotional violence does not usually result in the death of the individual, he says; it results in the death of the human soul. Simply put, violent children come from violent homes. Indeed, the neurobiological adaptations focused on survival may later result in an increased tendency toward violence.

Perry makes clear that if nurturing and appropriate social experiences are provided for a child, coupled with appropriate sensory and emotional stimulation, the capacity to tolerate impulsivity, frustration, and aggression occur naturally. In some sense, the brain develops in a sequential fashion, with brainstem and mid-brain developing in a functionally appropriate proportion to the other areas of the brain, and the modulation of aggressive impulses developing appropriately. If, however, that proportion is disrupted by an overstimulation of the brain stem and mid-brain, then the proportion of lower brain to higher is disrupted and a predisposition toward aggressive and violent behavior develops along with it. Experience for a young child actually continues to shape brain structure. For children raised in an emotionally, psychologically, and physically toxic environment, the lower brain is overdeveloped in proportion to the higher, and an excessively active and reactive stress response results. For children who, in Perry's words, are "incubated in terror," aggression, overreactivity, and extreme stress responses are inevitable.

Partly, traumatized children suffer distortions of time and positive memory, and many will continue to respond to new events as if they were past events, to the degree that their behavior may even appear delusional, which can add to the diagnostic dilemma. It is the position of this chapter, however, that brain structure deviated by early trauma may be ameliorated by later therapeutic intervention. While any visible proof of structural change is unknown, behavioral change can occur. The plasticity and malleability of the human brain is beyond question. In fact, in recent medical advances, very large portions of the brain have been removed from the brains of children who have suffered severe neurological dysfunction, and they appear to be learning new ways of thinking and behaving—while missing half of their brain.

The memory systems of traumatized children are germane to the present chapter. Normal children rely on semantic, episodic, conceptual, and procedural memory. Traumatized children apparently have access only to procedural and episodic memory, and even procedural memory can be disrupted. Consequently, they are stuck with old behaviors, and cannot rely on memory systems to help them learn new ones. Clearly, this has an impact on therapy with such children.

THE PROCESS OF HUMAN MEMORY

Shiffrin and Atkinson (1969) have done substantial research on human memory. They describe the storage and retrieval process in human memory as an input/output process that eliminates the decay of information in long-term memory. Long-term memory, they propose, is permanent, and deficiencies in retrieval are more a problem of ineffective retrieval than of actual decay or loss of information. As therapists, it is our aim to position in the long-term memory of our young clients new information and new ways of dealing with the disruptions described in the preceding sections.

Shiffrin and Atkinson describe memory process in three stages: sensory register, short-term storage, and long-term storage. Transfer from one "area" to another does not imply the removal of information, but rather a copying of information from one store, or status, to the next. While their articles do not hypothesize about physiological loci, the application of memory theory, brain structure, and the play therapy process described below do.

The first register of memory, the sensory register, temporarily holds incoming sensory information while it is being processed and copied to the short-term store. Information available to sensory memory, which one might term the conscious present, includes perceptual material, sounds, color, shape, texture, and the like. The sensory register may hold information from perhaps three milliseconds to 750 milliseconds. It requires contact with stimuli, and it is lost if it is not rehearsed or attended to by the individual. When sensory stimuli are worked with or manipulated, portions of it are copied to the short-term store, or short-term memory.

The short-term store serves a number of useful purposes. It includes phonological items, patterns, geometrics and the like, and in it, manipulations may take place on a temporary basis. It may also serve to separate information from the sensory register. Further, the manipulation process allows storage and retrieval from the long-term store. This short-term memory endures approximately forty seconds, and may hold up to seven plus or minus two items. The use of tools serves to economize the manipulation process (Shiffrin and Atkinson, 1969).

Long-term storage, or long-term memory, is relatively permanent, it is infinite in capacity, and it is in constant flow. Long-term storage is constantly occurring for the information working its way into short-term memory, and being copied to long-term memory. Long-term memory deals with semantics, episodes, concepts, images, gestalts, and affectively laden arrays. In a situation where a large amount of information—implying a near-overload of the sensory register—is being input to short-term memory, the capacity of the entire system is taxed, and the individual "chooses" what information it stores and what is lost. The severity of sensory stimulation, leading to an overload of short-term memory, perhaps results in the most painful or damaging material being stored in long-term memory, or conversely may result in the obliteration of such memory. Easily stored information is given preference. For example, visual information is more easily stored than auditory. The short-term memory then acts as a sort of "window" for the long-term memory.

Working memory, according to Shiffrin and Atkinson, is a set of processes that overlap short-term memory and long-term memory—a window. The working memory defeats the limitations of the short-term memory, and is a sort of workbench for the volitional mind. The deeper the level of processing, the higher the probability of retrieval (remembering), and the higher the level of confidence in responding. Additionally, there is an inverse relationship in response time. Things may be retrieved from long-term memory instantaneously.

Long-term memory, put to use after passing through the "window" of the overlap between short-term and long-term memory, processes semantics, episodes, concepts, images, gestalts, and affectively laden arrays. The ability to choose lies in the long-term memory. The neocortex, or higher brain, deals with the same issues. If we want change to occur in our young clients, it appears we must be aware of both sets of processes.

GROUNDED PLAY THERAPY PROCESSING

The list of symptoms and the potential diagnoses for the majority of foster children, based on research and practice, are lengthy. In light of a growing understanding of attachment disorder, its symptoms and behaviors, and its transgenerational perpetuation, we, in many cases, may have been addressing the wrong diagnoses in any case. Finally, based on the structure, function, and proportional growth of the human brain, many therapists may have been unwittingly contributing to the abysmal failure rate in treating conduct disordered and oppositional defiant disordered clients—especially so since their problems may be more attachment and brain related than simply chosen. First, we have been treating the wrong diagnoses. Compounding that problem, we have been addressing precisely the wrong parts of the human brain. The necessity for treating these children appropriately is clear, but the appropriate treatment may not be so. The following sections suggest a play therapy approach to these clients.

THE BASIC ASSUMPTIONS OF THE GROUNDED PLAY THERAPY APPROACH

It is the contention of the Grounded Play Therapy process that adolescents in foster care, and many of our clients, generally, are not *grounded*. Grounding in this approach to process implies at all stages that the child is in some sense adrift—separated from self, others, and existentially. Adolescents in foster care will present as separated or adrift from their own emotions, affect, mood, intellectual ability, self-esteem, and senses. It is the object of this approach to ground these children within themselves and in their own environments. In light of developmental theory and proportional brain development, the Grounded Play Therapy process attempts to meet the children where they are, and walk with them toward healing, growth, age appropriate maturity, and emotional balance.

There are four assumptions that form the basis of the Grounded Play Therapy approach to working with not only adolescents, but also with children in play therapy sessions:

1. Play is a symbolic activity for the child.
2. Play translates media properties into levels of activity, healing dimensions, and emergent functions.
3. The progress of therapy often appears erratic, but results in increasingly healthy relationships and the decay of unwanted behaviors, attitudes, and images.
4. The progress of therapy will follow a predictable set of processes.

PLAY AS SYMBOLIC

Therapists may be prone toward a set of fairly standard interpretations of the use of play therapy materials in working with children. Often, airplanes do represent a need for escape or freedom for instance, but not always. Guns may be instruments of control, aggression, or protection, but not always. In this approach to play therapy, it is important for the child to assign meaning to his or her own symbols. Dr. Byron Norton (1997) has proposed an excellent description of typical symbolic meanings for toys and environments.

It is fairly safe to say that most play in a therapy situation is symbolic of the child's internal and external worlds. However, based on the brain functions noted, it might be more accurate to say that cognitive processes begin experientially. Not only have the clients' development and environment shaped cognitive experiences, but also those experiences may be worked out and worked through in the therapeutic milieu. On some level, the child wants to share his or her life experiences with a trusted other, but according to Norton, verbal validations may not occur (Norton, 1997).

The purpose of the child's behavior, and its expression in therapy, may be primarily defensive and protective. The therapist must validate the child's behavior, and no defense mechanism should be removed before the need for that defense has been eliminated. As play develops, a symbolic theme will develop along with it. Symbols may represent the events themselves, or some dissociated safe haven. In some sense, fantasy play empowers the child and through it he or she may conquer (gain mastery over) those symbols. The therapist provides symbols that allow the child to externalize trauma, affect, or behavior, and over which the child may gain mastery.

Norton (1997) says that any violation of self will show in subsequent behavior. He also suggests that children who will not cycle through the process may still be living in circumstances requiring the embedded defenses, and may, therefore, not permit the removal of those defense mechanisms, no matter how injurious these may be. However, healing occurs on a symbolic level, whether or not the trauma and embedded affect are ever brought into consciousness and reality.

THE IMPORTANCE OF RELATIONSHIP

There are at least five issues to be considered in the building of appropriate relationship with our clients: limits and boundaries, time, exclusivity, safety, and confidentiality. Specific techniques for building relationship quickly and appropriately will follow.

Freud said, "There is little that gives children greater pleasure than when a grown-up lets himself down to their level, renounces his oppressive superiority, and plays with them as an equal" (Schaefer and Kaduson, 1994, p. 28).

Recently, a ten-year-old boy was in my office for his first session following a suicide threat. He definitely did not want to be there. As I gave him a tour of the play area, we sat together on the floor and examined the puppets. He looked at them curiously, and asked what they could do. I took a witch, whose arms allow the insertion of our hands, pretended it was a teacher, and she wrote on the blackboard in her worst printing "SCHOOL SUCKS!" He laughed until his face was red. "That's it!" he said! "You understand!" Later he asked his mother if he could come back the next day.

Limits and boundaries in therapy must be clear, consistent, rehearsed, rewarded, and consequenced. Limits tie us to reality and make for safer inner and outer worlds. In the very first session, make it clear to the children that no one will touch them without their permission, that they will be protected while they are in session, and that no one gets to know what is discussed without their and their parent's permission. Boundaries, which in the lives of foster adolescents have so often been so badly violated, increase that sense of safety, and allow the child to begin to work. Time is one boundary. Try very hard to begin and end sessions on time, and tell the child this. Also give warnings before the session is coming to an end, which gives young clients a sense of closure and allows the therapist to ready them for their next visit.

It is important for the adolescents to know that their time with their therapist is exclusively their own. If sessions with family or foster parents are necessary, try to schedule them separately from the child's time. Further, so many teenagers feel that no one has ever listened to them at all. The child-centered focus is critical. Often, they feel as if they have no voice; not only have they not been heard, they have been unable to tell their own stories. Appropriate therapy will allow both the speaking and the hearing.

Confidentiality is coupled closely to the preceding issue of being heard. Foster children have had their lives spread among social service agencies, foster agencies, social workers, placement personnel, medical personnel, and others for the entire time they have been in the foster care system. These disclosures have been made without the knowledge or permission of the adolescent, and the violations they feel are painful. In the very first session, emphasize that there are limits on confidentiality: harm to self, harm to others, or harm to the child being or having been perpetrated on them requires disclosure by the therapist to the appropriate authorities. (My promise to the children is that, with those exceptions, I will not discuss with anyone what they say to me without their permission.) Teenagers have active private lives, and this author's estimate is that parents or foster parents know only somewhere between 10 percent and 15 percent of what actually goes on in a child's life. He or she loves others the parents do not know. They have been involved in activities they do not want their parents or surrogate parents to know about. Keep their confidence, explaining to them that confidentiality is a sort of "one-way secret": They can tell anyone they want anything they want about what we do or discuss; the therapist is not permitted to tell anyone. (I have never had a child object to this arrangement. I have had some parents object to it, and will not treat the adolescent unless the parent can come to agree.)

Closely aligned with confidentiality and the other limits and boundaries is the issue of safety. No one is allowed to get hurt, neither the client nor the therapist. Some toys and other items may get broken, but we understand that accidents happen. In fact, it can be of therapeutic importance to note the things that a child might break on purpose when the symbolism of that object is clear. It may even be beneficial. (I also insist that we put things away when we are finished, but I confess that this boundary gets a little vague after a particularly active session.)

Therapists must also be concerned about the use of touching in therapy with all children, but especially so with abused and neglected children. With children who have been sexualized at early ages, and with all youngsters who are sexually active, even the most innocuous touch by a therapist may be misinterpreted by the child as a sexual touch. On the other hand, based on the brain processing and therapeutic needs of attachment disordered children, appropriate touch can be an important tool for healing. Choices in the use of therapeutic touch are personal, but critical. Competency in therapy necessitates clear supervision, observation with any child who may question the use of touch, parental or foster parent inclusion in or observation of therapy sessions, and extreme care on the part of the therapist. Typically, physical contact between therapist and child happens only with the permission of the child, and usually only when initiated by him or her.

THE PROGRESS OF
GROUNDED PLAY THERAPY

Grounded Play Therapy typically progresses through four stages: relationship, process, empowerment, and closure. These are not discrete stages of therapy, and may overlap one another, with the child frequently cycling back and forth through them, not only in the course of therapy, but also occasionally in the course of a single session. The therapist must be sensitive to the place where the child finds himself or herself, and adjust sessions accordingly.

In the first stage, relationship and trust are established. This is a delicate and artful part of the therapeutic process. Some communicators say that we have approximately three minutes to engage a child, or lose him or her for the entire course of therapy. While this may be slightly exaggerated, it is an important point. Engaging the child almost immediately is very important. The strategic placement of entertaining and curiosity provoking toys in the office, especially while the parent, social worker, or foster parent is present, can help the engagement process enormously. During the relationship and trust building stage of treatment, immediate, significant, but often temporary improvement may occur. Parents and other caregivers should be made aware of the fact that this immediate improvement is most often temporary.

The second stage is the Process Stage. Here, the adolescent expresses needs and works through issues in his or her own time, at his or her own pace, in relationship with the therapist. Various re-enactments may involve evoking responses familiar to the child. In a sense, he or she will show the therapist how his or her world often responds to his or her behavior. It is most important that the therapist's response is compassionate, understanding, and gentle. While the therapist may wish to respond to a particular behavior with anger, irritation, disgust, or even revulsion, the child is offering valuable information in this activity. They may be waiting to see if the therapist responds just like everyone else in their life has. Appropriate and understanding responses by the therapist will engage the child quickly and effectively.

It is also in the Process Stage that the adolescent will begin actually to work through the issues and emotions he or she brings to therapy. Deep feelings, memories, tissue memories, realizations, and insights may occur, and they may necessitate some behavioral acting out on the child's part. Parents and other caregivers should be warned that behavior that had begun to improve might deteriorate. In some sense, it is a good sign if the child begins to behave badly after having improved almost dramatically!

Following the Process Stage, the child will enter the Empowerment Stage of the Grounded Play Therapy process. Having offered to our clients appropriate symbols over which they have learned to gain mastery, a real sense of empowerment will follow. Here, the child will learn appropriate compensatory behaviors instead of the inappropriate compensations he or she has used in the past. During the Empowerment and Closure Stages of the Grounded Play Therapy process, behaviors may be somewhat erratic, but the "lows" will never be as low as they were at intake. In fact, over time, the low points in behavior and affect will be better than previous high points ever were.

The last stage of the Grounded Play Therapy process is Closure. As the child reconnects with self, with others, and existentially, the process for closure occurs. In the Closure Stage, consider offering transitional objects to the child, so that in some symbolic way the improvements gained in therapy will travel back to the real world with the child.

Within the overall Grounded Play Therapy process, there are six subsets of processes occurring. Evolving from the work of Lusebrink (1990), Maslow (1970), Piaget (Piaget and Thompson, 1974), and Moustakas (1992), these subprocesses include homeostasis, animation, trust, vesting, potency, and preservation. The following section discusses each subset, and table 11.3 presents a set of activities the author has found useful and practical in each subset.

GROUNDED PLAY THERAPY
THEORETICAL BASIS

The Grounded Play Therapy process represents a synthesis of important research, resting on the legs of pioneers in the fields of therapy and psychology. Lusebrink (1990) described the characteristics of the different levels of what she calls the Expressive Therapies Continuum (ETC), and noted both healing dimensions and emergent functions on each level of expression. She also described media properties for two and three-dimensional media. The Grounded Play Therapy approach uses her research, and notes that the movement in media properties may happen within a single session, as well as during the entire course of therapy. In essence, she says that the use of two-dimensional media will move from most resistive to least resistive media, for example, from pencils to magic markers, to chalk, to poster paint, to watercolor, and to finger paint. (My own experience adds finger painting with vanilla pudding colored with food coloring past the most fluid media, finger paint.) In three-dimensional media, she sees the process from most resistive to most fluid as potentially including stone, wood, oil clay, and water clay. (Again, through my own experience, we may add making our own silly putty from Elmer's Glue and a Borax solution.) Table 11.4 illustrates the levels of expression, the healing dimensions, and the emergent functions that Lusebrink provides.

Akin to Lusebrink's levels, dimensions, functions, and resistive/fluid continuums, Maslow (1970) proposes a five-level model of human need, from physiological needs, to safety needs, to belonging, to esteem, and to self-actualization. Piaget (Piaget and Thompson, 1974) adds the sensorimotor level, followed by preoperational levels, concrete operational levels, and formal operational levels. Moustakas (1992) proposes a therapeutic continuum from diffuse and pervasive anxiety and fear, to generalized anxiety and fear, to focused hostility and fear, to ambivalence, to preservation. The author developed the Grounded Play Therapy process in light of both Lusebrink's continuums and the theoretical bases of Maslow, Piaget, and Moustakas.

SIX SUBPROCESSES OF THE GROUNDED
PLAY THERAPY PROCESS

Homeostasis represents the ability of an organism to maintain balance in living by adjusting to its environment. All clients present with an existing homeostasis, and the aims of the initial clinical assessment and other assessments are to determine what that is. When we know where a client is, we can learn how he or she got there, and help the client determine a course for the future. This is the first subprocess.

Second, a period of animation enters into the child's play, which is characterized by kinesthetics, perception, and the conscious present. In this phase, it is important for the adolescent to begin to explore both self and surroundings, which may include his or her history using the symbols available through play therapy. Some of the requirements for this phase include limit setting, boundaries, family history, suicide inventories, noninjury contracts, and the like.

The levels of trust must develop in all sessions. Certainly, trust is a continuing issue in working with clients, and some level of it must be built very quickly. However, in the trust phase of the Grounded Play Therapy, which is a continuation of the sensory and perceptual activity of the animation phase, some sense of sanctuary must begin to develop in the sessions. The child gains mastery over feelings of assurance and security. That assurance and that security may include interventions in the home, in the school, in contacts with the extended family, and in the child's sense of self.

Following trust, the next phase of Grounded Play Therapy is vesting, where the child develops a sense of residence within the self. This is an affective phase, and begins to lead to cognition and cognitive reconstruction. It must be remembered that techniques addressing the cerebral cortex and cognitive areas of the brain are at best limited in the foster children we see. Attempting too much too quickly is futile.

At this point in the therapeutic process, the child will begin to develop a sense of potency. Here he or she is experiencing effective interactions with the environment. This is a phase full of energy, symbolism, and creativity.

Finally, attempts at preservation account for the final and closure phases of the therapeutic process. In this phase, transitional objects become very important, and the client learns to perseverate appropriate behaviors beyond the boundaries of the play therapy sessions. Often, school checks and parental conferences for follow-up are important. With the advent of the World Wide Web, the therapist's email address may be given to the client in order to provide the concept of continued contact availability. Transition to group sessions, community involvement, and occasional telephone follow-ups may be beneficial.

It must be noted that attempting to implement techniques and activities inappropriate to the phase of therapy within which the child emerges is futile and potentially damaging to the child. Some overlap may occur as the child cycles through the phases. Some phases he or she will revisit until mastery of appropriate symbols has been achieved. Regularly, however, the child will participate with the therapist in externalizing embedded affect, memory, and behavior, gaining mastery, and moving on.

SELECTION OF TOYS AND MATERIALS

Toys and materials are not randomly picked for the playroom, but chosen with a purpose. Selection of toys is made to encourage the expression of the child's feelings, needs, and personal life experiences. Toys are selected that facilitate and encourage the following:

1. Enhance the relationship with the child;
2. Provide an opportunity for the child to project a wide range of feelings, conflicts, wishes and fears;
3. Provide safety and nurturance for the child;
4. Promote creativity and the use of the imagination;
5. Develop self-identity and self-esteem;
6. Allow for the reenactment of real-life experiences;
7. Allow the child to go into fantasy to communicate indirectly;
8. Promote contact with the environment, with others, and with the self;
9. Promote the expression of feelings, attitudes, and needs through metaphor;
10. Promote tactile, auditory, and visual awareness and expression. (Adapted from Norton and Norton, 1997)

FROM THEORY TO PRACTICE: THE PROOF IS IN THE PUDDING

Does anyone truly understand why play therapy "works?" Indeed, it may be that we do not understand why *any* approach to therapy works. We just know that it does. It may be brain chemistry, or cognitive restructuring, or divine intervention. However, the proof, ultimately, is in the pudding. We know that it works, simply because it works. In part, we must learn to trust our tools to do the work that they do, even when we do not understand it.

Using the Grounded Play Therapy approach it is important to bear in mind the primary underlying principles at all times: providing a symbol that allows externalization and mastery, and moving from conscious present to long-term memory. Following that, the premise that a client will move from most resistive to least resistive media, either in a single session or during the course of therapy, is a constant. Finally, addressing the brain stem and mid-brain and limbic systems are the preludes to the neocortex and cognitive functioning.

CASE EXAMPLE AND IMPLEMENTATION

The next section of this chapter describes the process of therapy with a single adolescent in foster care. In doing so, it reflects both an outline for implementation and a case illustration. Further, due to the length of time spent in therapy with this child, a session-by-session description is impractical for this brief chapter. The case description follows the outline of Grounded Play Therapy described previously. While this is an actual case, all names and other identifying information have been changed to protect the confidentiality of the client.

Homeostasis

While testing is listed in a separate section in table 11.3, it is nevertheless an important part of the process. Often, a great deal of information is necessary to understand where a child actually "is." In Brian's case, I used the BTFI, the Children's Depression Inventory, the RCMAS, the WISC-III, and the House Tree Person projective screening process. Brian scored 88 percent on the BTFI, which allowed me to address abuse issues almost immediately. His foster mother had had him for several months by the time I met him, and knew a great deal about him, especially because her sister had Brian's brother as a foster child, and she was familiar with the biological family.

The boy was twelve, soon to turn thirteen, and he had a history of severe sexual and physical abuse. His father and two other men raped him, and his mother had at one point "ironed" his arm, leaving a scar from his wrist to above his elbow. He self-mutilated with pins, hid urine in his closet, had nightmares, hoarded food, performed poorly in school, had sleep problems, and experienced frequent nightmares. More symptoms emerged during the process of Homeostasis.

We began working the self-mutilation immediately, with him noting that it made him feel alive somehow. Use of a genogram, an ecomap, and the boundary exercises seemed to help with this very quickly. We connected with telephones, used playing catch as a conversation starter, and frequently tossed the Hoberman spheres back and forth to establish connection. Games with rules were very difficult for him, especially since he had almost no knowledge of children's games. Checkers, on a two-foot by four-foot cloth playing board helped, and when I insisted we play a few times without rules, he got the message immediately. In the early sessions, Brian was afraid to be touched by anyone, including his foster parents, and certainly by me. I did not insist on it in any way.

Animation

As we progressed through the Animation stage of the process, Brian began to move closer to me and to others. His play was characterized by more energy, and I focused on his sensory deprivation. We ate fresh cherries together, did balloon tossing, threw the crash dummy at the wall with pleasure, allowing it to become his father and others, and built towers with foam blocks, knocking them all over the play room and beginning again. He particularly enjoyed shooting the toy soldiers with rubber bands, setting them up as separate armies, and insisting that he win the war. I, of course, let him. Later, the armies joined at his insistence, and he and I fought the dinosaurs together. At one point, I taught him how to break a pine board with a single punch, and he was thrilled when he succeeded. I do not recommend this activity for anyone without proper training, but it was a great experience for this boy and many others. We also exploded film canisters using vinegar and baking soda, discussing how emotions held in caused explosions, but emotions released led to relief.

When he first came into foster care, he was disheveled, never brushed his teeth, had no clothes that fit, and had never used deodorant. We talked about bodily changes, using the *What's Happening to My Body Book for Boys* (Madaras and Madaras, 2000), and he began to clean himself up. By the end of our time together, he was ironing his own clothes—a significant activity for a boy who had been burned by an iron—and insisting on haircuts and clean fingernails. This did not become compulsive behavior, which I feared for him, but became more appropriate self-care as his self-esteem climbed. Food hoarding stopped in time, and his revulsion for vegetables turned into a genuine taste for them.

One key issue for Brian was sleep deprivation due to nightmares. He could recite the entire late-night line-up to me. Using a relaxation training tape, he learned to fall asleep easily, and began to sleep dreamless through the night. Referrals to doctors, optometrists, dentists, and dermatologists through his state funded health card cleared up his need for glasses, dental problems, and rashes. A psychiatric referral led to the prescribing of a drug to help with bedwetting, and one for hyperactivity, both of which were to some degree helpful.

Trust

Building trust with Brian was an effort. It began with boundaries and consistency. I also arranged for a visit from his brother whom he had not seen in two years, and waited patiently for him to initiate touch with me. In time, he did. By the end of our sessions, he would frequently and spontaneously hug me in front of his foster mother before he left. Art therapy, including the "rose bush technique" (Oaklander, 1988) and anger management exercises involving large muscle activity with no injury to either of us, helped. He enjoyed toys that connected to each other, such as building blocks and Lego, and we often used them. As he grew older, his circle of friends grew, and trust grew with it.

Vesting

In the Vesting stage of the process, we moved to activities that are more fluid. I outlined most but not all of his body on butcher paper and he enjoyed making a full-body drawing, the inside of which he illustrated with bones and a heart. We made our own silly putty using Elmer's™ glue and Borax™, which is a particularly fluid activity. At one point in the process, the glue resembles some bodily fluids, and is difficult for sexually abused children. He noticed it, but drove through the fluidity to a more firm texture. We also made a flour and salt concoction for play dough, built a volcano, erupted it with vinegar and baking soda, and I gave it to him to take home as a transitional object.

Testing in the earliest sessions of therapy indicated that Brian was intelligent, but lacking in fund of knowledge, which is not uncommon for many foster children. Verbal and performance IQ difference was statistically significant. As his grades improved right along with his school behavior, that fund of knowledge grew, and he discovered both music and his own voice. That was a milestone for the boy.

During this stage of the process, we were able to discuss sexuality more completely. He was afraid he was homosexual because of what happened to him, but was reassured when I told him that this was not necessarily so. People are born homosexual, I told him, and what was done to them does not make it so. These sorts of questions are extremely common among young male survivors of childhood sexual abuse.

Potency

The sense of empowerment that Brian had been gaining during the course of therapy made this portion of his progress a joy. When we discussed his strengths and weaknesses on a chart we made, and that I had him take home for his room, he was easily able to identify strengths and had difficulty finding weaknesses. Due to the fluidity of the activity, and the concurrent food difficulties emergent early in therapy, pudding painting was a distinct pleasure for Brian.

In many sessions, I let him choose the activity for the hour. He returned often to the armies and rubber bands, and frequently to activities that brought us into appropriate physical contact with each other. At one point, early in our time together, I had marked his height on the wall of the playroom. He often checked it, and as he hit the post-pubescent growth spurt while we were still in contact, the physical growth in the boy was dramatic. It is an interesting fact that children who are regressed emotionally and developmentally, often seem to be regressed physically as well. As the boy became more settled within himself, his physical growth began to match his emotional and psychological growth. Anger management exercises were interspersed throughout our sessions together, as were sessions with his foster parents. With the child's permission, as well as legal authorization, I often checked in with his school counselor, and regularly rewarded his good grades and better behavior with small treats.

It was also at this point in therapy that we participated in reenactment of abusive events in his young life. Using a four-foot soft doll, we reenacted the physical and sexual abuse, but reconstructed the outcome so that the child was powerful and self-defensive. At one point, we set up the family therapy room to represent his home, placing stuffed animals where adults might have been, and allowing him to triumph over them all. Not only was it fun, though difficult for him, but it also allowed him access to both the limbic and neocortical areas of his own brain to gain closure on the abusive events.

Preservation

In time, continuing sessions became redundant, and Brian often came to simply talk and tell me about his weeks. We terminated sessions with transitional objects, including an inexpensive set of toy soldiers that I bought for him, and I offered him my email address. His foster mother knew where to find me, and knew to call if it was necessary.

Closure

Brian did call me at my office a few times following termination. The conversations were friendly and lacked the pressured speech and frantic nature of his earlier talks. The calls quickly faded.

I saw him in therapy for approximately three years, weekly at first, then twice monthly for the last six to eight months. He was able to remain with the same, experienced, licensed therapist for a long period of time, partly due to his enrollment in a state funded healthcare program. He remained in the same foster home for the entire time, and was later adopted by that family. Not only did we focus on the Grounded Play Therapy process, but we also focused on therapeutic processes that emphasized his disrupted attachment, the sexual and physical abuse he suffered, and the severed family ties he had experienced. While drugs and alcohol were not problems for this client, they were a serious component in his removal from his biological family, where crack cocaine addiction was rampant. In most respects, he was a typical foster child.

When Brian first presented for therapy, the Behavioral True False Inventory showed an 88 percent "true" set of responses. During the writing of this chapter, I called his foster parents, who have since adopted Brian, and asked if they would complete it again for me. Brian himself, who is now seventeen years old, answered the telephone when I first called, and was obviously pleased and surprised to hear from me. I questioned him about the activities he remembered from our time together. He quickly recalled making the "gloop," playing with the soldiers, and playing with a giant rubber band I have that flings the child up to me as an exercise in trust and closeness. His grades are mostly As and Bs, he is active in his church, he has a large number of friends, and his mother told me he hugs her when he comes in from school every day automatically. He never sees his brother, who has had continuing drug problems. Today, Brian is a happy, healthy, and charming young man.

When his foster parents completed the inventory this year, Brian scored at 24 percent "true" responses. I noted to his mother and father that they deserve most of the credit for that, and her response was that they could not have done it without a good counselor.

There are no guarantees in the use of any therapy process. More research is certainly needed in the areas of attachment and play therapy approaches to it. And, more needs to be learned and published concerning the pressing needs of foster children, many of whom are adolescents. Perhaps this chapter will encourage that research and those approaches.

Table 11.2   Illustration of Summary Statements from All Data Sources

Foster Care Professionals	Foster Parents	PIC	RADQ
anger	anger	hostility	anger
	arguing		arguing
attention seeking		attention seeking	attention seeking
communication problems	communication problems		
confusion		confusion	
cruel to animals	cruel to animals	cruel to animals	cruel to animals
depression	sadness	unhappy	
destroying property	destroying property		destructive
detachment	attachment issues		attachment issues
family issues	family issues/visits		
few friends	few friends	poor peer relations	few friends
fire setting	fire setting		fire setting
food problems	food problems/starvation	eating difficulties	food problems
grief	sadness	depression	
inability to love	hyperactivity	hyperactivity	impulsive
	unable to love		inability to love
	lack of guilt		lack of guilt
loss	loss of family		loss and separation
lying	lying	lying	lying
	mood swings		

Table 11.2 (Continued)

Foster Care Professionals	Foster Parents	PIC	RADQ
neglect	neglect		neglect
	need for order		need to control
parental drug abuse	parental drug abuse		abuse and neglect
physical abuse	physical abuse		
poor hygiene	hygiene problems		
poor parenting			
school problems	school problems	school problems	school problems
	self-mutilation	dangerous activity	dangerous activity
sexual abuse	sexual abuse	sexual problems	abuse and neglect
	sexual perpetration		
spitting	spitting		
splitting parents	splitting parents		
stealing	stealing	stealing	stealing
unable to trust	unable to trust		
	withdrawn	poor social skills	poor social skills
		short attention span	impulsive
		developmental delay	
		motor skill problems	

Table 11.3   Phases of the Grounded Play Therapy Process with Suggested Activities

Phase	Suggested Activities
Testing at the Discretion of the Therapist	Children's Depression Inventory; State-Trait Anger Expression Inventory; Revised Childhood Manifest Anxiety Scale; Wechsler Intelligence Scale for Children; Kaufman Brief Intelligence Test; Adolescent Psychopathology Scale; Minnesota Multi-Phasic Personality Inventory—Adolescent; Personality Inventory for Children; Draw A Person Test; Bender-Gestalt; Substance Abuse Subtle Screening Inventory; Randolph Attachment Disorder Questionnaire; House-Tree-Person Projective Test; Jessness Inventory; Adolescent Sexual Concerns Questionnaire.
Homeostasis	Genogram; ecomap; noninjury contract; thorough initial clinical assessment; family history; behavioral check list; testing; suicide inventory; referral to psychiatrist if it appears necessary; parental interviews; Velcro paddles and balls; Hoberman spheres; boundary exercises and explanations; space phones; telephones—even make one with tin cans; games with rules.
Animation	Exploratory and nondirective play; puzzles, continuing disclosures; emphasize safety concerns; systems interventions as necessary (CSB, police, housing, food, clothing, etc.); chalk boards; commercial silly putty; pencil drawings; balloons; crash dummy; large doll; foam blocks; toy soldiers and dinosaurs; cars to crash; puppets; blocks; tea sets; plastic foods; bubbles; relaxation training; exploding canisters.
Trust	Rule rehearsal; slingshot, if the child wishes to do so; rose drawing; lake drawing; school interventions; family sessions; parenting training; drums; musical instruments; doll houses; continued anger management exercises; Leggos and Connex; other trust exercises as the child is able to manage them; finger traps; commercial play dough; sticky balls; drawing with markers.
Vesting	Full body drawing; make play dough; make silly putty; begin finger painting; poster paints; mood drawings using only colors and shapes; dummy to hit; explain that emotions → thoughts → actions; dominoes; review childhood photos.
Potency	Strengths and weaknesses charts, pudding painting, redo activities of choice; family sessions; reenactment and abreaction; letters to offending others; reframing; MORE anger management; house diagrams; ball-makers; finger painting; painting with pudding.
Preservation	School checks; parental conferences; email to the therapist if appropriate; group activity; community involvement; occasional follow-up via telephone; transitional objects.

Table 11.4   Characteristics of Different Levels of Expressive Therapies Continuum and Healing Dimensions and Emergent Functions on Each Level of Expression

Level	Healing Dimension	Emergent Function
Kinesthetic Motor movements, gestures, acts of doing, exploration of materials	Energy release, rhythm	Form, perception, affect
Sensory Tactile explorations, focus on inner sensations	Slow rhythm, awareness of internal sensations	Formation of internal images, affect
Perceptual Emphasis on form, formal elements, concrete images	Organization of stimuli, formation of good gestalts	Interactions of schemata, verbal labeling, and self-instructions
Affective Expression of feelings and moods, emphasis on color	Awareness of appropriate affect	Verbal labeling of feelings, internalization of affective and symbolic images
Cognitive Concept formulation, abstraction, verbal self-instructions	Generalization of concrete experiences, spatial relationships	Creative problem solving using verbal and imaginal interaction
Symbolic Intuitive and self-oriented concept formation and abstractions, synthetical thinking	Resolution of symbols through personal meaning; generalization of concrete personal experience	Insight leading to discovery of new parts of self, integration of repressed or dissociated parts of the self

Note: Adapted from Lusebrink, V.B. 1990. *Imagery and Visual Expression in Therapy.* New York: Plenum Press.

REFERENCES

American Psychiatric Association. 2000. *Diagnostic and Statistical Manual of Mental Disorders*, 4th ed., Text Revision. Washington, DC: American Psychiatric Association.

Aldgate, J., A. Maluccio, and C. Reeves. 1989. *Adolescents in Foster Families.* Chicago: Lyceum Books.

Bowlby, J. 1982. *Attachment and Loss. Vol. 1: Attachment.* New York: Basic Books. Originally published in 1962.

Cabe, N. 1997. A Pilot Study: When Chili Becomes Finger Food, or Understanding the Counseling Needs of Foster Children. Unpublished manuscript, Kent State University, Kent, Ohio.

———. 1999. Abused boys and adolescents: Out of the shadows. In *Handbook of Counseling Boys and Adolescent Males: A Practitioner's Guide*, ed. A. M. Horne and M. S. Kiselica, 199–215. Thousand Oaks, CA: Sage Publishing.

————. 2002. Exploring the Counseling Needs of Foster Children: A Qualitative and Quantitative Study of the Perspectives of Foster Parents and Foster Care Professionals. Unpublished doctoral dissertation, Kent State University, Kent, Ohio.

Fanshel, D., and E. B. Shinn. 1978. *Children in Foster Care: A Longitudinal Investigation.* New York: Columbia University Press.

Fanshel, D., S. J. Finch, and J. F. Grundy. 1990. *Foster Children in a Life Course Perspective.* New York: Columbia University Press.

Farrington, D. P. 1990. Implications of criminal career research for the prevention of offending. *Journal of Adolescence* 13: 93–113.

Fine, P. 1985. Treatment needs of children in foster care. *American Journal of Orthopsychiatry* 50(2): 256–63.

General Accounting Office. 1995. Foster care: Health needs of many young children are unknown and unmet. Letter report, GAO/HEHS-95-14, May 26, 1995. Available at http://home/rica.net/rthomas/fosref04.htm.

George, R., F. Wulczyn, and D. Fanshel. 1994. A foster care research agenda for the '90s. *Child Welfare* 73(5): 525–49.

Holman, R. 1973. *Trading in Children.* Boston: Routledge and Keegan Paul.

Lacher, D. 1990. *Multidimensional Description of Child Personality: A Manual for the Personality Inventory for Children.* Los Angeles: Western Psychological Services.

Levy, T. M. 1996. Attachment: Biology, Evolution and Environment. *Attachments Newsletter* (Spring/Summer). Evergreen, CO: The Attachment Center at Evergreen.

Lusebrink, V. B. 1990. *Imagery and Visual Expression in Therapy.* New York: Plenum Press.

Madaras, L., and A. Madaras. 2000. *The What's Happening to My Body Book for Boys,* 3rd ed. New York: Newmarket Press.

Maslow, A. 1970. *Motivation and Personality,* 2nd ed. New York: Harper and Row.

Moustakas, C. E. 1992. *Psychotherapy with Children: The Living Relationship.* Greeley, CO: Carron.

Norton, B. 1997. Play therapy with sexually abused children. Training event, Akron, Ohio, 1997.

Norton, B., and C. Norton. 1997. *Reaching Children through Play Therapy: An Experiential Approach.* Denver: The Publishing Cooperative.

Oaklander, V. 1988. *Windows to Our Children.* Highland, NJ: Center for Gestalt Development.

Pearce, J. W., and T. D. Pezzot-Pearce. 1994. Attachment theory and its implications for psychotherapy with maltreated children. *Child Abuse and Neglect: The International Journal* 18(5): 425–38.

Perry, B. D. 1995. Incubated in terror: Neurodevelopmental factors in the "cycle of violence." In *Children in a Violent Society,* ed. J. D. Osofsky, 124–49. New York: Guilford.

Piaget, J., and C. Thompson. 1974. *The Psychology of the Child.* New York: Basic Books.

Randolph, E. M. 2000. *Manual for the Randolph Attachment Disorder Questionnaire* (RADQ). Evergreen, CO: The Attachment Center Press.

Randolph, E., and R. Myeroff. 1997. Does attachment therapy work? Results of two preliminary studies, 2nd ed. Available at www.attachmentcenter.org/ articles/article02.9.htm.

Richards, I., and A. Sullivan. 1996. Psychotherapy for delinquents? *Journal of Adolescence* 19(1): 63–73.

Schaefer, C., and H. Kaduson. 1994. *The Quotable Play Therapist*. Northvale, NJ: Jason Aronson.

Shiffrin, R. M., and R. C. Atkinson, 1969. Storage and retrieval processes in long-term memory. *Psychological Review* 76(2): 179–93.

Tatara, T. 1993. *Characteristics of Children in Substitute and Adoptive Care, Fiscal Year 1989*. Washington, DC: American Public Welfare Association.

Van der Kolk, B. A. 1989. The compulsion to repeat the trauma: Re-enactment, re-victimization, and masochism. In *Handbook for the Treatment of Attachment-Trauma Problems in Children*, ed. B. James, 389–406. New York: Free Press.

———. 1997. Van der Kolk, Part II. *Attachments Newsletter* (Winter 1998). Evergreen, CO: The Attachment Center at Evergreen.

———. 1998. Dr. Van der Kolk at ATTACh Conference. *Attachments Newsletter* (Winter), Evergreen, CO: The Attachment Center at Evergreen.

·12·

Therapy Making Use of "Games of Rapport," "Games of Courtesy," and "Good Habits"

Thomas M. Nelson

$\mathcal{F}$ew things elicit greater support on the part of the public than programs promising to counter antisocial behavior and reduce human conflict. Interest is especially strong when attention is given to juvenile delinquency, a problem which is widespread everywhere and cries for therapeutic treatment.

Focus upon "play techniques" as a possible therapeutic intervention has expanded in recent years as interest in individual circumstance and emotional duress has mounted (Carroll, 1997). Board games are represented in this expansion and have sometimes been accorded an important role in treatment of troubled adolescents. However, they are not used as frequently as they might be. In the belief that widespread use should be promoted, this chapter describes how playing of specially designed board games can assist the therapist who treats the troubled adolescent.

The history of our games goes back twenty-five years. At that time, Social Services in the City of Edmonton, Alberta, found juvenile delinquency threatening to overwhelm the treatment resources they had available. In response, they engaged in an active search for alternative ways to deliver therapy to their juvenile caseload.

In course, Social Services contacted the Department of Psychology at the University of Alberta because they were aware that a research project to improve relations between residents, nurses, volunteers, and recreational staff of a geriatric hospital had been successfully concluded. This project had led to development of a specifically created board game called *Angels and Devils* (Corbin and Nelson, 1980). The hope they voiced was that similar game procedures might be adapted by Social Services and pay dividends in short-term therapeutic sessions. The therapeutic sessions projected were to involve family members and significant others, as well as the delinquent. The challenge laid down was accepted. Marianne Johnson, who was then a thesis student, was engaged and assigned to coordinate research in a Social Services unit specializing in treatment of juvenile delinquents.

A considerable period of time ensued before therapeutic gaming was attempted. Much of the time was devoted to Johnson taking the role of participant observer in existing therapeutic programs. By small steps this led to the design of a set of three games named *Roles*, *Justification*, and *Penalties* (Johnson and Nelson, 1978). These games were successfully tested and subsequently used by Social Services in delivering therapeutic interventions to counteract comparatively major juvenile violations. Violations were such as breaking and entering, possession of stolen property or proscribed substances, shoplifting as well as more serious instances of truancy, chronic lying, and mischief.

The original therapeutic games were then once more revised, expanded, and eventually made available as *Games of Rapport*. These games are to be the major focus of this chapter. Secondary attention will be given to *Games of Courtesy* and *Good Habits*, which address conduct problems that usually surface at elementary school level. These also provide a play therapy option applicable in cases where the adolescent client is developmentally challenged and can not derive full benefit from playing *Games of Rapport*.

PROLOGUE TO THERAPEUTIC BOARD GAMES

The word *game* names a fuzzy concept and is not a name attached to a restricted set of features. We are helped here by *Philosophical Investigations* (1953) where Ludwig Wittgenstein, the great philosopher of language, goes to some length to argue that no one thread runs through all things called *games*.

While it is true that dictionaries define games as a bundle of features, it is also true that understanding at this level is only a gloss over the real situation. Closer inspection of actual things called games shows that some of the set of defining features are incompletely present in any given game. According to Wittgenstein, games bear the same relationship to one another as do members of a family to one another. One family member may have a distinctive chin dimple, a long thin nose, eyes set wide apart, ears that stick out from low on the head, but other members, except for an identical twin, will have some but not all of these singularities. When the overlap between members is great enough, it creates a "family resemblance."

Games are a particular set of family resemblances. There are features within the family of therapeutic games that are strong. For example, all accept the idea that client progress will be affected by the attitudes of the therapist, that treatment will be most effective when it takes place in a nonthreatening atmosphere, that the client should be unconditionally accepted by the therapist, and that the client ought to have input as regards how therapeutic sessions are conducted. All agree, too, that effective treatment will be manifested in cognitive, social, behavioral, and emotional changes in the client. However, sharp disagreements surfaces as attention shifts to therapeutic procedure. A basic issue is whether to proceed with directive or with nondirective intervention. These define polar extremes that therapy can take and are reflected in the forms of game play a therapist decides to adopt.

Nondirective therapy is, of course, guided by Carl Rogers' concept of psychotherapy. Thus, in nondirective types of play therapy the therapist seeks to clarify the clients thought and emotion without interfering with the course it takes. In effect, the rules are of the client's making and issues entering therapy are also defined by the client. The adolescent guides the therapist into an environment which is, initially, a "mystery theatre." The therapist is there to help the client search this environment to find new awareness of self. The client is both subject and object and exploration takes place slowly and cannot be time bound.

The client entering nondirective play therapy embarks on a journey. This journey is analogous to that undertaken by Charles, sister Meg, and friend Calvin, heroes created by Madeline L'Engles in *A Wrinkle in Time* (1962). Their journey takes them to dangerous regions of paradox where they at last locate and exorcise an enchanted member of the family. This very long trip is successful only because it is counseled in a nondirective way by powerful neutral forces, such as the "Happy Medium."

Nondirective play is most useful when it is delivered in the period of life where self-discovery is proceeding vigorously and in a permissive supportive environment. Nondirective play becomes a less attractive option when therapy is undertaken as the result of expulsion from school or court action. At this point vigorous and less subtle intervention has to be considered.

Games of Rapport find greatest use in directive play therapy although they are of value as ice-breakers in propaedeutic "getting to know you" stages of all types of adolescent therapy. Reliance is put on strong protocol and unambiguous structure to create a psychological reality within which adolescent and therapist meaningfully interact. An asset of this game world is its familiarity. Every adolescent already understands the protocol and general structure of board games. Therefore, the appearance of a game board fosters a stress-reducing signal benefiting client–therapist interaction.

Therapy involving *Games of Rapport* transports the adolescent offender into a less threatening world where rules are defined clearly and expected to be voluntarily honored. Entering the therapeutic game board environment, the adolescent is analogous to Alice in *Through the Looking Glass* (Carroll, 1946). Characters encountered in Wonderland are real to Alice and those encountered in board game sessions are more than game players to the adolescent. Guided by the therapist they become fresh people—familiar faces that house different persons. The uncle, the principal, the storeowner are heard anew; they become renewed as persons and better understood. The adolescent may still say they are "out of it" but accept their usefulness in defining the reality they must make peace with.

The therapeutic game is a circumscribed world that is safe. Problem areas are quickly identified. Resistance is reduced. Players instinctively adapt new identities when game rules require player roles to be alternated. When every participant takes on the role of every other, a well-rounded understanding is created within the therapeutic group. And things that must change often become transparent. *Games of Rapport* are a great tool for informing players about themselves and to bring value systems of other persons into relief. By means of repeated play the therapist is helped in charting the extent to which the adolescent is deepening their understanding, accepting the need of others to be better treated, and taking steps to improve their own behavior.

GAMES OF RAPPORT

This section will describe the visual appearance of the games, the rationale governing game designs and accompanying materials, how games are introduced into therapy, and how play is conducted. In doing this, we will provide a brief example of the use of several *Games of Rapport*. These are the games *Playing It Like It Is, Straight Talk,* and *Staying Ahead of the Game*. The use of a fourth game called *Tradin' Places* in preventative therapy will be touched upon, as well.

Appearance

Game boards are printed in color on paper and this paper is attached to a stiff backing. Most boards fold in the center but this is necessary only when it needs to be packed. Boards have courses laid out for players to advance on with a pawn toward a final goal (figure 12.1). In these respects, our therapeutic games are visually reminiscent of "race" games that every adolescent has played at one or another time. Games such as *Snakes and Ladders* and *Steeplechase* represent basic patterns.

Familiarity

The familiar design of game boards gives a friendly appearance which is a comfort to the participants. A client and other players can relax slightly when holding a belief that they know to some extent what is about to happen. Familiarity enhances confidence and helps those targeted to become more open-minded. A defensive client can feel empowered when the game to be played is known. Familiarity makes it easier to break down whatever ego protective barriers have been erected against the essentially anxiety provoking situation.

An unfamiliar appearance, particularly an "artsy" design, should be avoided. An unfamiliar appearance can put persons who feel discomfort in a therapy environment on edge, possibly by suggesting that they may be incompetent to carry out their responsibility as a player. Overall, the best designed boards have a fresh look at the same time that they display strong family resemblances to simple parlor type game boards.

Games of Rapport and *Games of Courtesy* and *Good Habits* depart in several respects from convention. In order to motivate clients to increase personal, interpersonal, and social insights, and to foster prosocial attitudes and behavioral tendencies, these games take pains to invite players to "join in" with other players in taking turns to advance individual pieces toward the "common goal."

Consider the use of the term *join in* rather than *compete* and *common goal* instead of *win*. Both rewordings serve to avoid the unfortunate association parlor games can have with winning versus losing. A therapeutic game must never suggest to a player that he/she could again become a "loser" in the eyes of others. Competition is inherently in a race game and does not need further highlighting.

The obvious object of *Playing It Like It Is* is to be the first player to reach home square. Directly or indirectly the therapist conveys other purposes. The first is to establish a calm atmosphere that is secure enough to draw players into meaningful relationships. The second is to confront the adolescent with what others regard to be positive constructive social attitudes and behaviors, and to unambiguously reject the opposite. The third is to identify game players who can be relied on to make useful contributions to therapy over the long term.

The initial roster of game players can be extensive. This is because any combination of individuals the therapist discovers to be suited to function as role players can be retained in later stages of game therapy. The remainder need not be continued. Except for the adolescent client, the players need not be the same from session to session.

All games provide four roles. These are named *Client, Professional, Family*, and *Significant Other*. Attitude cards associated with these roles are coded on the card face by *C, P, F*, and *S*, respectively. Each player takes one of the roles. This is determined by rolling a die. The player with the highest number takes the role of Client. The player with the second highest number takes the role of Professional. The third highest becomes Family. The fourth highest takes the Significant Other role. Tied players roll the die again.

There are two packs of Attitude cards for each role. Each card contains a short projective type of Attitude statement. One pack of each set is marked "—" and consists of negative statements that could be made by a person in that role. These cards contain statements which put down the role-self or other role-selves, are self-centered, and are not friendly. The following are examples of negative C assertions: "I should be allowed to make up my own mind," "you always put me down," "the devil made me do it." Negative P attitudes include "you're not being fair to your family," "you really don't want to change," "take the consequences and don't whine so much." F negatives are "I'm fed up with you," "you need a good beating," and "nobody gets something for nothing." S negatives are "people are always making things sound worse than they are," "you never had a chance," and "it seems like the system is trying to screw him."

The other packs are marked " + " and consist of positive statements which could be made by a person in that role. These Attitude cards contain statements which show insight into the role-self or other role-selves, indicate confidence in the role-self or other role-selves, and are friendly and compassionate. The C examples are "sometimes I wonder why people do things," "I'm trying to understand where you're coming from," and "I'll buy some gas for the car." P positives are "I know I expect a lot from you," "this has given me confidence," "my job is difficult so I would appreciate your help." F positives include "I'm not always right,"' "I enjoy being with you," "sorry I reacted that way." S positive assertions are "you need help," "I want to be fair to everyone," and "being young is a great time for learning."

Before the therapeutic session commences every player shuffles their two packs of Attitude cards and places them face down in front of him/her on the game board. Negative and positive cards are kept in separate piles. Game play is started by C who throws the die and moves the pawn to the indicated number of squares. If C lands on a negative square, he/she draws a negative Attitude card, reads it to the other players, and moves the pawn back two squares.

If C lands on a positive square, he/she draws a positive Attitude card and moves the pawn forward two squares. The Players draw only one Attitude card a turn.

The person, who is sitting to the right of the C, has the next turn. This player rolls the die, moves the pawn, and so forth. When one of the players reaches home that round is finished. Players then move one seat to the right and assume a new role during the second round. The game session ends when every player has taken each of the different roles. The therapist encourages and directs postgame discussion.

Playing It Like It Is is normally used on the first therapeutic day. On this day players simply read the Attitude cards they turn up. They are allowed to comment but the therapist may be wise to discourage extended discussion. She/he can explain that the first day is an icebreaker—just for becoming comfortable with the game.

At the point the therapist decides it might prove productive to challenge the adolescent, the rules become those of *Straight Talk*. In this game when any player lands on a positive or a negative square and draws an Attitude card, he/she must do more than report what the card says. The player must read the card and then justify why he/she in that role would have reason to express such feelings. The player can explain (1) why this statement was made, or (2) what exactly is meant by the statement, or (3) how the role-self would feel about making that statement, or (4) what behavior, attitude, or circumstances would make the role-self say that. Importantly, the player must justify the Attitude to the satisfaction of the other players. If the majority of other players are not satisfied, the player must move back two squares when the Attitude is negative and is prevented from moving forward two squares when a positive Attitude is not dealt with satisfactorily. If the majority of other players are satisfied, the player can move forward the two squares when on a positive square and does not move back two squares on a negative.

Keeping Ahead of the Game follows the same rules as *Straight Talk*. In this game, however, the penalty for not being able to justify an Attitude is more severe. If a player cannot justify a positive or negative statement to the satisfaction of all the other players, he/she must "Go to Jail." This means that the player misses their next turn and must start the game over again. *Keeping Ahead of the Game* is symbolic of real world happenings. The therapist explains this at the start although the parallel is grasped spontaneously by most adolescents.

CASE HISTORY

Mark was fifteen years old when game therapy was initiated. At the time of referral he was attending school irregularly and in danger of failing most subjects. He had been referred to Social Services by the court due to suspected involvement in criminal and near criminal activity. More specifically, referral occurred as a result of police investigation of instances of minor theft (shoplifting), vandalism (destruction of washroom facilities, defacing of surfaces with marker pen) and complaints of rowdyism at a mall. Management also had lodged a complaint that Mark's presence in the mall constituted a nuisance. The specific complaint was that his behavior was detrimental to mall patronage.

Mark's family was largely although not entirely dysfunctional. The father and mother had separated two years before. His parents were on poor terms.

Mark's father was currently employed as an off-highway driver by a company engaged in oil exploration in a remote place north of the city. Low oil prices and economic recession had reduced company activity, causing family income to be uncertain. A younger sister still in elementary school restricted the mother to part-time janitorial work that paid poorly. The mother said she was lonely and admitted she spent time away from home in evenings. Mark said she got together with acquaintances three times a week in BINGO parlors. The result was that there was little in the way of family life. Visitors were a rarity except during the Christmas period. Aside from breakfast, the family did not regularly eat together.

On the positive side, Mark was emotionally attached to both parents. He defended his mother as "doing her best" and eagerly looked forward to his father's returns to the city. The father returned at regular intervals and Mark and his sister sometimes attended National Hockey League games or minor-league baseball with the father and his friends. Also, an elderly aunt and uncle of the father would invite the trio to visit. The mother's brother lived in the city as well. He and Mark were friends. However, this uncle operated a dry-cleaning business which, he said, gave him little free time to socialize with his sister's family.

The therapist handling the case was experienced in use of *Games of Rapport*. Accordingly, she made immediate contact with both of Mark's parents and the other relatives living in the area, inviting them to attend therapy sessions that could be spread over a month. The mother assented and the father did too, but said that he would not be able to attend some sessions. Two uncles volunteered to appear. To this list the therapist added a social worker, an "Uncle at Large," the assistant mall manager, a retired teacher and a friend of Mark's choosing. In addition, she had back up from office secretarial staff who had helped on other occasions.

Three game sessions of one hour were held the first week. The therapist chose not to become directly engaged at this stage in *Playing It Like It Is*. She decided to sit back and function as an observer. She intervened occasionally but only to keep the game play on track. The therapist used this period to select the players best suited to play *Straight Talk* and *Staying Ahead of the Game*.

The latter games were played on four occasions in weeks two and three. Only *Straight Talk* was played on week two and only *Keeping Ahead of the Game* on week three. The therapist acted as a player all four of these game meetings. The mother attended two of these sessions. The father and Mark's friend attended one each. The remaining spaces at the table were filled by significant others who attended one game session each.

The therapist counseled the mother and talked to the father by phone in the postgame period. Mark was seen several times on a follow-up basis. In the months following therapy, he phoned the therapist on a number of occasions "just to talk."

Family members said Mark derived benefit from game discussions and seemed better behaved. The assistant mall manager reported Mark was in the mall less frequently and had not caused further trouble. She said she was never pleased to see him, however. School attendance had improved but continued to be unsatisfactory. Mark reported spending more time at home with his sister watching TV and that he had developed an interest in cooking and was sharing meal preparation with his mother. He claimed to have been promised part-time employment in a restaurant. The mother and father continued as before. In the therapist's eyes, the game intervention was as successful as could be expected. She saw little to be gained at this point from re-establishing contact or starting a new series of treatments.

Tradin' Places is intended for home use. It is played in a way similar to *Playing It Like It Is* despite having a different appearance. Its purpose is to increase social understanding in the family by increasing communication and rapport within the family. The game board accommodates a maximum of four players. Adolescent attitudes are the focus of the game, but persons as young as twelve are potential beneficiaries.

The game is of the race type and contains four sets of Attitude cards relevant to the life situations of family members. One pack is marked "—" and consists of negative statements which could be made to any other player. These cards make statements which put down the role-self or other role-selves. They are self-centered and unfriendly. The other pack is marked " + " and consists of positive statements which could be made to any other player. These cards contain statements which show insight into the role-self or other role-selves. They indicate self-confidence and are friendly and compassionate.

The Attitudes expressed on these cards are identical to those accompanying *Play It Like It Is*. However, the fronts of the cards are marked differently. The *P* card is marked *A1* a designation used for *Adult One*. *F* cards become *A2* the code for *Adult Two*. The *C* card is changed to *C1* for *Child One* and *S* becomes *C2* for *Child Two*. Before the game starts, the parents or guardians stress that the *A1* and *A2* cards can be either a real or imaginary mother or father and that *C1* and *C2* a real or imaginary brother or sister. Some families remove cards that they find "too crude."

Participants are reminded that this is only a game and 'not for real.' Emphasis is given to the fact that play is to be fun. Also, players are told that they do not have to like the Attitude on the cards they turn but should try to imagine why such a thing might be said. In this game a player can "help the imagination" of another player so long as they are kind and helpful in so doing.

Tradin' Places starts with each of the family players rolling the game die. The highest number starts the game and play continues in clockwise direction around the board. The highest number also chooses their role on the first round of the game. The next highest number chooses from the remaining three sets, and so forth. Players shuffle their positive and negative decks before the game begins.

It is recommended that the game be played for about forty-five minutes, and play should not exceed two hours. The time period should be determined by all players before starting *Tradin' Places*. Also, any player should be allowed to drop out at any point without argument.

GAMES OF COURTESY AND GOOD HABITS

This name is applied to a group of three therapeutic games used largely with problem children in school environments. The game cards suit the needs of elementary school children but also are useful in therapy with adolescents with poor social skills and/or limited developmental potential.

Each game has its own board and two decks of Attitude cards. Concentration is on misbehaviors in classroom, cafeteria, washroom, and library settings. They also contain some content that counters bullying behavior on playing fields and discourages the occasional savagery emerging during inter-school competitions.

Tigers and Monkeys is of the *Snakes and Ladders* type, as can be seen in figure 12.2. The deck having the Tigers printed on it has cards that are drawn and read when a player lands on a Tiger circle. Tiger cards deliver positive messages. Monkey circles lead the player to read the Monkey negative messages.

The third game is *Plus and Minus*. The board for this game features an

Figure 12.1. *Playing It Like It Is* game board

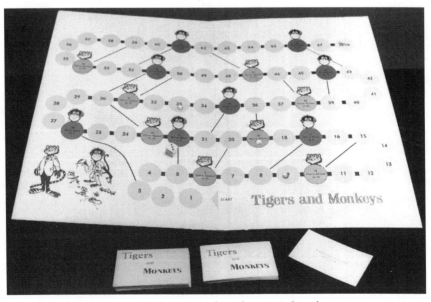

Figure 12.2. *Tigers and Monkeys* game board

endless loop reminiscent of those on playing boards for the parlor games *Clue* and *Monopoly.* The stopping squares are more varied and include "kind heart" squares that confer special benefits. The endless loop means that play continues until players lose interest in continuing.

    Brain and Numskull is very similar to *Tigers and Monkeys.* Both games are suited to two or three players. *Plus and Minus* accommodates four players. In any of the games, one of the players customarily is a school counselor, principal, or teacher. Sometimes the school makes the games available to students on a recreational basis.

    The Games of Courtesy and *Good Habits* provide a way to communicate the rules and attitudes schools would like students to embrace. It is regrettable when a student is punished or reprimanded for violating an expectation of which they were not fully aware. In every school, entering children represent a range of cultural, family, and educational backgrounds. There is an obvious need to make the institutional expectations explicit to all and these games serve this need.

    If a dozen copies of *Tigers and Monkeys* or *Brain and Numskull* are made available to the teachers responsible for deportment in grades one to three, and if students from grades four to six are paired with students in the earlier grades to read the game cards and counsel the younger students on school rules, the school environment will improve significantly. Institutional values are shared across the school and tend to be norms. The benefits reaped in classrooms, hallways, and schoolyards are enormous. The effort and cost of this yearly preventative effort is minute.

REFERENCES

Carroll, J. 1997. *Introduction to Therapeutic Play.* Oxford: Blackwell Science.

Carroll, L. 1946. *Alice's Adventures in Wonderland* and *Through the Looking Glass.* New York: Grossett and Dunlop.

Corbin, S., and T. M. Nelson. 1980. Using angels and devils: A board game developed for play in nursing homes. *International Journal of Aging and Human Development* 11: 243–50.

Johnson, M., and T. M. Nelson. 1978. Game playing with juvenile delinquents. *Simulation and Games* 9: 461–75.

L'Engle, M. 1962. *A Wrinkle in Time.* Toronto: Ambassador Books.

Wittgenstein, L. 1953. *Philosophical Investigations,* 2nd ed. Oxford: Blackwell.

· *13* ·

Play in the Therapy of Adolescents with Eating Disorders

Lisa Rogers and Hal Pickett

This chapter will present ideas for working with adolescents with eating disorders from a play therapy perspective. We should note here that the majority of adolescents with eating disorders are female, and, for simplicity, we will use "she" throughout this chapter. However, any of the discussion here could also apply to males. It should also be noted that play therapy should only be a component of the treatment of an eating disorder. Adolescents with eating disorders often require a team approach to treat effectively these serious and potentially chronic disorders. Play can be a useful component in this multimodal therapy. As play therapists are well aware, play in therapy can often serve to engage resistant clients. Adolescents with eating disorders can be quite resistant to direct strategies designed to change a behavior they may experience as ego-syntonic. In addition, play may encourage an overly controlled or pseudo-mature adolescent to begin to learn to enjoy some experiences again.

Any adolescent being treated for an eating disorder should have a complete medical evaluation in order to rule out possible medical causes for symptoms as well as to determine the medical stability of the client. Some clients will require hospitalization or intensive medical treatment to ensure medical stability. In addition, these adolescents should continue to be followed as needed to monitor for ongoing health concerns. For an extensive review of health issues related to assessment and treatment of eating disorders in adolescents, see Nicholls, de Bruyn, and Gordon (2000). It is important that the medical provider be experienced with eating disorders in adolescents. The provider needs to be aware of which complications to monitor and common medical consequences of eating disorders. In addition, a medical provider familiar with eating disorders will be better able to talk with clients and their families and work cooperatively with the treatment team.

There is research to indicate that for adults with bulimia nervosa, medication may be beneficial (American Psychiatric Association, 2000a). The research on anorexia and medication is less convincing, and there is a dearth of research on adolescents with eating disorders and medication. However, many psychiatrists with experience treating eating disorders will recommend a trial of medication for some adolescents. This can be managed either by the same medical provider who is following the client for general medical stability or by a psychiatrist. Who will follow the client for medication can be determined on a case-by-case basis. For a review of research on psychotropic medications and eating disorders, see Crow and Mitchell (2001b).

Many adolescents will also benefit from an evaluation and treatment by a nutritionist. For adults and older adolescents, the nutritionist generally works with the client individually, evaluating nutritional strengths and weaknesses in the client's diet and making recommendations for change. The experienced nutritionist can also provide information and support for the eating-disordered client who is gaining weight or afraid of change. However, when working with younger adolescents, it is likely that the nutritionist will need to work collaboratively with the parents as well. Parents may be able to supplement a younger adolescent's report of what she is eating. Certainly with younger adolescents, changes in available food choices will require parents' involvement. If parents understand the rationale for recommended changes and suggestions, they are more likely to help the adolescent comply and support the recommendations between sessions. In addition, the nutritionist can help to educate the parents regarding appropriate expectations for eating and exercising for their child. For a review of key points for nutritionists working with eating disorders, see Brunzell and Hendrickson-Nelson (2001).

Another valuable member of the treatment team may be a family therapist. This chapter will include a section of play techniques for families. The individual therapist may use some of these techniques, but it may also be important to have a separate family therapist. This person can help to support the family through the treatment and help to change patterns and relationships that contribute to the symptoms' maintenance. There is a growing body of research that suggests that family therapy is an important component of treatment for adolescents with anorexia nervosa (Eisler, et. al., 1997). Some research has indicated that family therapy can be effective as the sole form of therapy for young adolescent girls with anorexia (Lock, et al., 2001).

HISTORY OF ANOREXIA NERVOSA

The earliest recording of disordered eating behaviors date back to the teenage son of the Khalifah of the Islamic Empire in the ninth century (Sibley and

Blinder, 1988). Since that time, eating disorders have intrigued and mystified the general public and professionals. As early as 1689, there is documentation by Dr. Richard Morton of the treatment of two anorexic adolescents, one male and one female (Silverman, 1997). Descriptions of anorexia became more abundant throughout the nineteenth century because of two physicians working independently. Charles Lesegue of Paris and Sir William W. Gull of London gave the first detailed descriptions of Anorexia in 1873 (Silverman, 1997). Since that time, there has been a wide range of treatment approaches that emerged, from forced feeding, to isolation, to intense nurturance, to removal from the family for appropriate ego development, or even massage (Silverman, 1997). Dr. Louis-Victor Marce, a Parisian physician, documented in 1859 the need to change the patient's surroundings to aid healing that led to the flurry of causes that became the battleground for the turn of the twentieth century.

The debate that began over whether anorexia was a psychological, social, family, biological, or medical disorder still continues today. In 1911, Pierre Janet described two types of this "obvious" psychological disorder, hysterical and obsessional (Silverman, 1997). In 1914, Morris Simonds attempted to refute this theory by identifying pituitary gland abnormalities. This remained the accepted cause into the 1930s when Berkman refuted this cause and reintroduced anorexia as a psychogenic abnormality. Clarification was added by John Ryle with his article in 1936 where he "described in definitive and microscopic detail, the clinical picture found in anorexia nervosa" and presented treatment as a "highly structured, empathic refeeding program" (Silverman, 1997). The 1940s brought the psychoanalytic hypotheses, which had a strong influence until the 1960s when the developmental models emerged "rooted in the physical and psychological experiences of attaining adult weight" (Silverman, 1997), with starvation creating regression to a prepubertal state. As the selective serotonin reuptake inhibitors came to the market with their decrease in side effects, use of psychopharmacological intervention, as an adjunct to therapy became popular, targeting comorbid depressive, anxious, and obsessive symptoms.

The description of anorexia nervosa has changed and evolved through the series of Diagnostic and Statistical Manuals from II to IV-TR. The present diagnostic criteria from the DSM-IV-TR are listed in box 13.1. Anorexia nervosa is now categorized into Restricting and Binge-Eating Purging types, and lifetime prevalence is recorded as 0.5 percent in females with the occurrence in males being one-tenth that of females (DSM-IV-TR). Just as the description of the disorder has evolved over time, the treatment focus has changed from the pre-1960s psychoanalytic approaches. Most practitioners treat patients collaboratively with individual and family therapies, dietary management and medical consultation. Treatment intensity varies from individual therapy to day treatment to inpatient to long-term residential programs. The course and outcome fluctuate with some individuals experiencing a full recovery, some exhibiting a pattern of weight gain and relapse, and others experiencing a long chronic course of deterioration over time. Herzog et al. (1999) found in their seven-year follow-up that 43 percent had recovered, 28 percent had improved, 20 percent were unimproved, and 9 percent had died. When medically stable, patients often receive outpatient treatment involving a combination of Cognitive-Behavioral Techniques, Interpersonal, or Narrative Treatments.

Beyond the clinically diagnostic psychiatric case, the subclinical patterns of disordered eating have begun to intrigue many researchers. It seems the numbers of adolescents who are dissatisfied with their bodies and try excessive dieting to deal with it have increased. The sociocultural extremes in present day society are confusing to youth, from the increased number of overweight children who exercise less than at any time in our history, to the popular actresses who frequent the magazine covers, fighting to lose weight and fit into size zero gowns. Franko and Omori found in their 1999 research on female college freshmen that the continuum was 9 percent meeting criterion for an eating disorder, 23 percent described as intensive dieters, 17 percent described as casual dieters and 21 percent nondieters.

BULIMIA NERVOSA

In contrast to the lengthy historical attempts to define and describe anorexia nervosa, the term *bulimia* may have been coined as recently as the 1970s, and "therefore has no true historical era available for study" (Russell, 1997). Regina Casper in 1983 was the first to research and meta-analyze accounts of anorexia to determine the presence of overeating and vomiting "so as to identify patients whose case histories might resemble those of contemporary bulimia nervosa" (Russell, 1997). From her research, she deduced that the evidence supports that bulimia nervosa, as it is recognized today, "was virtually unknown until the later half of the twentieth century" (Russell, 1997). Theories have been proposed, such as the Anorexia Initiation Theory, in which bulimia basically emerges out of the anorexic failing to starve, setting up a binge-purge cycle that constitutes a continuous struggle of losing and regaining control over one's eating. Another theory that had gained some popularity was the theory of bulimia compensating for internal or family chaos. The adolescent, attempting to control her sense of ineffectiveness or attempting to control the world around her, limits what she eats but eventually eats ravenously, reinforcing the feelings of lack of control, and she attempts to regain control by purging. The purging makes the adolescent feel out of control instead of in control and so she returns to bingeing. The cycle becomes self-reinforcing and compulsive. The present description of diagnostic criteria for bulimia nervosa as documented in the DSM-IV-TR is seen in box 13.2.

The lifetime prevalence is 1 to 3 percent, with prevalence in males again representing one-tenth that of females. There is some evidence that bulimia is more responsive to treatment than anorexia nervosa (Garner, Vitousek, and Pike, 1997). Most research has focused on Cognitive Behavioral Therapy.

RATIONALE FOR USING PLAY THERAPY TECHNIQUES

Though little has been written on the use of play therapy with adolescents affected by eating disorders, there are many therapeutic advantages to using play with this population. One primary reason for using play therapy with adolescents with eating disorders is that play may make the therapy more effective by decreasing resistance and enhancing communication. Most adolescents entering treatment for an eating disorder are quite defensive about their symptoms. Adolescents rarely present for treatment independently and often do not see their behaviors as problematic. Addressing symptoms directly through verbal therapy may only increase this defensiveness. Adolescents come into therapy expecting to be told to change their eating habits and gain weight. Both of these directives can be quite threatening to an adolescent with an eating disorder. Addressing these symptoms and distorted thinking less directly through play can help to decrease this defensiveness.

Play therapy may also be beneficial because play itself challenges an adolescent to engage in activities that are therapeutic. When we explore Schaefer's fourteen "Therapeutic Powers of Play" (Schaefer, 1993), each one targets an issue with which many adolescents with eating disorders struggle. Play therapy provides a natural therapeutic space for working on some issues that are classic presenting traits of clients with eating disorders: emotional constriction, lack of self-connectedness, concrete cognitions, pseudomaturity, and rigidity. Play requires an adolescent to engage in a new manner and to experience herself and her environment in a new way.

As play therapists are aware, there are as many well-developed schools of theory and practice regarding play therapy as there are on verbal therapy. As O'Connor (1991) notes, play in therapy has been viewed as both an expressive outlet and as a teaching tool and has been adapted by practitioners from almost every theoretical field. Many of these approaches can be utilized in the therapy with adolescents with eating disorders. Some of these will be reviewed here.

AFFECTIVE EDUCATION AND RETRAINING

One of the more profound limitations in anorexia nervosa, which often impedes treatment, is the presence of alexithymia. The direct translation for *alexithymia* is "without words for feelings," but the clinical presentation of the cognitive-affective deficit is "(a) difficulty in identifying and describing feelings, (b) difficulty in distinguishing between feelings and the bodily sensations associated with emotional arousal, (c) restricted imaginative processes (few dreams or fantasies), and (d) thinking that is concrete and reality based" (Faulkner and Clopton, 2001). There is strong evidence that those with anorexia nervosa experience some degree of alexithymia, but research has also identified its presence in those with bulimia nervosa and obesity as well (Davis and Marsh, 1986; Legorreta, Bull, and Kiely, 1988). The extent of the deficit can be striking when the adolescent is asked to report how "happy" and "sad" feel different and the response is a blank stare with a rather flat "I don't know." The general restriction in affective and emotional display seems to be globally generalized. These adolescents struggle with identifying any somatic signal of hunger, pleasure, and sadness. Their cognitions become very black-and-white and rigid: right or wrong, good or bad. An adolescent with bulimia nervosa may be one who is out of control of her feelings and cannot grasp a connection between herself and her emotions. Emotions seem random at times and often incongruent with the situation.

From the perspective of a Play Therapist, these issues of emotional constriction, concrete cognitions, and lack of self-connectedness naturally suggest the therapeutic powers of play as appropriate treatment for the eating-disordered adolescent. Several play therapy techniques are useful when addressing the alexithymic deficits, which range from basic affective education and remediation to more complex release techniques once the restricted feelings are unearthed. Though we are working with adolescents, the basic Color-Your-Life Technique (O'Connor, 1983) and derivatives of this popular technique can be a valuable assessment and treatment tool to use with those affected by eating disorders. The initial instructions are for the adolescent to identify the color of four basic feelings and to color on a piece of paper to show the different feelings she has in her life. The adolescent can also be given specific triggers, images (e.g. a body outline), or thoughts to respond to in a drawing. Sometimes those with alexithymia may struggle with even this simple task and require more affective remediation.

In affective remediation, the goal is to try to instill internal representations of the feelings to which the client may connect. First colors are chosen by the client to represent four basic feelings: happy, sad, mad, and scared. The client can then color a feelings chart with cut outs for the facial expression of each of these feelings. Next, the client is asked to pick an animal from the sand tray miniatures, or a picture either drawn or cut out of a magazine to represent each of the feelings. Finally, the therapist teaches relaxation skills and encourages the client to visualize her body. The client is then asked to determine how each of these feelings might be felt in different parts of her body. For example "How does sad feel in our hands? Stomach? Face? Head?" The attempt is to use as much sensory input as possible to help instill the concept of each feeling for the client. Each of these steps can give insight into the level of alexithymia or affective chaos that the client is experiencing and the level of remediation needed.

RELEASE THERAPY

Sometimes release techniques can provide the environment that opens the psyche for learning and affective education. Release Play Therapy was introduced by David Levy (1938), and is based on the premise that directive situations can be set up that can create the therapeutic release of emotion. The following techniques described by Heidi Kaduson (1999) seem to engage a more primitive level of emotionality. They can be effective in identifying the eating disorder as the target toward which negative emotions can be released. Examples of these techniques include the dart gun target, destruction of the balloon persona, and the wet toilet paper bomb. In the dart gun target release, a target is drawn with rings that have increasing points and increasing significance of the negative emotion the closer they get to the bull's eye. An example might be three rings with "playing with my food," "obsession about exercise," and "afraid of getting fat." The adolescent is asked to shoot the dart gun at the target while yelling out a phrase such as "I hate obsessing about exercise." Processing how the release feels afterward is important. The balloon and the water bomb are similar techniques. A balloon of "anorexia" or "bulimia" or consequences of the eating disorder is created and inflated. The creation or decoration can be as elaborate as the adolescent chooses. The goal is then to practice attacking the eating disorder by pouncing on the balloon. Another verbal release technique is the water bomb technique. A large drawing of the eating disorder is created (this in itself may be therapeutic) and wet toilet paper bombs are thrown at the picture with verbal release. In indoor facilities Play-Doh, sticky toys, or other less messy substitutes may be used. This technique has the added advantage of challenging the tendency toward hyperneatness of many clients with eating disorders.

As the adolescent becomes more comfortable with emoting, increasing levels of difficulty can be achieved by adding more feelings to the affective education. As competency is advanced, complex feelings that might be a combination of two others might be explored. An example might be "furious," which can be a combination of "angry" and "frustrated."

FAMILY PLAY THERAPY

Since Salvadore Minuchen's work at the Philadelphia Child Guidance Clinic and Selvini-Palazzoli's work at the Milan Center in the 1970s, family therapy has been an integral part of the standards of treatment for those suffering from eating disorders. Minuchen and his colleagues in their practice of structural family therapy identified the anorexic family as psychosomatic in their enmeshment, rigidity, overprotectiveness, and use of the child to maintain the family system. In comparison, the Milan group depicted the family system as "rigidly homeostatic" and in need of empowering to develop problem solving (Selvini-Palazzoli, 1974). Strategic family therapy adds the perspective of family symptoms, feminist therapy demystification, and supporting the therapist in becoming a partner in change. Family therapy research at the Maudsley Hospital in London is based on Christopher Dare's theoretical framework that during treatment the family needs to be in control of the adolescent's eating because the adolescent is incapable of doing so (Dare and Eisler, 2000). Lock and LeGrange have expanded on this work with continuing research and a treatment manual for family therapy with adolescents with Anorexia Nervosa (Lock et al., 2001). This appears to be very promising research. As is typical in the history of treatment for eating disorders, the family techniques differ dramatically but continue to provide evidence that the family is integral to the treatment of adolescents with eating disorders. So, as family therapy is important, Family Play Therapy offers a perspective that uniquely fits the treatment of eating disorders. This setting provides an "opportunity for the therapist to join, to observe, to model, to teach, and to be present for all family members" (Miller, 1994). In working with those affected by eating disorders, play techniques can fit into any of the family models of care.

As with individual play techniques used in the treatment of eating disorders, the specific use of play with families can be the first therapeutic hurdle that these overly constricted families confront. Moving these families toward interacting in a playful manner can be an accomplishment in itself. Drawing a family genogram together is an alliance building technique that can be used initially as it is not too threatening. This can lead to a willingness to participate in more free drawing exercises. One task that can be helpful in assessing communication style is the double family drawing in which the family is first asked to draw a picture together of anything they would like. On the second drawing, the family is given the same instructions except they are not allowed to talk. Insight often emerges about how communication can interfere with function; family members observe others to get their cues instead of depending on words. Words can create power struggles, manipulations, or silent refusals to participate.

Game play can also be a nonthreatening form of play and interaction in family therapy if it is a known game to the family. There are rules and expectations that are predictable; but these games can provide insight into hierarchy, competition, and interpersonal dynamics. Another technique that can provide this insight but that may be slightly more threatening is the family sculpture. Family sculpting is a psychodrama technique in which each family member is asked to pose the family in a "sculpture" that represents how they see the family, relationships, or specific events in the family.

Other techniques, which provide opportunities for the family to play out their interpretations of the family dynamics, are family floor games or family sand trays. In these techniques, the family is given free reign of the sand play miniatures, and is asked to build a tray with figures that appeal to them. When the instructions are given in a less directive manner, more projective information is potentially produced. The Family Play Genogram, a more directive technique using sand play miniatures was created by Deborah Buurma (1998). In this technique, a large genogram is created on the floor. Each member of the family is asked one at a time to pick a miniature that symbolizes each of the other family members. No discussion takes place while members are choosing their miniatures. Some therapists ask if the family would like to comment on the experience and how it felt. Others may ask more specific questions about how family members might feel about the choices.

COGNITIVE-BEHAVIORAL TECHNIQUES

Cognitive-Behavioral Therapy (CBT) has been the most widely researched treatment for eating disorders, particularly for bulimia nervosa (Crow and Mitchell, 2001a). Research on CBT for anorexia has been less promising

(Mussell, Mitchell, and Binford, 2001). Traditional CBT focuses on having a client report her thoughts and behaviors related to her eating behaviors. CBT for eating disorders has three primary stages. The first is focused on changing the pattern of eating behaviors. The client is given direction about how to change her eating behaviors and asked to begin eating three meals a day and snacks. The client is provided with information regarding the importance of eating regularly and the negative impact of restricting and purging. The client is also asked to log her food intake in order to monitor changes and learn patterns. In the second stage, the client begins to monitor her cognitions related to eating and weight. Cognitions that trigger problematic eating are addressed through cognitive restructuring and problem-solving skills. The client is also asked to begin reintroducing "forbidden foods." In the third stage of treatment, relapse planning is done to plan for future triggers and difficulties with eating.

This form of traditional CBT is built on two premises. The first premise is that the client comes into therapy with a certain level of motivation. This therapy requires a client to do significant work outside of the therapy, and a client with little motivation for change may be unlikely to do the homework required for change. Many (if not most) early adolescent clients are brought into therapy by parents, and may have little or no motivation to focus on changing eating or gaining weight as a primary goal. Second, CBT requires the client have the ability to report cognitions and behaviors in a linear manner. The mean age of onset for anorexia nervosa is seventeen, with a bimodal distribution at ages fourteen and eighteen (American Psychiatric Association, 2000b). This means a great number of girls with anorexia nervosa are not likely to have the abstract cognitive abilities to collect information and address their cognitions in a way consistent with CBT. Younger clients with bulimia nervosa are also unlikely to be able to follow through on the demands of this therapy.

The principles underlying CBT for eating disorders may be important for adolescents to address. The challenge for the clinician is to adapt these underlying principles to a language and modality that will be more effective for a child or early adolescent.

In the first stage of traditional CBT, the adult client is presented with information to help her guide her eating choices and her understanding of the importance of eating enough to meet her energy expenditure needs. Adolescents may be less likely to accept this information from an adult and may have trouble understanding the idea of long-term impact on their bodies and health. They may have internalized all the mixed messages they have heard about dieting to mean that they can simply will themselves to eat as little as they want. In her work on prevention of eating disorders, Kater (1998) describes one method to make the concept of compensatory eating clear to children. She tells the children that they all have been getting far too much air and that if they really wanted to they could cut back on air intake and be healthier and more attractive. The children are given straws and told they can only have as much air as they can breathe through a straw. After a short time, the children inevitably grow too short of breath and compensate by dropping the straws and taking big gulps of air. This can then be used as a jumping off point for how the body takes care of itself in the face of restricting diets.

In the chapter on cognitive-behavioral therapy, Christie (2000) describes adaptations of CBT techniques. For example, the author describes turning work traditionally done in a verbal manner into art projects. One of the tasks of the second stage of CBT is frequently to address the list of forbidden foods. Clients have told themselves that certain foods are "bad," and they cannot eat them. However, these often are foods that are highly desirable and needed for a healthy diet (such as any foods with fats). As part of therapy, these foods are listed and ranked and then gradually reintroduced into the diet. Christie (2000) describes making a visually rewarding art project out of this task by turning each new food tried into a petal of a flower. The flower grows and blossoms as the child tries more and more. It provides a visual and rewarding reminder of progress.

Cognitive restructuring activities, which are an essential part of CBT, may also be adapted for younger clients. Younger clients will require far more coaching in order to be able to use this technique. Young adolescents may have difficulty taking the outside perspective necessary to generate alternatives to their beliefs or to challenge their thoughts. This change in perspective can sometimes be triggered or taught through role-playing. Rather than simply trying to generate a list of arguments to support a thought, a client can be asked what another person might say in response. Often, if therapy has gone well thus far, the adolescent will use the therapist as reference and say, "I know you would say such and such." Or the adolescent may be encouraged to seek out others' input about thoughts. A more active approach such as asking the child to create a representation of the eating disorder and then practice "arguing" with it in your office may also help trigger this process. She can create this representation in whatever art form she is most comfortable (painting, drawing, clay, or collage). This task can also help to externalize the eating disorder and help the adolescent to begin separating her identity from the eating disorder. The adolescent is more likely than an adult to need to challenge thoughts out loud rather than simply writing out ideas on paper. In addition, she is likely to need input from others on how they think about these ideas. Encouraging input from parents about such ideas as comparing oneself to others and judging others based on appearance is developmentally appropriate and may be an important part of family therapy.

BODY IMAGE

Improving body image may be one of the more difficult tasks of treating eating disorders. In adolescence this task may be even greater. Early adolescents are acutely conscious of how they appear to others. This may be even more difficult for adolescents whose bodies have been changing dramatically and who are likely to be in social environments that are very focused on appearance. The dramatic shift from seeing one's body as useful and functional to seeing it as something primarily for impressing others is highlighted in adolescents. In a short time these adolescents have gone from using their bodies as an instrument of enjoyment and activity to an object to be disparaged and criticized. The activities of childhood, running, riding bikes, jumping rope, playing tag, and so forth are not contingent on a particular body type or slimness. However, within a few years adolescents have come to see their bodies as something to be molded and denied. When asked, these adolescents struggle to remember times they have played and when they have enjoyed their bodies. Rebuilding this relationship and helping an adolescent to reconnect with her playfulness can be critical.

During this time an adolescent's ability to think and reason is also going through dramatic changes. These changes allow her to take others' views and imagine how others perceive her. This can be a positive development; however, for an adolescent at risk for an eating disorder, it may contribute to even greater self-consciousness and social discomfort. Finding ways to reduce critical comparisons with others and the perceived ideal is essential. In addition, helping girls to expand the basis on which they judge and evaluate themselves is important. If girls are primarily valuing themselves based on appearance, they will continue to be at risk.

Art Projects can be useful in helping adolescents to be aware of assets other than appearance. A girl may be asked to make a collage of all the things she is good at or would like to be good at. Many girls with eating disorders will have trouble with this type of assignment because they are not in the habit of calling attention to their own positive qualities. Many will only be able to list a few positive traits such as "nice," "take care of my sister," "good grades." When this happens, the girl may be asked to engage her parents in helping to build her list. This should only be done when the clinician is sure that the parents will actually be able to help the girl add to this list. Sometimes parents can be primed to contribute to this. For example, the week before the parents can be asked to note each day a few things they appreciate about their daughter and then share this with the therapist. The therapist can help to make sure the things noted are actually helpful and then ask the parents to share the list with the child. Girls can also be asked to ask a favorite teacher, relative, or other important adult. The girls should be directed to look for pictures for the collage in magazines other than fashion magazines. The completed collages can be reviewed with the therapist and then hung in the child's room to help remind her on a daily basis of why she wants to get strong and healthy. Assigning an adolescent to play in between sessions is likely to evoke rolling eyes and looks of disdain. Nonetheless, it can be a vital task. However, "play" may need to be carefully defined for these adolescents. Play should not include adding additional practice time to sports or dance. Exercising with the goal of weight loss clearly is not play. For the purpose of this assignment, play is an activity done with no overt purpose other than enjoyment. Most adolescents will need prompting. Possible suggestions are swinging on swings at the playground, running through fallen leaves, blowing bubbles, drawing, having pillow fights with friends, dancing in the living room to fun music (for those not on activity restriction). Often, adolescents will be embarrassed about this type of task and may take a while to follow through. However, most end up enjoying an "excuse" to play.

In addition to helping a client to enjoy the physical experience of her body, the process of trying to find time to play and engaging in an activity with no clear success criteria can be therapeutic. Negotiating this "assignment" can help address a client's rigidity and achievement needs. Finding time to engage in playful activities can help to introduce some flexibility into a rigid and overly scheduled week.

Another related homework assignment that is helpful to many adolescents is completing a play history with a parent. The adolescent is asked to review (either verbally or with photo albums) what her favorite games were as a child. She may be given a list of specific questions related to body such as "When did you first learn to run?" "Did you like bubbles in your bath as a child?" "What helped you sleep as a child?" The purpose of this task is twofold. The adolescent is reminded of pleasurable physical activities that were not contingent on appearance, and she and her parent spend time talking about a more relaxed, enjoyable time in their relationship.

For some adolescents, the disconnection from their bodies may be so marked that play techniques are needed to help them reconnect with their bodies. This needs to be addressed cautiously as many adolescents with eating disorders (particularly Anorexia Nervosa) may be quite uncomfortable with touch. The therapist may play guessing games with texture and later on smell and possibly taste. The adolescent is asked to close her eyes and a series of textures is introduced. She is asked to describe these or identify preferences about them. The goal is to have her attend to the physical cues and experience positive physical sensations. The same games can be played with smell as she becomes more comfortable with a variety of odors (severely restricting clients may have difficulty with this task). Much later in therapy, tastes may also be introduced or the adolescent may be asked to search out different types of tastes on her own.

CONCLUSION

Treatment of eating disorders in adolescents can be quite complex and challenging. This chapter is not meant to be a comprehensive overview of treatment. Rather, it is intended to present a perspective on treatment and options that may prove beneficial to the clinician treating an adolescent with an eating disorder. Many of the techniques presented here are not unique to treatment of eating disorders; rather, the techniques target symptoms that those with eating disorders may have in common with other clients. For example, teaching affective expression and regulation is not unique to eating disorder therapy. Many play therapy techniques designed for other populations may be

---

BOX 13.1
Criteria for Diagnosis of Anorexia Nervosa

1. Refusal to maintain body weight at or above a minimally normal weight for age and height (weight loss leading to maintenance of body weight less than 85 percent of that expected or failure to make expected weight gain during a period of growth, leading to body weight less than 85 percent of that expected).
2. Intense fears of gaining weight or becoming fat although underweight.
3. Disturbance in the way in which one's body weight or shape is experienced, undue influence of body weight or shape on self-evaluation, or denial of the seriousness of the current low body weight.
4. In postmenarcheal females, amenorrhea, i.e., the absence of at least three consecutive menstrual cycles.

BOX 13.2
Criteria for Diagnosing Bulimia Nervosa

1. Recurrent episodes of binge eating. An episode of binge eating is characterized by both of the following: (a.) eating, in a discrete period of time (e.g., within any two-hour period), an amount of food that is definitely larger than most people would eat during a similar period of time and under similar circumstances, (b.) a sense of lack of control over eating during the episode (e.g., a feeling that one cannot stop eating or control what or how much one is eating).
2. Recurrent inappropriate compensatory behavior in order to prevent weight gain, such as self-induced vomiting; misuse of laxatives, diuretics, enemas, or other medications; fasting, or excessive exercise.
3. The binge eating and inappropriate compensatory behaviors both occur, on average, at least twice a week for three months.
4. Self-evaluation is unduly influenced by body shape and weight.
5. The disturbance does not occur exclusively during episodes of anorexia nervosa.

---

adapted to work with eating-disordered clients. However, the clinician should always keep in mind the client's heightened sensitivity about body image and appearance when selecting techniques. It is also likely that direct work on changing eating habits and monitoring of these changes will be necessary for many of these adolescents. Long-term prognosis for these adolescents is guarded, and therapy should be approached with a respect for the importance of multimodal treatment.

REFERENCES

American Psychiatric Association. 2000a. *Diagnostic and Statistical Manual of Mental Disorders*, 4th ed., Text Revision. Washington, DC.

———. 2000b. Practice guidelines for the treatment of patients with eating disorders (revision). *American Journal of Psychiatry* 157: 1–39.

Brunzell, C., and M. Hendrickson-Nelson. 2001. *In The Outpatient Treatment of Eating*

Disorders: A Guide for Therapists, Dietitians, and Physicians. Minneapolis: University of Minnesota Press.

Buurma, D. 1998. Family Play Genogram. Paper presented at the Association for Play Therapy, Phoenix, Arizona.

Christie, D. 2000. Cognitive-behavioural therapeutic techniques for children with eating disorders. In *Anorexia nervosa and Related Eating Disorders in Childhood and Adolescence, 2nd Edition.* United Kingdom: Psychology Press.

Crow, S., and J. E. Mitchell. 2001a. Bulimia Nervosa. In *The Outpatient Treatment of Eating Disorders: A Guide for Therapists, Dietitians, and Physicians.* Minneapolis: University of Minnesota Press.

———. 2001b. Pharmacotherapy. In *The Outpatient Treatment of Eating Disorders: A Guide for Therapists, Dietitians, and Physicians.* Minneapolis: University of Minnesota Press.

Dare, C., and I. Eisler, eds. 2000. Family treatment for Anorexia Nervosa. In *Handbook of Treatment for Eating Disorders, 2nd Edition,* ed. D. M. Garner and P. E. Garfinkel. New York: Guilford Press.

Davis, M. S., and L. Marsh. 1986. Self-love, self-control, and alexithymia: Narcissistic features of two bulimic adolescents. *American Journal of Psychotherapy* 40: 224–32.

Eisler, I., C. Dare, G. Russell, G. Szmukler, D. Le Grange, and E. Dodge. 1997. A five-year follow-up of a controlled trial of family therapy in severe eating disorders. *Archives of General Psychiatry* 54: 1025–30.

Faulkner, T., and J. Clopton. 2001. Characteristics of alexithymia and eating disorders in women. Unpublished doctoral dissertation, Texas Tech University, Lubbock.

Franko, D. L., and M. Omori. 1999. Subclinical eating disorders in adolescent women: A test of the continuity hypothesis and its psychological correlates. *Journal of Adolescence* 22: 389–96.

Garner, D., K. Vitousek, and K. Pike. 1997. Cognitive behavioral therapy for anorexia nervosa. In *Handbook of Treatment for Eating Disorders, 2nd Edition,* ed. D. M. Garner and P. E. Garfinkel. New York: Guilford Press.

Herzog, D. D., D. J. Dorer, P. K. Keel, S. E. Selwyn, E. R. Ekeblad, A. T. Flores, D. N. Greenwood, R. A. Burwell, and M. B. Keller. 1999. Recovery and relapse in anorexia and bulimia nervosa: A 7.5 year follow-up study. *Journal of the American Academy of Child and Adolescent Psychiatry* 38: 829–37.

Kaduson, H. 1999. Short-term Play Therapy with disruptive children. Educational Conference, Minneapolis, Minnesota.

Kater, K. 1998. *Healthy Body Image: Teaching Kids to Eat and Love Their Bodies Too!* Seattle, WA: Eating Disorders Awareness and Prevention Press.

Legorreta, G., R. H. Bull, and M. C. Kiely. 1988. Alexithymia and symbolic function in the obese. *Psychotherapy and Psychosomatics* 50: 88–94.

Levy, D. 1938. Release therapy for young children. *Psychiatry* 1: 387–89.

Lock, J., D. Le Grange, S. Agras, and C. Dare. 2001. *Treatment Manual for Anorexia Nervosa: A Family-based Approach.* New York: Guilford Press.

Miller, W. 1994. Family Play Therapy: History, theory and convergence. In *Family Play Therapy.* New Jersey: Aronson.

Minuchen, S., L. Baker, B. L. Rossman, R. Liebman, L. Milman, and T. C. Todd. 1975. A conceptual model of psychosomatic illness in children. *Archives of General Psychiatry* 32: 1031–38.

Mussell, M., J. E. Mitchell, and R. Binford. 2001. Anorexia Nervosa. In *The Outpatient Treatment of Eating Disorders: A Guide for Therapists, Dietitians, and Physicians.* Minneapolis: University of Minnesota Press.

Nicholls, D., R. de Bruyn, and I. Gordon. 2000. Physical assessment and complications. In *Anorexia Nervosa and Related Eating Disorders in Childhood and Adolescence, 2nd Edition.* United Kingdom: Psychology Press.

O'Connor, K. 1983. The Color-Your-Life technique. *Handbook of Play Therapy.* New York: Wiley and Sons.

———. 1991. *The Play Therapy Primer: An Integration of Theories and Techniques.* New York: John Wiley and Sons, Inc.

Russell, G. F. 1997. The history of Bulimia Nervosa. In *Handbook of Treatment for Eating Disorders, 2nd Edition,* ed. D. M. Garner and P. E. Garfinkel. New York: Guilford Press.

Schaefer, C. 1993. *The Therapeutic Powers of Play.* New Jersey: Aronson.

Selvini-Palazzoli, M. 1974. *Self Starvation from the Intra-psychic to the Transpersonal Approach.* London: Chaucer.

Sibley, E., and B. Blinder. 1988. Anorexia Nervosa. In *The Eating Disorders: Medical and Psychological Basis of Diagnosis and Treatment.* New York: PMA Publishing.

Silverman, J. 1997. Anorexia Nervosa: Historical perspective on treatment. In *Handbook of Treatment for Eating Disorders, 2nd Edition,* ed. D. M. Garner and P. E. Garfinkel. New York: Guilford Press.

· 14 ·

Group Therapy for Adolescents with Anger Problems

Karen Snyder Badau and Giselle B. Esquivel

A significant amount of work has been accomplished over the past decade on the treatment of children and adolescents with anger management problems. Clinicians and researchers are rising to the occasion, along with educators, parents, and others, as violence becomes an increasingly salient issue across our nation.

—Evans and Rey, 2001; Wodarski and Feit, 1997; Yung et al., 1998; Zeman and Shipman, 1997

Anger management problems are imbedded in larger problems such as lack of self-control. Many of the children and adolescents who have anger problems also lack skills for impulse control, patience, and delay of gratification. They want what they want, and they want it *now*. Youths who learn to interact this way may resort to bullying, fistfights, or verbal aggression towards their peers (Dodge et al., 1990; Margolin and Gordis, 2000; Mulvey and Cauffman, 2001). In a fast-paced society with a growing emphasis on immediacy, many youths seem to have only a tenuous grip on values of self-control (Schleser and Thackwray, 1982), the ability to think things through before acting, personal accountability, and the simple consideration of others (for example, Raspberry, 2001 and Whitten, 2001).

The overt nature of problems stemming from anger dyscontrol may offer a sort of in-road for addressing some of the larger, more abstract issues described previously. Excessively angry behaviors are usually so obvious that they can be identified easily as problematic. Through the process of acquiring anger management skills, it is our hope that the other related, broader skills also may begin to develop. This might include stopping and thinking before acting impulsively (e.g., see appendix 14.1, the S.T.E.P. procedure), considering alternate views of a situation, listening to others (and perhaps increasing empathy skills), and accepting feedback about their own behaviors.

A number of techniques for anger control have been developed throughout the country over the past several years. They have varying degrees of theoretical bases and empirical support. The technique presented here, Anger Management Group Training for Adolescents, is characterized by a very brief (four-session) cognitive-behavioral approach that was developed over the years by a group of clinicians in a psychiatric hospital setting who were treating inner-city adolescents with anger problems. In the following sections, an historical and theoretical background of anger, the therapeutic rationale, research support, the implementation of this particular treatment package, and a case illustration are provided.

HISTORICAL AND
THEORETICAL BACKGROUND

> The man who is angry at the *right* things and with the *right* people, and, further, *as* he ought, *when* he ought, and *as long as* he ought, is praised.—Aristotle, circa 330 B.C. (emphases added)

Anger is a fundamental emotion with survival value in the presence of threats and danger (Lang, 1993). Even in civilized society, anger tempered with self-control has its place (Dollard and Miller, 1950; Kramer, 1971) and can lead ultimately to positive consequences in spite of momentary social awkwardness or unpleasantness. However, when anger is intense, chronic, and linked to poor impulse control, it is inevitably maladaptive. As with many of the adolescents in our clinical practices, intense anger mixed with tenuous impulse control can lead easily to aggressive behaviors.

Although anger has received only limited scientific attention compared to other emotional constructs, such as depression and anxiety (Averill, 1983, p. 1153), there are some basic theories to guide our current understandings of anger. The next section will present the various theories on anger.

THEORIES ON ANGER

The Single Dimension of Anger and Fear

Many theorists in the mid-twentieth century believed that anger and fear were fundamental emotions on a single dimension. Angry and fearful behaviors were probably adaptive for enhancing survival (e.g., dominance, protection of offspring, securing a food supply). The organism had limited choices in extreme situations: attack or escape. Thus, anger and fear were seen as rooted in our basic human existence and survival needs (Darwin, 1872/1965; Miller and Kozak, 1993). Even now, with increasing sophistication in research and in technical equipment for studying such phenomenon, the physiological difference between anger and fear/anxiety is not entirely clear (Berkowitz, 1993; Lang, 1993). The weakness of this perspective, however, is that it does not account for the *human cognition* involved in the process of choosing between angry and fearful responses (e.g., thinking about and interpreting the meaning of the situation before deciding how to respond).

The Cognitive-Neoassociationist Perspective

The cognitive-neoassociationist perspective takes into account the cognition involved in the interpretation of events. It views anger as a daily experience that is triggered automatically by unpleasant, aversive events. That is, all aversive events (everything from small annoyances to major frustrations) automatically begin the process of becoming angry (Berkowitz, 1993). The aversive event leads to the primitive processing of negative affect through basic associations, and the negative affect elicits either aggression or escape related tendencies. These tendencies then are processed into either rudimentary anger or primitive fear. As higher-order processing takes over, the mind considers attributions, rules, and consequences of behaviors. Rudimentary anger is differentiated into its subtle derivatives, such as irritation and annoyance.

> People who are feeling bad, whatever the reason . . . are theoretically apt to feel angry, have hostile thoughts, and be disposed to attack a suitable available target. . . . [This perspective] assumes that feelings of irritation, annoyance, and anger have much in common, although they differ in their felt intensity, and can therefore, be regarded as initially the same emotional state. . . . The more intense and more agitated these negative sensations are, the more likely it is that they will generate recognizable feelings of anger and activate hostile thoughts and aggressive inclinations. (Berkowitz, 1993, pp. 10–11)

Thus far, this explanation may sound similar to the early perspectives on anger and fear described previously. However, this theory places relatively more emphasis on the cognitive processes. The criticism of this theory is its assumption that once an aversive event occurs, there is little choice but to follow the designated path towards the ultimate endpoint of anger, hostility, and possibly aggression. This may describe some portion of our experience of becoming angry, but it does not account for the higher levels of cognitive control that we can have over the interpretation of aversive events. For example, therapists frequently decide not to become angry when their patients produce direct, hostile verbalizations (aversive event) due to the therapists' deeper interests in comprehending the angry patient's frustrations and fears. In fact, most therapists are able to take these angry, provocative behaviors in stride, pouring all of their effort into maintaining a high level of tolerance and understanding for their patients, and being careful not to show any annoyance elicited by the patient's direct provocations—at least on the good days.

The Frustration Aggression Hypothesis

In the late 1930s and for several decades thereafter, the frustration aggression hypothesis dominated the professional literature in this arena (Dollard et al., 1939; Feshbach, 1964). This hypothesis attempted to merge Freud's psychoanalytic theory (1895/1966, 1920) and Hull's drive-reduction-reinforcement theory (e.g., see Hull's classic cumulative publication, 1951), two distinct and apparently opposed theories.

Freud's assumption was that aggression was an innate drive, an instinctual and destructive biopsychological energy that had to be spent so that the organism could return to a state of quietude (Freud, 1895/1966, 1920). In order not to direct this destructive energy towards oneself, the aggressive energy had to be displaced outwardly onto other people. The major problems with this explanation of aggression are (1) the logical absurdity of a "death instinct" that is counterproductive to the survival of the organism and/or the species, and (2) the instinctual "pool" of aggression is not necessarily reduced by cathartic expenditures of the aggressive energies. Indeed, the aggressive "pool" sometimes grows when expressed or experienced vicariously through observation, such as in the watching of a violent movie or newscast (Bandura, 1973; Fromm, 1973; Hughes and Hasbrouck, 1996).

The group of psychologists who developed the frustration aggression hypothesis (Dollard et al., 1939) proposed the ideas that frustration invariably stemmed from the thwarting of a person's goal attainment, that frustration then caused aggressive behaviors such as inflicting injury on the responsible individual, and that this action reduced the aggressive drive. Thus, a blocked goal caused frustration (a negative sensation) and resulted in an aggressive act. The frustration aggression hypothesis did offer a viable explanation for human aggression, but the problem remained that "frustration arouses an aggressive drive that can be reduced only through some form of aggressive behavior." It also begged the question of whether frustration "is a necessary and sufficient condition for aggression" (Bandura, 1973, p. 53).

Berkowitz (1989) reformulated the frustration aggression hypothesis to shift the focus onto the decision-making process of the person experiencing frustration. The person processes the negative experience cognitively; the personal meaning of the frustration becomes central to the interpretation of the situation (1989, 1993). Berkowitz reformulated the hypothesis to indicate that if hostile intent is attributed to the stimulus person (i.e., if the person intended to insult, disrespect, or provoke), then aggression results. The research studies by Dodge and his colleagues on the hostile attribution biases of aggressive children (Dodge, 1985; Dodge and Frame, 1982) support this view.

Every theory has its weaknesses, and the weakness of the frustration-to-aggression assumption is that the hypothesis does not explain the lack of aggression where there was obvious hostile intent. There are instances where frustration does not lead to aggressive behavior, even when hostile intent is perceived. Consider the definitively nonaggressive responses of leaders such as Martin Luther King who were surrounded by hostility, or the mother whose good parenting skills allowed her to rise above the aggressive kicks of her angry two-year-old child in a tantrum, and to respond to him with tolerance and calmness. Likewise, the school psychologist who tolerates the hostile verbalizations of an angry parent does not respond with aggression to the parent's hostile intent because other personal meanings and interpretations of the situation are more important than the ensuing frustration or the expression of aggression.

There are also circumstances where frustration does not precede aggression. Instrumental (psychopathic) aggression is one example (Dodge, 1991; Feshbach, 1964; Furlong and Smith, 1994). Some sports seem aggressive for the sake of competition rather than as an outlet for frustration (e.g., boxing, wrestling, karate). Playful aggression or "horse play" among children is not commonly associated with frustration or anger (Asarnow and Callan, 1985; Dodge et al., 1990). Nevertheless, the recent developments of the frustration aggression hypothesis by Berkowitz (1989, 1993) and others served to clarify the cognitive aspects of the original hypotheses.

Social Learning Theory

Bandura's social learning theory emerged from his criticisms of the frustration aggression hypothesis (Dollard et al., 1939) and from Dollard and Miller's (1950) concept of learning through social imitation. Bandura (1973) explained that there are social factors that steer aggressive behaviors. For example, aggression frequently has a functional value to the user; aggression may offer an array of reinforcing social contingencies such as to gain access to resources, to change the rules in his/her favor, to gain control over others or to change their cognitions and future behaviors, and to remove barriers from immediate goal attainment. Bandura (1973) also noted that various physiological factors could lead to aggressive behaviors, such as chromosomal defects, hormonal factors, and brain trauma. He asserted that these aggressive behaviors could not be explained by psychoanalytically based instinctual drives or by the frustration aggression hypothesis. Bandura also broadened the definition of aggression to include the destruction of property and the infliction of injuries that were not only physical but also psychological in nature, such as devaluation or degradation. In his analysis of aggressive behaviors, he proposed the idea that a variety of aversive experiences, coupled with personal meanings and the individual's prior history and experience of behavioral contingencies, produced a general state of emotional arousal that led to a diverse array of behaviors (Bandura, 1973). The specific behavior displayed varied with the individual, and was not necessarily overtly aggressive. In fact, some of the responses were constructive.

> When distressed, some people seek help and support, others increase achievement strivings; others show withdrawal and resignation; some aggress; others experience heightened somatic activity; still others anesthetize themselves against a miserable existence with drugs or alcohol; and most intensify constructive efforts to overcome their adversities. (pp. 53–54)

Social learning theory (Bandura, 1973) also emphasized the patterns of family interactions. Parents with poor management of their own emotions served as models for the children in that family, and thus the children failed to develop skills for self-control. In such a familial context, it was more likely that frustration led to physical displays of aggression, rather than to a more constructive way of coping with frustration and distress. Studies also indicate evidence for the social learning of impulsivity and violence within the family (e.g., Herrenkohl and Russo, 2001; Pallone and Hennessy, 1996), and the "hidden cycles of family violence" that perpetuated aggression and violence through neglectful/abusive parenting practices (Widom, 1992, p. 2).

Cognitive-Behavioral Theories

Due to the growing emphasis on the role of cognition and the increased use of behavioral contingencies, a new wave of cognitive-behavioral treatments began in the 1970s. Novaco (1975) developed an anger control intervention for adults based upon Meichenbaum's (1977) work on internal dialogues (a kind of cognitive "self-talk" that we use to monitor and control our own behaviors). Other researchers later adapted Novaco's cognitive strategies for child and adolescent populations (Camp, 1977; Feindler, Ecton, and Iwata, 1984; Saylor, Benson, and Einhaus, 1985). These strategies placed a growing emphasis on the application of new skills to real social situations, where the provocations are most likely to occur. Cognitive-behavioral techniques continue to offer the most promise for teaching anger management skills to children and adolescents, as they were found to be the most effective (Averill, 1983; Feindler, 1991; Goldstein and Pentz, 1984; Kazdin, 1987).

THERAPEUTIC RATIONALE

Cognitive and cognitive-behavioral interventions continue to remain in the forefront of the best practices for treating anger management problems in adolescents (Hemphill and Littlefield, 2001). Drawing upon the literature in this area, the current intervention takes a cognitive-behavioral approach, with an emphasis on the importance of the adolescent social context and the importance of social support for the newly learned skills.

This cognitive-behavioral group treatment for adolescents places the most emphasis on three main areas. These areas are: (1) cognitive restructuring (i.e., modifying initial interpretations about provocative situations, decreasing hostile biases, increasing attention to a wider range of environmental cues, generating alternate explanations for apparently hostile/provocative behaviors from peers); (2) self-management strategies (i.e., learning to lower physiological arousal, attending to internal cues for interpreting situations hostility, thinking through the various solutions and behavioral responses); and (3) the understanding of consequences for behaviors.

It is imperative that efforts be made to allow the adolescents to generalize and maintain their new skills for managing anger. This can be done through behavioral contingencies and/or other methods. First, the intervention should be a good "fit" within the existing therapeutic environment (Martens and Witt, 1988; Mulvey and Cauffman, 2001), such as home, the classroom, or the day treatment center. It should be in accord with the approaches used in the surrounding environments so that the adolescents receive the same message about needing to control their anger consistently in each of the settings. Second, the anger management treatment series can be linked more directly to a behavior contingency system in one or more of the surrounding environments. Third, generalization of anger control skills is promoted within the treatment series by the use of the peer group format; in a peer group, adolescents are generally less resistant and more engaged in the therapeutic process as compared to being in individual therapy (Kymissis, 1997). Fourth, a variety of techniques and strategies may be used to move increasingly toward the practice and individualized use of anger management skills.

The series is designed so that it begins with psychoeducational discussions (which are less threatening), then moves gradually into specific techniques for anger control and increased self-disclosure. It ends with structured role playing via a game board with token rewards and guided resolutions of naturalistic conflict situations. Finally, generalization and maintenance may be promoted by incorporating adults in the adolescents' daily lives (e.g., teachers, counselors, child care staff) into the group therapy sessions. With some review of the treatment series in advance, and plenty of opportunity for discussion, these dedicated paraprofessionals are frequently the ones who make the most difference in the moments of stress and high conflict for the adolescents when they are faced with provocations in their social worlds. Typically they are also the ones who know the most about the current status of each adolescent and what is on their minds lately. It would be a mistake to underestimate these adults' impact or to undervalue them because of their lack of formal training as clinicians. Rather, they may be seen as the valued counterbalance to the trained clinician's role in the co-leadership of the group.

If the group members are adolescents who continue to interact within the same social environment after the group therapy sessions (i.e., hospital units, schools, group homes), then a set of contingencies that apply to all group members equally should be considered. The adolescents may have some say in the details of the contingency system, although the basic structure of the behavioral contingency system and what constitutes the scenario for earning or losing points should be worked out by the adults ahead of time. For example, when an adolescent uses good anger management skills during a social interaction, he/she should receive praise and some predetermined amount of points from an adult who is nearby. Obviously, this requires some prior work with the participating adults who are readily available in the adolescents' social worlds (e.g., teachers, paraprofessionals, parents, relatives, and counselors). The good news is that most adults who work with youngsters tend to be open to, and even enthusiastic about, helping to teach anger management skills to adolescents. It is important that these adults understand the structure and the main ideas of the anger management group treatment. Perhaps they may even co-lead a group series (which can be simultaneously an enlightening, empowering, and humbling experience for the co-leaders). In the original treatment series on the psychiatric in-patient hospital unit, the involvement of the nursing staff was critical to the linkage between the adolescents' participation in the training series and their application of anger management skills on the hospital unit after the group therapy sessions.

By contrast, if the group members are meeting once a week and do not see each other outside of the group, then it may be more feasible to have an overall plan of points that are earned (or lost) for specific behaviors. It would be important to tailor the rewards (and punishments, if applicable) to reflect those reinforcers that are of value to them. The families and the adolescents themselves are the most helpful in deciding what should constitute a reward for using consistently good anger management skills throughout a day and what should be lost if good skills are not used. For example, an adolescent who is successful at controlling anger may receive individualized verbal praise and extra points on the behavior modification system. Likewise, incidents of poorly managed anger are discouraged either by verbal commands or whatever intervention suits the behavior. After the angry episode, when the adolescent is calmer and better able to think about what occurred, a discussion with an adult is warranted. These discussions might explore the triggers for anger in that situation, the adolescent's angry response, and some of the preferred (more appropriate) behaviors for future incidents. When adults engaged in this process, the adolescents seemed to make great strides in learning the anger management skills. In essence, these angry episodes served as windows of opportunity. Thus, the adolescents' skills generalized more readily to the immediate social environment of the contained hospital unit and, perhaps, to social settings beyond as well.

One aspect of a contingency system was developed as part of an anger management system in the context of a residential treatment center (Snyder, McMorrow, and Payne, 2000). The administrators and clinicians developed a form titled *Problem Ownership*. This form was given to each adolescent who was restricted from activities due to a behavior problem. The adolescent was asked to write about the behavior problem and what had occurred. The adolescent was asked whether or not he/she would accept responsibility for his/her own behaviors, and to write how he/she could have handled the situation differently. Most notably, they found a balance between setting limits on out-of-control behaviors and making the acceptance of responsibility "the cool thing to do" on adolescent terms. These administrators/clinicians succeeded in increasing responsible behaviors and decreasing angry/aggressive incidents on their campus, thus the activity proved to be a good addition to the anger management treatment and a strong, consistent contingency system. Specifically, this kind of activity may facilitate the adolescents' clear understanding of consequences and ownership of behaviors.

RESEARCH SUPPORT

Overall, the research literature in this area supports anger management group therapy programs with the use of cognitive-behavioral approaches. However, the reviews raise questions about the "transferability" of such skills into real life social situations. The acquisition of skills alone, usually demonstrated through self-report measures, is not enough to demonstrate the social utility of such interventions. Skills have to generalize to the social settings where the provocative, anger-eliciting situations actually occur among adolescents, and must be maintained so that they have some lasting usefulness for the adolescents (Averill, 1983; Feindler, 1989, 1991; Goldstein and Pentz, 1984; Kassinove and Eckhardt, 1995; Kazdin et al., 1987). For these reasons, the Anger Management Group Training treatment presented here emphasizes the ways in which skills may be generalized and maintained after the group series has been completed.

The results from several pilot studies and a formal study on this intervention (Snyder, 1999; Snyder, Kymissis, and Kessler, 1999) indicated that the adolescents who go through the four-session Anger Management Group Training series, indeed, benefit from the treatment in spite of its brevity. They can acquire anger control skills within the four-session series. After the treatment, they report feeling significantly less angry as compared to control subjects. Furthermore, others rate them as being less angry and less behaviorally disruptive after the treatment as compared to control subjects (rated by adults—teachers and nursing staff—who observe all of the adolescents' social behaviors among peers, blind to the study). Thus, these studies suggest that anger management skills can be learned in a condensed, very brief treatment package, that is, a four-session group therapy series, if the treatment is delivered within a supportive system. One of the critically important features of this intervention is its emphasis on the adult support in the surrounding therapeutic milieu. The daily support of the nursing staff and teachers, and occasionally from various clinical staff members, seems to have the effect of extending the treatment session into the real world. Perhaps this reproduces the effect of a longer treatment series. If adults are not available for this kind of support beyond the group therapy sessions, then the conservative choice is to use one of the longer and more complex treatment series (e.g., Evans and Rey, 2001; Feindler et al., 1986; Goldstein and Glick, 1987; Lumsden, 1994; Pratt and Laiose, 2000). The longer treatment series may afford more opportunities for structured practice and individualization of strategies. However, in the current, rather stringent atmosphere that imposes increasingly brief treatments, this type of focused, very brief group treatment may be all that time allows. Again, clinical judgment must prevail.

IMPLEMENTATION OF THE TREATMENT

The current treatment package is developed to meet the need for an intervention to be administered within a two-week time frame. The cognitive components of anger control include skills for reframing and altering the initial interpretations of situations, decreasing hostile biases, and making self-statements. The behavioral components of this intervention may include the rewards that should be tailored to the nature of the group members according to age, gender, emotional maturity, and any other relevant variables. During the group sessions, the behavioral components may include rewards such as verbal praise, acknowledgment of effort, tokens, and/or points for attending the group, showing appropriate behaviors during the session, maintaining a positive attitude in spite of frustrations, and willingly engaging in the learning process. After the group therapy sessions, it is highly recommended that a behavioral contingency system with points be used for behaviors such as staying calm when provoked, or using one of the anger management strategies taught in the treatment series. Additionally, there are supplemental play therapy activities (see appendix 14.2) that might be useful for engaging the adolescents in the process of change in-between sessions and beyond the four-session treatment series.

A structured manual was developed (see appendix 14.1) for the co-therapists to use in this series (Snyder, 1997, 1999; Snyder, Kymissis, and Kessler, 1999). It begins with a more structured approach so that the basic concepts of anger and related topics can be presented. This is important, as adolescents tend to be defensive, shy, awkward, and/or threatened when they hear the title of the group (some will envision a group full of intensely angry, out-of-control teenagers). A bit of a didactic approach in the beginning seems to ease these fears quickly, and soon the group gets rolling and each person usually finds a point that describes them or interests them. Very little pressure should be given initially for group members to participate actively. Indeed, we frequently found that the seemingly passive, quieter group members often absorbed much more than we expected. It is recommended that two co-leaders run this group series (the same two leaders for all four sessions within a series). Not only is there a lot of material to cover, but also the material can be intense, and the group members' progress can occur quickly. The presence of two co-leaders also gives the adolescents two different adults with whom to "connect."

The treatment manual is structured, but it allows for the co-leaders to have flexibility within each session. It is more important to handle situations realistically than to worry about presenting the points in a sequential order, as long as the co-leaders cover all the conceptual points indicated for that particular session. Within this framework, the co-leaders may follow the contours of the adolescents' participation in the group to elicit the most meaningful involvement from each group member. After the four treatment sessions are described, a case illustration is presented.

Session I

Session I of the anger management series begins with the group members and co-leaders introducing themselves by name. Next the co-leaders present a brief review of the basic rules for group participation (e.g., no cursing, one person speaks at a time, anyone who feels that he/she cannot handle the discussion may ask to leave—rather than behaving aggressively). Next, the co-leaders explain how the intervention fits into the behavioral contingency system and how many points are earned (if applicable). Co-leaders may want to allow the adolescents to earn some points for attending the groups and for complying with the basic group rules. At this point, if clinical judgment warrants it, the co-leaders may allow each person to state his/her own view of being able—or not being able—to benefit from this treatment group. This allows the co-therapists to gather a preliminary view of each group member's level of comfort in the group. Some defensiveness and resistance to the group is likely to emerge at this point, but the co-leaders should take this in stride and proceed as planned. The adolescents, even the resistant ones, will join in if the co-leaders are perceived as firm but gentle.

This first session is more structured and directive, as it lays the groundwork for the rest of the treatment series. Essentially, it teaches the basic ideas about anger and gives everyone a common language with which to discuss anger and related emotions. Most children and adolescents do not know how to talk about emotions, especially anger, and they may feel overwhelmed, anxious, or defensive when put into a group that requires them to discuss exactly this topic. Therefore, the initial session with its presentation of anger concepts is best delivered in a nonthreatening, matter-of-fact way. By the end of the first session, they should have a framework for understanding angry feelings that may be explored further in the later sessions, and they should have several opportunities to give brief answers to some of the nonthreatening questions that are asked (see appendix 14.1).

Specifically, Session I presents a description of anger as an emotion. It raises the group members' awareness of various triggers for anger, such as social provocations, misinterpretations, beliefs and hostile biases, and sensitivity to personal issues. Emphasis is placed on the cognitive perceptions of social situations, as the literature shows that this is the primary component of anger and anger control. The co-therapists suggest to the group members that management of emotions is frequently learned from role models (e.g., older siblings, parents, and peers in the community). The co-therapists present anger not as a negative emotion, but rather as a normal part of human experience when handled reasonably. They briefly explore with the adolescents some effective ways of handling anger.

Then the co-therapists initiate a discussion of the experience of anger in the body to sensitize the group members to their own physiological responses. Group members respond to the question, "How does anger feel to you in your body?" The co-therapists might offer examples such as, "Does it feel like a volcano, a pounding headache, or maybe a slow boil? One activity that has been used with this discussion offers a concrete way of drawing out the responses. By using a poster-sized blank sheet of paper and a dark marker, a co-therapist can write the group members' responses in a list, scattered over the page, or within the boundaries of a circle. It offers a visual aide for the adolescents who might benefit from this approach, and it may serve as a reference point for a discussion later in the session.

Session I then moves into a discussion of the expression of anger through behaviors and the consequences for various angry behaviors. Group members are given a framework for defining their usual ways of responding to anger, including the directing of angry feelings inward or outward, the tendency to generalize anger to all situations versus focusing it on one, narrow situation, and the intensity of the anger expression. One activity that proved to be useful was to use a large poster-sized sheet of blank paper to display some of these ideas. For example, a co-therapist might draw a line to represent a continuum, with "directing angry feelings *inward*" on one end, and "*outward*" on the other end of the continuum. Together with the group members, the co-therapists can fill in examples along the continuum of the behaviors that constitute directing anger inward (e.g., depression, isolation, excessive guilt or anger at oneself) and the behaviors that constitute directing anger outward (e.g., overt displays of anger, disruptiveness, hostility, defiance, aggression). Likewise, a blank sheet of paper can serve as a way of displaying the intensity of the anger expression on a simple thermometer, with the low intensity expressions at the bottom, and the high intensity expressions rising towards the top like heated mercury. The important aspect of these activities is not in the details, but rather in the process of engaging the adolescents to think through the idea of anger, its parameters, and the many possibilities of how to handle it.

The co-therapists then guide the group members to recall and acknowledge angry episodes and to explore their own thought processes during those episodes. For example, they are encouraged to recall angry self-statements and beliefs about having been treated unfairly. Then, the consequences of angry behaviors are discussed in realistic terms. The group co-therapists may want to acknowledge to the adolescents that sometimes they might need to be aggressive *momentarily* in order to defend oneself amidst many peer provocations, but the co-therapists guide the discussion toward the wide range of alternative solutions besides aggressive responses.

Although the treatment series becomes less directive and more open to verbal expression in the later sessions, it should never become as emotionally cathartic as a longer group therapies with the intense, sustained expressions of deep emotions. While it may be tempting and it may feel good at the time, the co-leaders are cautioned against "going too deep" with any particular adolescent during this group treatment series. There is not enough time within the parameters of this brief group treatment package to explore these deeper feelings appropriately. Ultimately, it may do more harm than good to lead an adolescent into a full, cathartic expression of intense emotions without having the necessary time to devote to this kind of therapeutic work. The dilemma is that deeper feelings and intense experiences are frequently elicited by frank discussions of emotions, and there will always be one group member who wants to indulge more than time permits. The recognition of emotions, and the willingness to share, should be praised. However, the co-leaders should intervene by offering, and even insisting, that the deeper, more intense discussion be saved for a private, individual discussion later with one of the co-leaders. In an individual session, the issue may receive the clinical attention it deserves. Other options include asking the adolescent to write about or draw/paint their experience, but these should be followed by opportunities to discuss the feelings. In sum, the emphasis should remain on the learning of anger concepts so that each adolescent is able to identify and acknowledge angry feelings, to recognize when anger can lead to aggression or other non-productive behaviors, and to build a repertoire of cognitive strategies and activities for managing anger.

Typically, by the end of the first session, the group members are less resistant and more willing to be part of the treatment group. The three remaining sessions build on the ideas introduced in Session I. They encourage increasing sensitivity and the learning of anger control through a variety of cognitive strategies and activities.

Session II

Session II begins with a review of the concepts from Session I, as most of the group members will need to refresh their memories. The co-leaders then introduce a specific four-stage strategy for managing anger wherein the adolescents learn to stop, think, evaluate the situation, and plan a response (see appendix 14.1). This gives the adolescents concrete methods for slowing their impulses to respond aggressively, for calming themselves, for asserting some control over their physiological responses, and for slowing their own pacing. It also gives them ways to observe their own thinking, to check for misperceptions, to consider alternative ways of responding, and, finally, to decide how to respond. The group members are asked to check the effectiveness of their behaviors and anger management strategies, and to listen to peer responses from the other group members. This is done first as a psychoeducational presentation, and then through the group members' personal examples of recent provocative situations. The co-therapists may facilitate this process. If an adolescent is not able to think of examples of recent angry episodes, a co therapist might gently remind him/her of a recently witnessed angry episode, and allow the adolescent to decide whether or not to use that particular angry episode as an example in the group. The adolescents then review the four-stage strategy for managing anger (stop, think, evaluate, plan), they put it into their own words, and they discuss the use of the four-stage strategy during angry episodes. Finally, the co-therapists should encourage the group members to practice the four-stage method of anger management outside of the group therapy sessions.

Session III

Session III may begin by briefly reminding the group of the four-stage method of anger management, and giving just a few minutes for group members to say how they may have used the new method since the last session. The remainder of this session should be devoted to The Anger Control Game (Berg, 1995). This board game offers structured role plays in which the adolescents can apply basic concepts of anger management to naturalistic social situations. It is a board game with individual game pieces and tokens for good responses to the conflicts described on playing cards. The social conflicts described on the cards, randomly chosen from a pile on the board game, mimic the kinds of conflicts and difficult social situations that adolescents face in their daily lives. The cards are quite varied; the co-leaders should decide in advance which of the cards to include in the pile for their group. The cards give them an opportunity to apply and strengthen their cognitive skills to various social situations in more objective ways without actually being in the situation. The cards also provide opportunities to practice skills and to receive feedback from peers and co-leaders. They receive a game board token and verbal praise if they gave an appropriate response or a good solution to the proposed conflict situations. Quickly enough, the adolescents become quite focused on who is earning the most tokens. Overall rewards at the end of the game are optional. All group members should be asked to take note of any anger-inducing situations that occur in their lives between the third and fourth sessions, as they will be asked about them in Session IV (see appendix 14.2 for alternate play activities).

Session IV

In Session IV, the co-leaders may begin by highlighting the basic concepts of anger, as well as the anger management techniques. In particular, it is important to review the four-stage strategy for managing anger (S.T.E.P.), and to ask for the adolescents' personal examples of having applied the strategy in recent anger-inducing situations. By this time, the adolescents are typically quite willing to discuss personal examples of angry episodes and their attempts to use the strategies.

In the fourth session, there is one concrete activity. Each group member receives a "hassle log" (Feindler et al., 1986). This is a simple one-page form for the adolescents to record what occurred in their angry episode (for example, who made them angry, why, how they handled it, and a simple rating system for how angry they felt). This encourages the articulation of thoughts about being angry (such as self-statements, interpretations of other's behaviors) and other important cognitive skills that help to consolidate and individualize the anger management techniques (for instance, correction of misperceptions, reduction of hostile biases, listening to peer feedback, and increased problem solving skills). Although this kind of feedback may occur in earlier sessions, it becomes increasingly focused, useful, and individualized by the fourth session. Time permitting, one or more of the angry episodes described by the group member(s) could potentially be used as material for a brief role play within this session with guidance from the co-therapists. This would give the group members an additional opportunity to participate and also to master, or to remaster, good anger control skills by reexperiencing the anger-eliciting situation within the safety of the therapeutic group. It also would allow for peer feedback. For the less shy group members, and if equipment is available, an audiocassette (or audio-video) recording of the role play may offer the adolescents a more objective vantage point of their own responses to provocations during the role plays (see also, Berg, 1997, and Lumsden, 1994).

The treatment series ends with opportunities for the adolescents to clarify various concepts and techniques from the treatment series, and the co-therapists should encourage them to use these skills in their real life situations. Finally, the co-therapists ask the adolescents for their opinions about what aspects of the treatment series were most helpful. This feedback may be used to develop more successful future group sessions.

CASE ILLUSTRATION

Leona (a fictitious name to protect confidentiality) is a fifteen-year-old female adolescent on an in-patient psychiatric hospital unit. She is somewhat more overtly angry and aggressive than the usual adolescent patient, but all the better to see more clearly the problematic behaviors and the behavior changes after treatment.

Leona has a history of angry, aggressive behaviors since age twelve. She was transferred by ambulance from a nearby smaller psychiatric hospital because of her uncontrollable behaviors. At the previous hospital, Leona had an altercation with another female patient over an earring and was subsequently sent to the "quiet room" for a time-out period. However, she defied the hospital unit staff's authority and came out of the quiet room prematurely, then began to yell at one of the nurses who was trying to work with some of the other patients. When Leona was told to stay in the quiet room for the remaining few minutes of her time-out, she ran screaming toward that nurse in an attempt to assault her, and was stopped by two nursing assistants. The hospital decided that Leona's frequent outbursts were too much for them to handle. Upon transfer, she carried the primary diagnosis of Conduct Disorder and was described as having "an extensive history of aggressive behaviors, faulty judgment, interpersonal deficits, questionable reality testing, and gross attention impairments." She had been taking 25 mg of Thorazine four times a day.

In our interview with Leona, she recalled her angry outbursts at the previous hospital fairly well and apparently with little remorse. For example, when she was asked why she tried to assault the nurse, she responded defiantly, "because I wanted to, and because I was scared."

Leona was adopted at age three and reported to have a good relationship with her adoptive parents in spite of some conflicts with her (adoptive) mother in recent years. Leona was the middle of five children, all of whom were adopted into this family, and none of whom were related biologically. Leona was placed into a residential treatment center (RTC) two years ago when her adoptive parents felt that her angry outbursts exceeded what they could tolerate in the home. Leona seemed to function adequately under the increased structure of the RTC, but at one point went to her adoptive parents' home without prior arrangements and then refused to return to the RTC.

Leona was doing well in the ninth grade of her school. In fact she was capable of being a very good student and listed mathematics and reading among her favorite subjects. Leona's school problems were reported to stem from her social interactions, as she often engaged in physical altercations with other girls. She was occasionally truant. Leona denied drug abuse, but admitted to drinking alcohol (beer) sometimes to the point of passing out. There was no known criminal behavior. She reported good sleep and appetite.

Psychological testing indicated that Leona had intact reality testing and an estimated average intelligence (Full Scale IQ = 93) with a nonsignificant difference between verbal and nonverbal skills. In the verbal domain, she showed a relative strength for concept formation when only short answers were required. Weaknesses emerged in her general knowledge and concentration for long verbal questions. In the nonverbal domain, Leona showed a relative strength in her capacity for attention to visual details requiring short-term memory. In general, her quick hand-eye coordination and somewhat impulsive style helped her to gain points on these nonverbal subtests for solving items fastidiously. She lost points, however, wherever the tasks also required concentration, long-term memory, and synthesis of parts into wholes. Her own soothing, encouraging self-statements helped her to regain control some of the time. Likewise, she had the beginnings of good social judgment but needed some work in this area; she clearly understood social situations and acknowledged how she should behave. Leona demonstrated an interest in rules and achievement by saying at one point, "I want to do it right, and to know that I did it fair." However, in many social situations, she reverted to a survival stance and did whatever she perceived as self-protective (fight or flight responses). Her academic achievement was slightly lower than her intellectual potential, but her desire to succeed academically and her budding abilities to control her impulses and slow herself down may have helped her to improve her scholastic and social skills.

When asked what she wanted to be "when she grows up," Leona responded with confidence that she wanted to be a criminal lawyer. In more immediate terms, Leona's three wishes were: (1) to go home and live with her family; (2) to have half of the money in the world; and (3) to live a normal life. For all of her explosiveness and external toughness, there was something quite vulnerable and workable in Leona. Indeed, this follows the pattern of our experience with many of the adolescents who initially present as extremely difficult, angry, and explosive. All except for the most severely conduct disordered patients tended to respond positively to the anger management treatment and to the therapeutic milieu.

There were several paper-and-pencil instruments given to all of the adolescents before and after the Anger Management group therapy treatment. On the *STAXI* Trait Anger Scale (Spielberger, 1988), a self-report measure used as a selection criteria, Leona endorsed seven out of ten items about being angry. For example, she said that she did have a fiery temper and that she felt the impulse to hit someone when she is frustrated.

On the *MMPI-A* Anger Content Scale (Butcher et al., 1992), a self-report measure given before treatment, Leona endorsed eight out of seventeen items dealing with angry behaviors such as feeling like breaking things, feeling irritable, and feeling angry when other people rush her. After going through the Anger Management group treatment, Leona endorsed only three of the seventeen items on the *MMPI-A* Anger Content Scale (Butcher et al., 1992); her score dropped from eight items to three items on this scale. While she still felt irritable (a low-level, chronic anger), she no longer felt like breaking or smashing things. Anger and sadness were less likely to be translated into aggression for her.

The adults also rated Leona's behavior as being more in control after going through the treatment (*SSBS*, Merrell, 1993; *HCSBS*, Merrell and Caldarella, 1997). The nursing staff on the hospital unit rated Leona as still being easily provoked by peers at times, and still likely to insult peers and to complain to staff, but much less likely to act impulsively without thinking. In other words, she was beginning to use words instead of fists. The teachers rated Leona as still somewhat argumentative with her classmates, but less likely to break or destroy things when upset, and more productive with her schoolwork.

Hence, with just a two-week treatment series Leona was able to acquire and utilize some of the basic skills taught to her in the Anger Management group treatment series. These are the kinds of subtle, yet important, changes that many of the adolescents demonstrated after going through the treatment. In the end, it was the lack of aggressive behaviors in Leona that was most noteworthy. The violent assaults on staff members and the absence of fistfights with female peers diminished significantly in the phase after the treatment. It is not to say that we altered her entire outlook on the world, or that her attitude was completely changed. That would be unrealistic, especially within a few weeks! Rather, it seemed more like turning a corner with her, and with many of the adolescents in these group treatment series. They began to understand their own feelings of anger. Once we had captured their interest, they began to see the benefits of having more self-control over their own anger and more strategies in their repertoire, and they began to seek out the information and to find ways to use the new skills. The treatment team did not believe that Leona's improvements in behavior were due primarily to her regimen of psychotropic medications. In fact, during the two weeks that she attended the anger management treatment sessions, there were several decreases in the Thorazine dosages. By the time she was ready for discharge from the hospital, complete discontinuation of the medications was under consideration.

Ultimately, we recommended Leona be discharged to a residential treatment center with individual and group therapy because of her needs for a structured environment, and because of her family's reluctance to allow her to come home. In an RTC environment, we hoped that she might receive continued support and structure to build the internal control to subdue her aggressive impulses. In particular we emphasized the need for her to be linked with a certain kind of therapist. If Leona could view the therapist as attuned to her social/manipulative maneuvers ("hip" enough), and the treatment as adaptive for her world, then she would be more likely to respect that therapist and to invest herself in the therapeutic process.

REFERENCES

Aristotle. circa 330 B.C./trans. 1947. *The Nicomachean Ethics*. Bk. IV, Ch. 5. New York: Random House.

Asarnow, J. L., and J. W. Callan. 1985. Boys with peer adjustment problems: Social cognitive problems. *Journal of Consulting and Clinical Psychology* 53: 80–87.

Averill, J. R. 1983. Studies on anger and aggression: Implications for theories of emotion. *American Psychologist* 38: 1145–60.

Bandura, A. 1973. *Aggression: A Social Learning Analysis*. Englewood Cliffs, NJ: Prentice-Hall.

Berg, B. 1995. *The Anger Control Game*. Los Angeles: Western Psychological Services.

———. 1997. *The Anger Control Workbook*. Los Angeles: Western Psychological Services.

Berkowitz, L. 1989. Frustration-aggression hypothesis: Examination and reformation. *Psychology Bulletin* 106: 59–73.

———. 1993. Towards a general theory of anger and emotional aggression: Implications of the cognitive-neoassociationistic perspective for the analysis of anger and other emotions. In *Advances in Social Cognition, VI: Perspectives on Anger and Emotion*. Hillsdale, NJ: Erlbaum.

Butcher, J. N., C. L. Williams, J. R. Graham, R. P. Archer, A. T. Tellegan, Y. S. Ben-Porath, and B. Kaemmer. 1992. Minnesota Multiphasic Personality Inventory-Adolescent. Minneapolis: University of Minnesota Press.

Camp, B. W. 1977. Verbal mediation in young aggressive boys. *Journal of Abnormal Psychology* 86: 145–53.

Darwin, C. 1872/1965. *The Expression of Emotion in Man and Animals*. Chicago: University of Chicago Press.

Dodge, K. A. 1985. Attributional bias in aggressive children. In *Advances in Cognitive-Behavioral Research and Therapy*. Orlando, FL: Academic Press.

———. 1991. The structure and function of reactive and proactive aggression. In *The Development and Treatment of Childhood Aggression*. Hillsdale, NJ: Erlbaum.

Dodge, K. A., and C. L. Frame. 1982. Social cognitive biases and deficits in aggressive boys. *Child Development* 53: 620–35.

Dodge, K. A., J. D. Coie, G. S. Pettit, and J. M. Price. 1990. Peer status and aggression in boys' groups: Developmental and contextual analyses. *Child Development* 61: 1289–1309.

Dollard, J., L. W. Doob, N. E. Miller, D. H. Mowrer, and R. R. Sears. 1939. *Frustration and Aggression*. New Haven: Yale University Press.

Dollard, J., and N. E. Miller. 1950. *Personality and Psychotherapy: An Analysis in Terms of Learning, Thinking, and Culture*. New York: McGraw-Hill.

Evans, G. D., and J. Rey. 2001. In the echoes of gunfire: Practicing psychologists' responses to school violence. *Professional Psychology: Research and Practice* 32: 157–64.

Feindler, E. L. 1989. Adolescent anger control: Review and critique. In *Progress in Behavior Modification*. Newbury Park, CA: Sage.

———. 1991. Cognitive strategies in anger control interventions for children and adolescents. In *Child and Adolescent Therapy: Cognitive-Behavioral Procedures*. New York: Guilford.

Feindler, E. L., R. B. Ecton, and M. Iwata. 1984. Group anger control training for junior high school delinquents. *Cognitive Therapy and Research* 8: 299–311.

Feindler, E. L., R. B. Ecton, D. Kingsley, and D. R. Dubey. 1986. Group anger-control training for institutionalized psychiatric male adolescents. *Behavior Therapy* 17: 109–23.

Feshbach, S. 1964. The function of aggression and the regulation of the aggressive drive. *Psychological Review* 71: 257–72.

Freud, S. 1895/1966. *Project for a Scientific Psychology*. Vol. 1 of *The Standard Edition*. London: Hogarth.

———. 1920. *Beyond the Pleasure Principle*. Vol. XVIII of *The Standard Edition*. London: Hogarth.

Fromm, E. 1973. *The Anatomy of Human Destructiveness*. New York: Holt, Rinehart and Winston.

Furlong, M. J., and D. C. Smith, eds. 1994. *Anger, Hostility, and Aggression: Assessment, Prevention and Intervention Strategies for Youth*. Brandon, VT: Clinical Psychology Publishing Company.

Goldstein, A. P., and B. Glick. 1987. *Aggression Replacement Training*. Champaign, IL: Research Press.

Goldstein, A. P., and M. Pentz. 1984. Psychological skills training and the aggressive adolescent. *School Psychology Review* 13: 311–23.

Hemphill, S. A., and H. Littlefield. 2001. Evaluation of a short term group therapy program for children with behavior problems and their parents. *Behavior Research and Therapy* 39: 823–41.

Herrenkohl, R. C., and M. J. Russo. 2001. Abusive early childrearing and early childhood aggression. *Child Maltreatment: Journal of the American Professional Society on the Abuse of Children* 6: 3–6.

Hughes, J. N., and J. E. Hasbrouck. 1996. Television violence: Implications for violence prevention. *School Psychology Review* 25: 134–51.

Hull, C. L. 1951. *Essentials of Behavior*. New Haven: Yale University Press.

Kassinove, H., and C. I. Eckhardt. 1995. An anger model and a look to the future. In *Anger Disorders: Definition, Diagnosis, and Treatment*. Washington, DC: Taylor and Francis.

Kazdin, A. E. 1987. Treatment of antisocial behavior in children: Current status and future directions. *Psychological Bulletin* 102: 187–203.

Kazdin, A. E., K. Esveldt-Dawson, N. H. French, and A. S. Unis. 1987. Problem-solving skills training and relaxation therapy in the treatment of antisocial child behavior. *Journal of Consulting and Clinical Psychology* 55: 76–85.

Kramer, E. 1971. *Art as Therapy with Children*. New York: Schocken Books.

Kymissis, P. 1997. Group therapy. *Child and Adolescent Psychiatric Clinics of North America* 6: 173–83.

Lang, P. J. 1993. The three-system approach to emotion. In *The Structure of Emotion*. Kirkland, WA: Hogrefe and Huber.

Lumsden, L. 1994. Class teaches students to cope with anger. *Oregon School Study Council Report* 34: 1–6.

Margolin, G., and E. B. Gordis. 2000. The effects of family and community violence on children, *Annual Review of Psychology* 51: 445–79.

Martens, B. K., and J. C. Witt. 1988. On the ecological validity of behavior modification. In *Handbook of Behavior Therapy in Education*. New York: Plenum.

Meichenbaum, D. 1977. *Cognitive-Behavior Modification: An Integrative Approach*. New York: Plenum.

Merrell, K. W. 1993. School Social Behavior Scales. Austin, TX: Pro-Ed.

Merrell, K. W., and P. Caldarella. 1997. Home and Community Behavior Scales: Research Edition for Ages 6–18. Available from the first author: Kenneth W. Merrell, Ph.D., University of Iowa, Iowa City, Iowa, 52242.

Miller, G. A., and M. J. Kozak. 1993. Three-systems assessment and the construct of emotion. In *The Structure of Emotion*. Kirkland, WA: Hogrefe and Huber.

Mulvey, E. P., and E. Cauffman. 2001. The inherent limits of predicting school violence. *American Psychologist* 56: 797–802.

Novaco, R. 1975. *Anger Control: The Development and Evaluation of an Experimental Treatment*. Lexington, MA: Heath and Company.

Pallone, N. J., and J. J. Hennessy. 1996. *Tinder-Box Criminal Aggression: Neuropsychology, Demography, Phenomenology*. New Brunswick, NJ: Transaction Publishers.

Poets in Public Service. 1993. *Dreams Painted on My Pillow*. New York, New York.

Pratt, D. M., and G. Laiose. 2000. The effectiveness of a cognitive-behavioral anger management program in a child and adolescent psychiatric facility. Paper presented at the Annual Meeting of New York State Office of Mental Health, Albany, New York, December.

Raspberry, W. 2001. Test scores tell only part of the problem. *The Natchez Democrat* (August 14). Natchez, Mississippi.

Saylor, C. F., B. A. Benson, and L. Einhaus. 1985. Evaluation of an anger management program for aggressive boys in inpatient treatment, *Journal of Child and Adolescent Psychotherapy* 2: 5–15.

Schleser, R., and D. Thackwray. 1982. Impulsivity: A clinical-developmental perspective. *School Psychology Review* 11: 42–46.

Seltzer, S., and J. P. Reifler. 1982. The use of drawings in outpatient process groups. *Social Work* 27: 277–79.

Snyder, K. 1997. Co-leader's manual for anger management: Group training for adolescents. Department of Psychiatry, Adolescent Unit, Westchester Medical Center, Valhalla, New York. Photocopied.

———. 1999. Anger management for adolescents: Efficacy of a short-term cognitive-behavioral intervention. Ph.D. dissertation, Fordham University. UMI number: 9923445.

Snyder, K., P. Kymissis, and K. Kessler. 1999. Anger management for adolescents: Efficacy of a brief group therapy. *Journal of the American Academy of Child and Adolescent Psychiatry* 38: 1409–16.

Snyder, K., D. McMorrow, and G. Payne. 2000. Angry, aggressive adolescents: How can we treat them? Paper presented at the Annual Meeting of New York State Office of Mental Health, Albany, New York, December.

Spielberger, C. D. 1988. *State Trait Anger Expression Inventory: Professional Manual*. Odessa, FL: Psychological Assessment Resources.

Webb, N. B., ed. 1991. *Play Therapy with Children in Crisis: A Casebook for Practitioners.* New York: Guilford.

Whitten, E. 2001. Schools strengthen discipline. *The Natchez Democrat* (August 8). Natchez, Mississippi.

Widom, C. S. 1992. The cycle of violence. *National Institute of Justice: Research in Brief.* Washington, DC: Department of Justice.

Wodarski, J. S., and M. D. Feit. 1997. Adolescent preventive health: A social and life skills paradigm. *Family Therapy* 24: 191–208.

Yung, B. R., W. R. Hammond, M. Sampson, and J. Warfield. 1998. Linking psychology and public health: A predoctoral clinical training program in youth violence prevention. *Professional Psychology: Research and Practice* 29: 398–401.

Zeman, J., and K. Shipman. 1997. Social-contextual influences on expectancies for managing anger and sadness: The transition from middle childhood to adolescence. *Developmental Psychology* 33: 917–24.

APPENDIX 14.1
Anger Management Group Training:
A Very Brief Cognitive-Behavioral Treatment for
Adolescents in Small Groups

SESSION 1

Introduction

- Names of participants (each person introduces self), review the basic rules of the group
- Brief rationale for the group, say how the anger management group fits into the surrounding milieu (if applicable)
- Each person's views on his/her own management of anger (expect some resistance, listen, and move onto the next sections which are likely to engage them gradually)

Discussion of Anger as an Emotion

- Anger has many triggers: Social, misperceptions, misinterpretations, beliefs, sensitivity to certain personal issues (give some examples)
- Anger is one of many emotions, and it can be expressed well or not well
- Some situations deserve angry responses, but it is important to think through the situation
- Ways of handling anger are learned from role models, family, peers, life experiences, and also from having been reinforced for behaving certain ways (give some examples)
- The physical experience of anger: How does it feel to you in your body? (as a volcano, a slow boil, bomb, pounding headache, or is it localized somewhere else in the body?) Allow each group member to comment—this is a safe way for each person to start to become engaged in the treatment

Expression of Anger

- How does each group member express anger? Directed inward or outward? Is it focused and ruminating anger, or more generalized anger towards everyone and everything? Does the intensity of the anger usually match the situation (or is there some overreaction)? Use concrete visual aids on poster paper as needed (described in the section, Implementation of the Treatment)

- Controlling the anger, instead of letting it control and overwhelm you
- What are you thinking, in the moment when you are getting angry?
- Are there less hostile ways to interpret someone else's behavior? Can you consider other explanations for that person's behavior?
- Possible thoughts during and *after* expressing anger: A momentary sense of power, cathartic relief, satisfaction, guilt, remorse, fear of retaliation, fatigue, simmering rage (any of these, alone or in combination, are possible)
- Negative consequences for inappropriate expression of anger (listen, prompt as needed)

SESSION 2

Review of Basic Concepts

- Anger is an emotion, and it has many triggers
- Misperceptions, hostile stances, angry frames of minds
- What anger feels like in the body (physiological arousal responses)
- Various ways of expressing anger (appropriate and inappropriate ways)
- Consequences of anger expressed inappropriately

Introduction to S.T.E.P.

- STOP—Take slow, deep breaths, count backwards 10 to 1, lower your physiological arousal to the situation, slow your pacing, make soothing self-statements such as, "keep cool," "chill out"

- THINK—What do you think about this situation? What are your perceptions, your impulses to respond? What is the situation, really?

- EVALUATE the situation: Are there alternate ways to interpret the situation?
    —Are you misattributing the other person's intentions?
    —Are there other reasons for the person's behavior toward you?
    —Is there anything else you could consider about the situation?
    —Is this the most effective way to handle the situation?
    —How will others perceive your response?
    —What *consequences* might occur?
    —What will you think of your behavior *afterwards?*
- PLAN what you will do next: How exactly will you respond?
    —Does your response match the intensity of the situation?
    —How will you keep in control, while responding?

—Use the self-statements that work for you in order to keep in control of yourself

SESSION 3

The Anger Control Game (Berg, 1995)

- Provides written descriptions on playing cards of various anger-provoking situations
- Structured for equal chances of participation
- The written descriptions of conflicts are prescreened by the co-therapists, then shuffled for random ordering, then placed in a pile for group members to chose from during the game
- The game provides opportunities for group members to practice new anger management skills and encourages the thinking through of behavioral responses in a safe, objective, structured way
- The emphasis should be on reducing hostile biases, reframing perceived provocations, modifying beliefs, considering all environmental (social) cues, problem solving together for situations that justify an appropriately angry response, and reviewing the possible consequences for behaviors

SESSION 4

Review of Techniques and Strategies

- Bodily cues for anger, and calming-down techniques
- S.T.E.P.:
  Stop—slow down, breathe deeply, stay calm
  Think—what do you think about this situation?
  Evaluate—the alternate views, responses, consequences
  Plan—your response, what exactly to do, and how to stay calm

Give Out Blank "Hassle Logs" (Feindler et al., 1986)
- Ask them to write down what happened in a recent angry episode in their lives (who made them angry, how they responded, how well they believe they handled the situation, and how they would like to handle it in the future)
- Review the S.T.E.P. procedure to help them to process the angry episode (in retrospect)
- Reframe the interpretations of situations, challenge the hostile biases
- Help them to consider alternative ways of responding, problem solving, negotiating

- Encourage objectivity and honesty from each person and constructive feedback from peers

Discussion, Opinions, and Generalization of Skills to the Real World

- Ask the adolescents: What did you think of the group treatment?
- What techniques were most helpful?
- Can they make the techniques their own (tailor them to their own styles)?
- Ask them which of the skills they would use in real life situations

APPENDIX 14.2
Additional Play Materials and Activities

Suggestions for additional play materials and activities that may be included *within* the Anger Management Group Training for Adolescents treatment package:

- Large-sized paper: Poster paper,[1] newsprint, or butcher paper (Webb, 1991)
- Things with which to write and draw: Markers, crayons, colored pencils (or a blackboard and chalk can be used in a classroom setting
- A simple drawing of a large thermometer on a large piece of paper, with an indicator in red to mark where the "mercury" would rise to (symbolizing how much anger was felt)
- Writing a group poem about anger (Poets in Public Service, 1993)
- Have the group develop *further* a list of individualized self-statements that would help to calm them, to refocus them, and to use the anger management skills in *their own language* (Novaco, 1975)

Beyond the group therapy treatment package: Play activities that may supplement the adolescents' growth experience *outside* of the group sessions:

- Journals to write in freely, to record thoughts, angry feelings, resolutions, etc.
- Paper or large blank books to draw in (see Seltzer & Reifler, 1982)
- Clay in small packets (about 5 lbs per person)
- Any materials that can be used to make collages or to build small sculptures
- Workbooks to learn and practice skills (see Berg, 1997)
- Other psychoeducational videotapes on conflict resolution, social skills, etc. (e.g., WNYC Foundation, 1997; Berg, 1997; and various videotapes from Sunburst, Inc., www.sunburst-store.com)

Note: 1. For low or nonexistent budgets, simple materials may be substituted. For example, plain copier paper may be substituted for large poster paper. Ten pages of plain copy paper may be stapled together along the left side to create a personalized "journal" for an adolescent, if necessary. Simple pens and pencils may be used instead of purchasing packets of markers and crayons. It is the *ideas*, here, that are most important; fancy supplies are not mandatory.

·15·

Cognitive-Behavioral Interventions for Bullies, Victims, and Bystanders

Berthold Berg

$\mathscr{B}$ullying at school involves the repeated intimidation of one child by another. Approximately 15 percent of the school-aged population engages in bullying or is victimized by bullies (Olweus, 1993). Forms of bullying vary. Direct bullying involves several behaviors, including teasing, taunting, hitting, threatening, and stealing. Indirect bullying involves spreading rumors about the victim and excluding them from social groups. Boys favor the more direct forms of intimidation while girls favor the more indirect methods (Banks, 1997; Crick and Grotpeter, 1995). For both boys and girls, teasing is the most common form of bullying.

Victims typically experience verbal and physical assaults over several years (Egan and Perry, 1998; Hodges, Malone, and Perry, 1997; Olweus, 1978). Bullies, too, evidence stability of their behavior over time. (Olweus, 1993; Pellegrini, Bartini, and Brooks, 1999). Bullying begins in the elementary grades and peaks during junior high. Bullying continues in high school although there is a reduction in the use of direct physical assault. Verbal assaults, however, continue throughout the high school years (Banks, 1997). The aggressive behavior of bullies tends to be proactive rather than reactive. They are children who act aggressively not out of anger but from a need to feel powerful and in control. They are typically physically or psychologically stronger than their victims (Banks, 1997; Beane, 1999). They often come from homes where physical punishment is common and where parental warmth and involvement is lacking. They also have problems with authority and pose disciplinary problems more often while in school. They are five times more likely to have a criminal record by age thirty than nonbullying children (Fried and Fried, 1996). Most experience little anxiety and have rather high self-esteem (Batsche and Knoff, 1994).

Victims often provoke or reinforce bullying (Hodges and Perry, 1999; Olweus, 1978). Externalizing victims provoke bullying by being disruptive, aggressive, dishonest, and argumentative. Internalizing victims are anxious and cry easily, are socially withdrawn, and submit passively to the bully's demands. Victims tend also to be physically weaker than other children in their class. Most have no friends because of rejection by peers or withdrawal from social contacts. The presence of friends has been shown to be a protective factor against bullying (Hodges, Malone, and Perry, 1997). Friends are more likely to come to the aid of the victim and are less likely to support or reinforce bullying behavior.

Intervention and prevention of bullying are typically school based and systemwide (Beane, 1999; Fried and Fried, 1996; Newman, Horne, and Bartolomucci, 2000; Olweus, 1993; Ross, 1996). Interventions include classroom education about bullying, the establishment and enforcement of rules against bullying, parent involvement, and individual counseling for bullies and victims.

BOARD GAMES

The *Bullying Game* (Berg, 2001) was developed to complement existing intervention methods in the schools and to provide a tool for practitioners working with bullies and victims both within and outside the school setting. The game shares the basic characteristics of other games developed over the last twenty years by the author for different problems. (See www.childpsychologygames.com for information on other games.) Board games are especially useful in working with adolescents because they effectively bridge the gap between dolls, puppets, toys, and art materials associated with play therapy and the "talking therapy" for adults. They allow the adolescent to play and have fun (through skill, chance, and competition) without the pressure of unstructured talk about personal problems.

Like play therapy, the games do not demand self-disclosure. They allow the player to talk safely about someone else's problems until they feel ready to talk about their own. The player responds to vignettes of attitudes and behaviors of a fictitious character. Players are asked to advise the character of better attitudes and behaviors in cases where they are dysfunctional, and to suggest other appropriate attitudes and behaviors where those held by the card character are functional. In this way, players learn to evaluate and modify the attitudes and behaviors that they share with the character. Changes in attitude are acquired more rapidly when players acknowledge this similarity.

Several features are common to all the games:

1. Cognitive-behavioral intervention principles
2. Identification of learning objectives based upon the clinical and research literature related to a problem type
3. Identification of individual needs using questionnaires and creating individualized stacks of game cards for each player
4. Application to both individual and group therapy
5. Suitability for use by parents and paraprofessionals when guided by the therapist's training and card selection
6. Guidelines for the objective evaluation of progress and outcome

THE BULLYING GAME

The *Bullying Game* is designed for work with bullies, victims, and bystanders. The therapist can play the game with an individual or in small groups of up to six players. Group composition may be homogenous (bullies, victims, or bystanders) or heterogeneous (bullies, victims, and bystanders).

Players roll a die and select and respond to a game card when landing on the *Take a Card* circle. The therapist awards two chips for a good response to a card. For group play, other players are awarded one chip for contributing another good response to the card. Several circles add chance elements to the game. When landing on *Give One Chip to Another Player*, the player gives one of his or her chips to the player on the left. A player takes one chip from the player on the left when landing on *Take One Chip from Another Player*. When landing on *Take Chips from the Bank*, a player rolls the die and takes the number of chips indicated. The player returns the designated number of chips indicated by the role of the die to the bank when landing on *Give Chips to the Bank*. Players continue around the game board until the end of the game. The game ends at a time established by the therapist at the start of play. Winner of the game is the player with the most chips.

One hundred and eighty cards are available for play. Cards are in three groups, fifty with a bully protagonist, one hundred with a victim protagonist, and thirty with a bystander protagonist. Cards may be selected for play according to these groupings as well as to the results of the *Bullying Checklist* completed by the player's teacher.

The cards describe a problem situation. Following the description, the first question on each card is, *What advice would you give* _____ *(the card character)?* This open-ended question permits a variety of good responses, generally involving better ways—or other good ways—for the character to think and act in the situation. Ideally, the player will give a response that addresses the specific learning objective of the card. If not, asking the second question will generally elicit an objective congruent response. The therapist might elect, of course, to ask questions and encourage discussion bearing other issues felt to be clinically relevant.

The following is a description of the learning objectives and card types associated with Bullies, Victims, and Bystanders. The selection of game cards (and the associated objectives) are guided by scores on the *Bullying Checklist*. The checklist consists of twenty-two common behaviors of bullies, victims, and bystanders and is completed by the player's teacher.

Bully Cards

Eight objectives and related card types are appropriate for bullies. Use of these cards facilitates insight into the motives and consequences of bullying behavior and encourages discussion of more appropriate ways of resolving the conflicts or meeting the needs of the bully.

Displacement   Bully's are often victims too. Cards illustrate their victimization within their family or by older children, their inability to react directly to the aggressor, and the displacement of their anger on their victim. Cards facilitate insight into one source of bullying behavior.

Bully—Displacement

Carl's mother criticized him constantly for not getting better grades. At school, Carl often picked on one of the slower kids, telling him that he was "stupid" and "worthless."
What advice would you give Carl?
What's a better way to deal with the problem?

Compensation   Bullying is sometimes prompted by a failure experience. Bullying behavior compensates for this failure by elevating the bully's self-worth. Cards encourage the player to discover that bullying is often compensatory behavior that does not solve the problem and only creates others.

Bully—Compensation

Wayne felt pretty down on himself after doing poorly on a test. Later that hour he picked on another kid and for some reason felt a lot better about himself.
What advice would you give Wayne?
What's a better way to deal with upset feelings?

Attention Bullying usually gets attention from peers that might not be achieved in other ways. Cards encourage the exploration of other, more appropriate ways to get attention. They might also address the issue that the need for attention may be excessive.

Bully—Attention

Todd was usually ignored by most of his classmates. But when he pushed around one of the weaker kids, he got the attention of the kids around him.
What advice would you give Todd?
What's a better way to get attention?

Status Bullies often believe that bullying will enhance their status among peers. That may be true for some peers, but others may view the bullying as cruel and immature. Cards offer the opportunity to correct the bully's misperceptions about what peers think. They also encourage discussion of other, more positive ways, of gaining status and recognition.

Bully—Status

Not many people looked up to Jane. But when she picked on one of the girls who always acted up in class she figured, "The other kids appreciate me now. They don't like her acting up either."
What advice would you give Jane?
What's a better way to get other kids to look up to you?

Prevention Bullies may themselves have been bullied or fear being bullied. They may believe that by becoming a bully they can avoid being bullied. Discussion of the cards might raise more appropriate alternatives that are suggested by the Victim cards.

Bully—Prevention

Mark had the reputation of being a bully. He thought, "When I bully someone it let's kids know they can't bully me."
What advice would you give Mark?
What's a better way to avoid being bullied?

Rewards Sometimes bullying is used simply to get what one wants. Threats and the use of force are common bullying behaviors. Cards stimulate discussion of the negative aspects of using bullying to get what one wants and alternative and more appropriate ways of getting what one wants.

Bully—Rewards

Ray didn't have any money for lunch. "I know where I can get some," he thought.
He then went over to bully a kid into giving him some money.
What advice would you give Ray?
What's a better way to get what you want?

Punishment　Bullies often fail to consider all the negative consequences of their behavior, particularly the long-term consequences. Cards encourage the exploration of both the short and long-term consequences of bullying.

Bully—Punishment

Jim liked picking on a kid in class who was known to lose his temper easily.
He thought, "I won't get into trouble. Everyone will figure it was his fault."
What advice would you give Jim?
What consequences should be considered?

Approval　Bullies often believe that peers approve of their behavior. Cards portray characters who wrongly believe that peers approve of their action and offer the opportunity to consider a more realistic appraisal of peer opinion.

Bully—Approval

Erin constantly teased Lisa, an overweight girl in her class, and excluded her from her small group. "I'm just doing what the other girls would do if they had the nerve. They appreciate it that I'm doing the job for them."
What advice would you give Erin?
What opinions are peers more likely to have?

Victim Cards

Victim cards are intended to make players aware of both functional and dysfunctional responses to bullying. Avoidance and blame are dysfuctional responses to bullying; the others are more functional alternatives. The cards are in nine groups:

Avoidance　These cards illustrate a common strategy among victims—avoiding school and social activities where the bullying takes place. The cards stimulate discussion of more functional alternatives to dealing with bullying.

Victim—Avoidance

Jake had started to hate recess. Out on the playground, he could count on being pushed around and bullied every time. He figured if he told his teacher

that he wasn't feeling well, or wanted to catch up on some work, she would let him stay behind when the other kids went outside.
What advice would you give Jake?
What could Jake do or say to himself to deal with the problem?

Prevention These cards address the observation that victims are often targeted because of their provocative behavior. One group often targeted are children who get angry easily and provoke others. Other groups are those who are socially withdrawn and who cry easily. Prevention cards illustrate the self-talk victims might use to reduce these provocative behaviors, and encourage discussion of other ways these behaviors can be changed.

Victim—Prevention

Linda would often get upset and cry in class. When she did, Karen would call her names like "cry baby" and get the other girls to laugh at her. Linda thought, "Getting upset and crying just makes other kids put me down. I'm going to try harder not to get so upset."
What advice would you give Linda?
What else could Linda do or say to herself to deal with the problem?

Blame The protagonists of these cards blame themselves for the bullying. They internalize bully's view that they are inadequate or worthless. This exacts a toll on their self-esteem and perpetuates the bullying. A vicious cycle is initiated: they are targeted because they feel inadequate, bullying increases their feelings of inadequacy, bullying increases, and so on. Self-blame is most common among children who are bullied because of physical characteristics that are difficult or impossible to change (e.g., overweight, frail and weak, poorly clothed). The victims of *Blame* cards (unlike those of the *Prevention* cards, whose behavior is the cause of bullying) are victimized because of their physical characteristics.

Victim—Blame

Jeremy was constantly pushed around by the bully because he was small and underweight for his age. "I'm a nobody and always will be," he said to himself.
What advice would you give Jeremy?
What could Jeremy say to himself that would be better?

Ignoring The victims portrayed by these cards respond appropriately by ignoring the bully. Getting upset gives bullies what they want; ignoring them reduces their motivation to bully. The situations portrayed by the cards involve teasing and name-calling, the kind of bullying for which this strategy is most likely to work. More extreme forms of bullying, such as threats and physical assault, require more forceful measures.

Victim—Ignoring

Jamie often ridiculed Sara for being overweight. Jamie would puff up her cheeks and waddle around the room pretending she was Sara. Sara ignored her, saying to herself, "If I get upset it will just give her the attention she is looking for."
What advice would you give Sara?
What else could Sara say to herself to help her ignore Jamie?

Distracting   These cards portray characters who use a variety of techiques to distract or frustrate the bully. Techiques include endless questions about the bully's accusations and responding with the "broken record" or "fogging" techniques. As with the *Ignoring* cards, the bullying situations illustrated are of a less extreme kind.

Victim—Distraction

Alexander liked to tease Jimmy in gym class for being small and for not being very strong: "Jimmy, you are so little and weak. You ought to be in the younger kids' gym class to keep up with everyone." Jimmy replied calmly, "Possibly," and walked away.
What advice would you give Jimmy?
How else could Jimmy distract Alexander?

Asserting   Assertion of one's rights (e.g., not to be bothered) with appropriate voice and body language, avoidance of provocation, and retaliation in kind (e.g., "I'm not going to stoop to the level of calling you names") characterizes the assertion cards.

Victim—Assertion

Chris spoke with a dialect different from the other kids in his class. As had happened almost every day during the past week, Dale began teasing Chris about his dialect. Chris said, "I've got more interesting things to do than to listen to this," and walked away.
What advice would you give Chris?
How else could Chris assert himself with Dale?

Disarming   These cards illustrate a variety of techniques that undermine the bully's objectives. Included is self-deprecating humor, agreeing with what the bully says, making an asset out of what the bully regards as a liability, giving "permission" to tease, and anticipating the bully's teasing.

Victim—Disarming

Adam did poorly on his test. Todd, sensing the opportunity, called Adam a "stupid idiot." Adam responded, "I can't help it. My entire family is stupid." Todd then left without saying another word.
What advice would you give Adam?
How else could Adam disarm Todd?

Punishing   Several techniques can be used to punish bullying behavior. The cards include techniques that make fun of the bully, reverse the teasing, highlight the bully's ignorance, and the like.

Victim—Punishing

Clarence was eating lunch by himself when James came by and called him a "loser" with no friends.
Clarence replied, "Yeah, takes one to know one. You're only calling me a 'loser' because you know you are one yourself. I'll go eat somewhere else so you can sit here by yourself and think about that."
What advice would you give Clarence?
How else could Clarence punish James?

Telling   These cards encourage victims to tell adults about the bullying. Many victims do not tell adults in authority about the bullying. They may fear retaliation if the bully found out, feel that the adult will blame them for their victimization, fear the adult will belittle them for allowing themselves to be victimized, or believe that adults are powerless to remedy the situation. The *Telling* cards address these fears by portraying characters who give voice to one of these fears.

Victim—Telling

Jack told Jim he would beat him up after school. Jim thought of telling the teacher but changed his mind. "There's nothing she can do to prevent it," he said to himself.
What advice would you give Jim?
How could Jim say to himself that would be better?

Bystander Cards

Peers play a role in perpetuating or preventing bullying. Three roles are illustrated by the cards. *Helpful* cards portray either intervention on behalf of the victim or confrontation of the bully. *Passive* cards portray characters that would like to be helpful but are deterred by one of four attitudes. *Hurtful* cards portray characters who reinforce bullying behavior.

Helpful

The *Helpful* cards model two ways in which a peer can help a victim. One is to offer emotional support; the other is to intervene on behalf of the victim. The cards illustrate ways of offering emotional support and intervening on behalf of the victim.

Bystander—Helpful A

Jane watched as Erin teased Amy about the blouse she was wearing. Amy was crying. Jane thought, "I'm going to tell Amy I think her blouse is pretty."
What advice would you give Jane?
What else could Jane do to help Amy?

Bystander—Helpful B

Mike overheard Joe threaten to hit Jason if he didn't give him a dollar. He then went over and told Joe that he was going to tell the teacher what he had heard.
What advice would you give Mike?
What else could Mike do to help Jason?

Passive

Passive cards illustrate four common beliefs underlying a passive response to bullying: (1) the victim is not really being hurt by the bullying, (2) the bully will pick on me if I stand up for the victim, (3) telling someone in authority does no good, and (4) the victim is bringing the bullying upon him/herself.

Bystander—Passive A

Sara listened as Erin mocked the way that Ann talked. Ann started to cry. Sara thought, "I could say something but she'll get over it in a minute."
What advice would you give Sara?
What could Sara think to herself that would be better?

Bystander—Passive B

Jack, along with some other kids, stood and watched as Joe cornered Bill and called him some nasty names. He thought, "Joe shouldn't do that. But if I say something, he might start picking on me."
What advice would you give Jack?
What could Jack think to himself that would be better?

Bystander—Passive C

Jill listened as Amy told her how they should give Sara the silent treatment. "If we don't talk to her she'll get the message and leave us alone," Amy said. Jill thought that was pretty cruel and that she should tell the teacher what Amy was doing. "But the teacher wouldn't do anything," Jill thought.
What advice would you give Jill?
What could Jill say to herself that would be better?

Bystander—Passive D

Kevin would regularly punch and shove Aaron, who disturbed the class by talking to himself during quiet time. In watching all this, Jerry thought, "I can't feel sorry for Aaron. He has it coming."
What advice would you give Jerry?
What could Jerry think to himself that would be better?

Hurtful

Hurtful cards are of two types: (1) the bystander reinforces the bully's behavior by laughing, attention, and the like; and (2) actively joins in the bullying.

Bystander—Hurtful A

As Amy imitated Jane's nervous habit of pulling at her hair, Jill and a group of girls laughed, while Jane was close to tears. "That's really funny," Jill said to Amy.
What advice would you give Jill?
What could Jill do that would be better?

Bystander—Hurtful B

Karl was pushing Ed, who was small for his age, into the lockers as they were walking down the hall. As Jim watched, he shouted, "Hey Ed, when are you going to stand up and fight?
What advice would you give Jim?
What could Jim do that would be better?

THERAPEUTIC PROCESSES AND INTERVENTIONS

The *Bullying Game* lends itself to interventions within a variety of conceptual frameworks. The client-centered therapist might use the game cards to stimulate discussion of an adolescent's concerns, with play of the game suspended to discuss those concerns at length. Psychodynamic therapists will view responses to cards as the player's projections of needs, wishes, and conflicts onto the character and explore those at length. The author works within a cognitive-behavioral framework and several cognitive-behavioral principles are prominent in the design and use of the game.

Reinforcement of appropriate responses, with game tokens and praise, facilitates the learning of more adaptive attitudes and behavior over time. For unambiguously good responses to cards, the procedure is straightforward: the player is awarded two chips coupled with praise. It is less straightforward for responses that that are partially correct or clearly wrong. It is tempting to reinforce inadequate responses because not to do so risks discouraging or alienating the player and doing so undermines learning. A solution is for the therapist to first help the player fashion a better response by building on the positive elements suggested by the player, or by questioning the player about their answer until they suggest a better one. This approach generally leads to a reinforceable response.

As a player of the game, that therapist has the opportunity to *model* a good response when responding to a card. This helps players to construct a good response when they encounter a similar card. Thinking aloud as the therapists prepares a response to a card question (e.g., generating and evaluating alternative responses) is also useful in illustrating the thought process involved in arriving at a good answer. The therapist may also wish to model a bad response. Using the devil's advocate technique, the therapist offers a clearly wrong response to the card and encourages the player (who generally doesn't require much encouragement) to debate the therapist and to prove him or her wrong. Besides being fun, this technique requires the player to think more about why a response is good or bad and so enhances learning.

Because the situations described by most game cards are problems that need to be solved, they permit the therapist to teach *problem-solving* skills (Elias and Tobias, 1996). Steps in problem-solving are (1) defining the problem, (2) generating potential solutions, (3) selecting the best solution, (4) implementing the solution, and (5) evaluating the outcomes. While steps 4 and 5 are not applicable in discussing the fictional situation described by the card, the first three are. Should a card stimulate disclosure of a similar real-life problem, the therapist can add the last two steps by obtaining a commitment to implement a solution and evaluating the outcome at the next session.

Behavioral rehearsal, or role play, can also be used in working with a game card. The situations portrayed by most cards can be acted out in order to rehearse alternative ways of responding to a problem situation. Players can learn from the reactions of the other role player to their actions. Role reversal after the initial role play is also useful in understanding the reactions of the other player. Role play is appealing to adolescents, particularly for those who prefer to act out rather than talk about their views.

Cognitive-restructuring of client's dysfunctional attitudes, assumptions, attributions, and beliefs is the essential feature of cognitive therapy (Beck, 1995; Zarb, 1992). Modification of these dysfunctional cognitive structures lays the groundwork for more functional behavioral and emotional responses Applied to the *Bullying Game*, the card character's self-statements (Meichenbaum, 1977)—insofar as they embody these dysfunctional attitudes, assumptions, attributions, and beliefs—are the targets of change.

Consistent with the cognitive-restructuring approach, four questions can be asked about a card character's dysfunctional self-talk. Taking as an example a victim's self-statement, "Telling my teacher about the bullying would just make it worse," the therapist could ask, *What evidence would be needed to convince you (the player) that the character's belief was true?* The player might cite evidence that the character's previous attempts to stop bullying by telling the teacher, or that of others he knows, resulted in an increase in bullying. The therapist might also ask, *What would be evidence against the belief?* Here the player might cite the fact that telling by others has not resulted in reprisal, assurances by the teacher that she will prevent reprisals and other evidence of that kind.

What's another way to look at it? is a question that might be asked when no strong evidence can be found for or against a belief, or when the belief is not factually based. This often applies to the attribution of motive in the behavior of others. A character who has no friends in the classroom and who says to himself, "No one wants to be my friend," is making an attribution that is admittedly consistent with the fact that he doesn't have friends but lends itself to other plausible explanations. Perhaps he hasn't made enough effort in making friends or lacks the social skills to do so.

What are the consequences of holding that belief? is another question that can be asked. For the example above, the belief that others don't want to be one's friend is likely to be a self-fulfilling prophecy. The alternative belief, that one has made little effort or lacks the skills, is more likely to change the situation if it motivates the individual to make a greater effort at initiating friendships or in developing the skills to do so. Similarly, the belief that informing on the bully will lead to retaliation increases the chances that the bullying will continue.

It is common in cognitive therapy to evaluate automatic thoughts of patients for the presence of *thinking errors* or cognitive distortions (Beck, 1974; Beck, 1995; Burns, 1980). The self-statements of the card characters, as well as those that might be suggested by players in discussing a card, are like automatic thoughts and can be subjected to the same scrutiny. Using

Burns' formulation, several cognitive distortions about self and others apply to the self-statements associated with play of the game:

> *All-or-Nothing Thinking.* Viewing events in dichotomous categories like right or wrong and success or failure. A bully might say to himself, "It is either pick on others or get picked on by them."
>
> *Overgeneralization.* Viewing a single event as a never-ending pattern. A child who wasn't asked to participate in a group says to himself, "They'll never ask me to join their group."
>
> *Disqualifying the Positive.* Dismissing positive experiences by believing that they "don't count" for some reason. A victim in successfully countering bullying behavior might say to himself, "I just got lucky. That's not going to happen again."
>
> *Jumping to Conclusions.* Making negative predictions without a basis in fact. A victim might say to himself, "I'll always be picked on no matter what I do."
>
> *Should Statements.* Associating words like "must," "should," and "ought" to one's own behavior and that of others. A bystander might say of a victim, "They should be able to stand up to the bully without my help."
>
> *Labeling and Mislabeling.* A form of generalization, this is a tendency to attach a highly pejorative label to self or others. A bystander failing to defend a victim might say to himself, "I'm just an uncaring person."

In the examples above, the therapist can encourage the substitution of positive self-talk for the negative self-talk illustrated. Positive self-statements can also be statements that guide behavior and prepare the individual for stressors (Michenbaum, 1985). They may be used to take credit for and to reinforce the successful enactment of those behaviors. For example, a bystander who is troubled by not having intervened in previous bullying behavior might prepare himself to intervene by saying, "I'm going to politely tell him (the bully) that what he's doing is wrong. I'm going to be a little scared doing that but I know I can say it in a way that will keep him from picking on me." Having successfully intervened, he might then say to himself, "Good for me. I did the right thing. It worked because I planned ahead—not because I was lucky."

APPLICATIONS

The interventions below illustrate different ways of working with the game cards. The first example illustrates a straightforward approach to exploring the motives of the card character and suggesting more functional ways of dealing with the problem. In the second, the therapist offers a poor response to the card—the devil's advocate technique—and engages the client to think about and defend a better response. The third is an example of questioning the evidence for and against a belief.

Bully (5) Displacement 1

Billy's dad often told him he was weak and that he was disappointed he wasn't tough like himself. At school, Billy liked to push around smaller kids and tell them how pathetic they were.

What advice would you give Billy?

What's a better way to deal with the problem?

C: I'd tell him to pick on someone his own size.

T: That would certainly be better than picking on smaller kids. What would happen if he picked on kids his own size?

C: He'd probably get beat up.

T: So he picks on smaller kids to make sure he wins. Why do you think he picks on kids in the first place? Why doesn't he just leave them alone?

C: 'Cause of his dad?

T: Yeah, I think so. So how is it related to his dad?

C: His dad thinks he's not tough.

T: So picking on other kids makes him feel tough?

C: Yeah.

T: Is there anything else about his dad that might make him act this way?

C: I dunno.

T: Well, I'm thinking that he may be angry at his dad. If I were a kid and my dad put me down I'd be pretty angry at him but be afraid to fight back. So I might take my anger out on someone else. And if a feel tough doing that I'd also be disproving my dad's opinion.

C: Yeah, but his dad will still put him down, and I wouldn't feel tough picking on smaller kids.

T: That's right! So what's a better way do deal with the problem? First of all, what is the problem?

C: Picking on smaller kids?

T: Yes, that is a problem. But from Billy's point of view, it's a solution to a problem. But like you said, it's not a very good solution. See, I think Billy's problem is how he feels. He feels very disappointed in himself and angry with his father for making him feel that way. He's probably saying something to himself like, "It's important to be tough, and I'm going to prove him wrong by acting tough." So what's a better solution to the problem?

C: To feel better about himself?

T: That's right! What could he say to himself that would make him feel better?

C: He could say to himself, "I'm tough."

T: Great! I would add a little bit to that and say, "I'm tough and don't have to prove it all the time by picking on other kids." I think that's what Billy should say to himself, or something like that, every time he's about to pick on another kid. What might he say to himself when his dad starts picking on him, calling him weak?

C: I'm not weak?

T: Good. Again, I would add something like, "I'm not weak, and I'm not going to let my dad convince me that I am. He just doesn't know me like I know myself." I would tell Billy to say that to himself whenever his dad says that to him. Is there anything that Billy could say to his dad?

C: Tell him to leave him alone.

T: What do you think would happen if he told him that?

C: He might hit him.

T: Okay, so saying something like, "Just leave me alone!" isn't likely to work. But I think the idea of letting him know he doesn't like it is something Billy should try. He just has to find a better way to say it. Is there a better way to say it?

C: Please leave me alone?

T: That's a lot better. I would add a statement of why Billy wants him to leave him alone and change the wording a bit. I might say, "It hurts me when you say you're disappointed in me." Do you think saying something like that will get his dad to leave him alone?

C: I dunno.

T: I don't know either. A lot depends on his dad. He may have to hear it from Billy several times before he changes his behavior. And maybe even then he won't. But I'm pretty sure by saying it the way I suggest isn't going to make him angry or think Billy is weaker than he already thinks. And if it doesn't work, Billy should still say something to himself like what we talked about a minute ago, like "It doesn't matter what my dad says. I know I'm not weak."

Victim (13) Avoidance 7

Jason started missing the school bus on purpose because Zach would tease him every morning.

What advice would you give Jason?

What could he do or say to himself to deal with the problem?

T: Well, I'd say that's okay. But I'd tell Jason to stay in touch with some kids in his class to find out whether Zach moved or something so he'd no longer be on the bus and so Jason could go back to school. What do you think?

C: Zach might never move. I'd tell him to get on the bus and sit far away from Zach.

T: Okay, but what if Zack just gets up and goes over and sits next to him?

C: Jason needs to go where some other kids are already sitting so there wouldn't be any room

T: Suppose he can't find a place where there's no room for Zack?

C: He could tell the bus driver to tell Zack to leave him alone.

T: Okay, but suppose the bus driver says he's too busy and Jason should solve his own problem. Or suppose he tells Zach in a loud voice to leave Jason alone, and all the other kids start teasing Jason 'cause he's a wimp?

C: Well, then maybe he could just ignore Zach.

T: How would he do that?

C: He could take out a book or something and start reading when Zach starts teasing him.

T: And what, he just keeps reading and doesn't look at Zach when he starts teasing him?

C: Yeah.

T: Okay. That's a great idea. I would add just one thing to help him stick to his decision to ignore Zach. I'd suggest that he talk to himself while Zach is teasing him. He might say something to himself like, "If I keep ignoring him it'll take all the fun out of it for him. Eventually he'll stop the teasing."

Bystander (3) Passive 2

Tanya was making fun of Christina for flunking her English test. Danielle overheard and thought to herself, "I don't need to say anything. I bet Christina isn't that upset; she's so smart and does so well on her other tests."

What advice would you give Danielle?

What could Danielle say to herself that would be better?

C: I'd say to tell Tanya to stop making fun of her.

T: Okay. What could she say to herself to help her do that?

C: Maybe say to herself that Christina really is upset.

T: Okay. But we don't really know whether Christina is or isn't upset. How could Danielle find out? What would be the evidence that she is upset?

C: If she cried or something when Tanya teased her.

T. Good. That would be pretty conclusive. But if she didn't cry, would that mean that she isn't upset?

C: No, she could be keeping it inside.

T: That's right. What would be good evidence that she *isn't* upset.?

C: Maybe if she tells Tanya to mind her own business.

T: Good, and maybe telling Tanya to put her time to better use by studying because she's the one who really needs it. The point is that Danielle shouldn't jump to conclusions without looking at the evidence. She should collect the evidence for and against before concluding the Christina isn't upset. Unfortunately, it's not that easy. For one thing, if Danielle is like most people, she's likely to look for evidence, or interpret facts, that support the belief she already has. And even if she overcomes this problem, she might still be left with a situation where the evidence for and against is about equal. What should she do then?

C: Nothing, I guess.

T: Well, unfortunately, that means doing the same thing that she's already doing based on her belief that Christina isn't upset. But there is something else she can do when there isn't enough evidence one way or the other. She could ask herself what the consequences would be of doing something or doing nothing. To put it another way, what would be the harm of assuming she is upset even if she isn't? It would only mean telling Tanya what she is doing isn't right or Danielle telling Christina that she doesn't agree with Tanya or that Tanya has no business talking that way. That would do some good even if Christina weren't upset.

EVALUATION OF PROGRESS AND OUTCOME

Design of the *Bullying Game* permits an objective evaluation of therapeutic progress and outcome. Methods may vary, but all should begin with a comparison of the adequacy of responses to game cards over time. Players who are making therapeutic progress should demonstrate better responses to game cards in later sessions compared to earlier ones (or pre- and post intervention). In other words, they should demonstrate that learning more appropriate attitudes and behaviors has occurred. One approach begins with the preparation of a questionnaire consisting of game cards (approximately ten) of the kind that the player will encounter in the course of play (different questionnaires may therefore have to be prepared for different players, or separate questionnaires for bullies, victims, and bystanders). Players then write their response to each item on two or more occasions. A five-point scale (*poor* to *excellent*) prepared earlier, and anchored by an example of a poor and excellent response for each item, is then used to score each response. Therapists may score the questionnaires themselves, or for a more objective assessment, enlist raters (blind to the identity of the respondents and to when the questionnaire was completed).

Learning more appropriate attitudes and behaviors is not, of course, the same as applying what is learned. To assess change in attitudes and behaviors, the *Bullying Checklist* might again be completed by the player's teacher. A comparison of pre- and post intervention ratings can then be undertaken, hopefully demonstrating a significant reduction in problematical attitudes and behaviors. To demonstrate that what was learned in the course of playing the game was the likely source of such change, a player's postintervention questionnaire scores should correlate positively with the change reported by his or her teacher.

For therapists wishing a more objective evaluation of game effectiveness, an experimental design including a control group is required. The nature of that group may vary, ranging from a discussion group about bullying to a group that plays a game unrelated to bullying. The groups, however, should control for the possible effects of an adult-lead group interaction as well as the potential teacher expectation and bias that positive change will result from intervention. Teachers and raters should, of course, be blind to group assignment of the individuals they are evaluating.

Appropriate statistical tests can be applied to evaluate the significance of change. Depending on the number of subjects involved and the interests of the investigator, more specific questions might also be addressed. For example, for which groups (bully, victim, or bystander) is change the greatest? And what specific attitudes and behavior are most and least resistant to change?

CONCLUSION

The *Bullying Game* is a versatile tool for intervening with bullies, victims, and bystanders. Based on the known cognitive distortions and behavioral deficits of these groups, the game can be played with the individual or small groups. A checklist for teachers also permits the selection of game cards that best represent the learning objectives for individual players. A variety of cognitive-behavioral techniques can be applied to attain these objectives, including (1) reinforcement of good responses to game cards, (2) modeling of good card responses by the therapist, (3) teaching problem-solving skills, (4) using role play to rehearse new behaviors and (5) facilitating cognitive restructuring. The design of the game lends itself to the evaluation of progress and outcome.

REFERENCES

Banks, R. 1997. Bullying in schools. ERIC Digest. ED407154.

Batsche, G. M., and H. M. Knoff. 1994. Bullies and their victims: Understanding a pervasive problem in the schools. *School Psychology Review* 23: 165–74.

Beane, A. L. 1999. *The Bully Free Classroom*. Minneapolis, MN: Free Spirit.

Beck, A. T. 1974. *Cognitive Therapy and the Emotional Disorders*. New York: International Universities Press.

Beck, J. S. 1995. *Cognitive Therapy: Basics and Beyond*. New York: Guilford.

Berg, B. 2001. *The Bullying Game*. Dayton, OH: Cognitive Therapeutics.

Burns, D. D. 1980. *Feeling Good: The New Mood Therapy*. New York: Signet.

Crick, N. R., and J. K. Grotpeter. 1995. Relational aggression, gender and social-psychological adjustment. *Child Development* 66: 710–22.

Egan, S. K., and D. G. Perry. 1998. Does low self-regard invite victimization? *Developmental Psychology* 34: 299–309.

Elias, M. J., and S. E. Tobias. 1996. *Social Problem Solving: Intervention in the Schools*. New York: Guilford.

Fried, S., and P. Fried. 1996. *Bullies and Victims*. New York: Evans and Co.

Hodges, E.V.E., and D. G. Perry. 1999. Personal and interpersonal antecedents and consequences of victimization of peers. *Journal of Personality and Social Psychology* 76: 677–85.

Hodges, E. V. E., M. J. Malone, and D. G. Perry. 1997. Individual risk and social risk as interacting determinants of victimization in the peer group. *Development Psychology* 33: 1032–39.

Michenbaum, D. 1977. *Cognitive-Behavior Modification*. New York: Plenum Press.

———. 1985. *Stress Inoculation Training*. New York: Pergamon Press.

Newman, D. A., A. M. Horne, and C. L. Bartolomucci. 2000. *Bully Busters: A Teacher's Manual*. Champaign, IL: Research Press.

Olweus, D. 1978. *Aggression in Schools: Bullies and Whipping Boys*. Washington, DC: Hemisphere.

———. 1993. *Bullying at School*. Malden, MA: Blackwell Publishers.

Pellegrini, A. D., M. Bartini, and F. Brooks. 1999. School bullies, victims, and aggressive victims: Factors relating to group affiliation and victimization in early adolescence. *Journal of Educational Psychology* 91: 216–24.

Ross, D. M. 1996. *Childhood Bullying and Teasing: What School Personnel, Other Professionals and Parents Can Do*. Alexandria, VA: American Counseling Association.

Zarb, J. M. 1992. *Cognitive-Behavioral Assessment and Therapy with Adolescents*. New York: Brunner/Mazel.

Index

active play therapy, 143

activity filial therapy (AFT): case presentation of, 63–65; contents of kit for, 56–57; creation of, 48; group format of meetings, 56; implementing, 55–56; process of, 57–63; research in, 50–55; therapeutic rationale for, 48–50

adolescent culture, 12

adolescent play, history of research in, 144–45

alcohol/drugs, 21, 25, 78, 121, 131, 178, 179, 181, 183, 203, 244, 255

alexithymia, 227

Allan, J., 160

Allen, F. H., 98

Angels and Devils (game), 210–11

The Anger Control Game (board game), 253

Anger Management Group Training treatment, 248–54; additional play materials/activities, 266; brief treatment for small group, 262–65; session I, 250–52; session II, 252–53; session III, 253; session IV, 254. *See also* anger problems, group therapy for; anger theory

anger problems, group therapy for: case illustration, 254–57; history of anger emotion, 240; overview of anger management, 239–40; research support, 247–48; therapeutic rationale, 245–47. *See also* Anger Management Group Training treatment; anger theory

anger theory: cognitive-behavioral theory, 244–45; cognitive-neoassociationist perspective, 241–42; frustration aggression hypothesis, 242–43; single dimension of anger/fear, 240–41; social learning theory, 243–44. *See also* Anger Management Group Training treatment; anger problems, group therapy for

animal phototherapy, 132

anorexia. *See* eating disorders

Anorexia Initiation Theory, 225

Arkema, P. H., 73

Atkinson, R. C., 189–90

Attachment Disorder, 184

Axline, V. M., 61, 97, 143–44

Bandura, A., 243–44

Bavin-Hoffman, R., 54

behavioral reversal (role play), 12, 49, 58–59, 60, 61, 62, 64, 73, 102, 114, 215, 232, 278–79. *See also* drama therapy

Behavioral True False Inventory (BTFI), 128, 136, 138, 203

Benson, R. M., 77

Berkowitz, L., 242–43

Berry, P., 160

best thing/worst thing about . . . activity, 131

Blos, P., 144

board game, therapeutic: Anger Control Game, 253; Brain and Numskull, 221;

287

About the Editors

Loretta Gallo-Lopez, MA, RPT-S, RDT-BCT, merges her experience as a play therapist and board-certified drama therapist and trainer in her psychotherapy practice in Tampa, Florida. She is a former adjunct professor in the drama therapy program at New York University. She has authored several chapters on play and drama therapy and has presented trainings nationally on topics related to sexual abuse and creative approaches to therapy with children, adolescents, and families.

Charles E. Schaefer, PhD, RPT-S, a nationally renowned child psychologist, is professor emeritus of psychology at Fairleigh Dickinson University in Teaneck, New Jersey. He is cofounder and director emeritus of the Association for Play Therapy and has written or edited more than sixty-five books on parenting, child psychology, and play therapy, including *The Therapeutic Use of Child's Play*, *Family Play Therapy*, and *Short-Term Play Therapy for Children*. Schaefer maintains a private practice in child psychotherapy in Hackensack, New Jersey.

Contributors

Steven C. Abell, Ph.D., University of Detroit Mercy, Detroit, Michigan.

Berthold Berg, Ph.D., Private Practice, Dayton, Ohio.

Dorothy Breen, Ph.D., Associate Professor, Counselor Education, University of Maine, Orono, Maine.

Christopher J. Brown, Ph.D., Assistant Professor and Clinical Director, Professional Counseling, Department of Educational Administration and Psychological Services, Southwest Texas State University, San Marcos, Texas.

Neil Cabe, Ph.D., Private Practice, Northfield, Ohio.

Giselle B. Esquivel, Psy.D., A.B.P.P., Professor, Fordham University, New York, New York.

Loretta Gallo-Lopez, M.A., RPT-S, RDT-BCT, Private Practice, Tampa, Florida.

Theresa Kestly, Ph.D., Director, Program Development and Training, Sand Tray Training Institute of New Mexico, Corrales, New Mexico.

Claire Milgrom, MSW, RSW, Private Practice, Winnipeg, MB, Canada.

Evangeline Munns, CPsych., RPT-S, Clinical Director, Blue Hills Play Therapy Services, Blue Hills Child and Family Services, Aurora, Ontario, Canada.

Thomas M. Nelson, Ph.D., University Professor and Professor of Psychology, Emeritus, University of Alberta, Edmonton, Alberta, Canada.

Hal Pickett, Psy.D., L.P. Assistant Professor, University of Minnesota Medical School; Associate Director, Outpatient Services, Division of Child and Adolescent Psychiatry, Fairview-University Medical Center.

Scott Riviere, MS, RPT-S, Founder and director, Kids Interactive Discovery Zone, Inc., Lake Charles, Louisiana.

Lisa Rogers, Ph.D., L.P., Psychologist, Emily Program, St. Paul, Minnesota; Private Practice, St. Paul, Minnesota.

Virginia Ryan, Ph.D., C Psychol, MBAPT, Director, MA/Diploma in Nondirective Play Therapy, Social Policy and Social Work Department, University of York, York, England.

Karen Snyder Badau, Ph.D., Psychologist, Crisis Intervention Services, Westchester Medical Center, Valhalla, New York; Clinical Instructor, New York Medical College, Valhalla, New York.

Johanna Krout Tabin, Ph.D., Chicago Center for Psychoanalysis, Chicago, Illinois; Private Practice, Glencoe, Illinois.

Andrew Taylor, M.A., University of Detroit Mercy, Detroit, Michigan.

Kate Wilson, B.A., DipSoc, DipCouns, Chair of Social Work, Head of Centre for Social Work, University of Nottingham, Nottingham, England.